MEXICOCITY

INSIGHT *City* GUIDES

Edited by Jutta Schütz
Photography by Christa Cowrie, Jutta Schütz and others
Managing Editor, English Edition: Andrew Eames

APA
PUBLICATIONS

MexicoCity

First Edition
© **1991 APA PUBLICATIONS (HK) LTD**
All Rights Reserved
Printed in Singapore by Höfer Press Pte.Ltd

ABOUT THIS BOOK

Following the success of Apa Publications' *Insight Guide: Mexico,* this CityGuide turns its attention to the country's capital, explaining, in words and pictures, the world's largest metropolis – a city which itself consists of many worlds. An expert team of writers and photographers tackled this challenging task, examining the Mexican capital from all sides: its history, problems, people, streets and plazas, its pulsating nightlife and possible day-trips in the vicinity.

The Team

It was in 1973 that this book's editor, **Jutta Schütz**, visited Mexico for the first time, working in a hotel in the capital. Since then, the country has never ceased to fascinate her. She has spent months at a time there, visiting even the most out-of-the-way Indian villages. She wrote her social science dissertation on handicrafts and tourism in Mexico, and has written other guides to the country.

An important factor in her visits to Mexico has been her Mexican friends. One of them, photographer **Christa Cowrie**, emigrated from her native Hamburg when she was 14. In Mexico Cowrie has worked for well-known newspapers and followed the election campaigns of three presidents.

Christa Cowrie provided most of the photographs for this guide. Other pictures are the work of the editor and contributors.

Andreas M. Gross studied art, archaeology and languages in Munich, Mexico and Brazil. He lived in Los Angeles for five years and has worked as a tour guide for various educational travel organizers, making use of his rich knowledge of North and Latin America. In this book Gross, who as a boy had always wanted to be an Indian, wrote the detailed chapters on the Indian history of pre-Spanish Mexico City, the Revolution and its famous protagonists, Zapata and Villa.

Hans Haufe also completed part of his studies in art history, history and archaeology in Mexico. He devoted his dissertation to 20th-century Mexican painting and his doctorate on 19th-century Mexican art, and is well qualified to write about Mexico during the Colonial epoch, the post-Revolutionary murals and modern architecture.

Gabriele Gockel took on the task of describing Mexico's bumpy road from colony to Republic. She lives in Munich and works as an author, translator and language teacher. As a supporter of the Third World movement, she takes a special interest in Mexico's historical and political development.

Erdmann Gormsen, geography professor at the University of Mainz in Germany, is a long-time Mexico specialist. Since 1964, the year of his first long stay in Mexico and his work with the major Mexico project of the German Research Society, he has visited Mexico repeatedly. In this book he writes about the urban development of the Mexican metropolis as well as the city of Puebla.

Elena Poniatowska was born in Paris and moved to Mexico while still a child. Today, as a journalist and author, she is one of the country's best-known writers. Her pen gives a voice to those who can no longer speak, the victims of the tragedy in Tlatelolco. In this book, she describes with biting humor her fellow residents of Mexico City, her artist colleagues and the sophisticated non-conformists in the Zona Rosa.

Anne Schumacher de la Cuesta worked

Schütz

Cowrie

Gross

Haufe

Poniatowska

for the Friedrich Ebert Foundation at the German embassy in Mexico City from 1963 until 1979. She has developed a particularly strong affinity with the country and its people through her two Mexican children. Since 1984, she has been director of the Mexican State Tourism Office in Frankfurt.

Austrian contributor **Sigrid Diechtl** switched from financial planning for multinational firms to anthropology studies in Mexico. Along with her field research with monkeys in sub-tropical rain forests, she has spent years studying the attitudes of Mexican drivers in the capital. In addition, she describes Coyoacán, where she lives and where in 1985 she survived the great earthquake.

Ernesto Riedwyl, a native of Switzerland, has adopted Mexico as his home since 1976. He studied the science of teaching and Latin American studies and has made many journeys throughout the country. For some years, his main objective has been to popularize Mexico as a tourist destination. He knows the best restaurants in the capital, and also loves to cook.

Roger Franz is a educational travel guide with a doctorate in journalism. He has studied ethnology, political economy, art history and archaeology. Since 1975, he has traveled throughout America. As his special interest is in the Indian roots of the country, he takes the reader through the Anthropological Museum in Tula.

The widely traveled journalist **Imogen Seger** has a doctorate in sociology. Her chapters on the Guadalupe cult and Teotihuacan reveal her fascination with Mexico.

The nightlife of Mexico City should really be described by an insider: **David Siller** was born in Mexico City. He has worked for several Mexican newspapers and in 1983 received Mexico City's first prize for journalism. His city reportage was published in book form (*Uno de estos días*) and he is now heavily involved in Mexican television.

The high volcanoes that surround Mexico City are presented by two mountain climbers and guides: **Wolfgang Koch**, who studies ethnology in Munich and **Till Gottbrath**, chief editor of the journal *Outdoor*, which covers every imaginable adventurous sport in the great outdoors.

Ursula Moser-Rasetti and **Jutta Schütz** translated the articles by Poniatowska and Siller from the Spanish. Travel Tips, the compilation of practical information at the back of the book, was prepared by **Maja Specht**, an experienced travel editor and Mexico specialist.

The Translation

Work on the English edition was coordinated by **Andrew Eames** in Apa Publications' London office; translators **Annette Bus**, **Wendy Reed** and **Susanne Pleines** worked on the main text. **John Wilcock**, himself the author of a guide to Mexico City, added expert editorial input from his base in California. **Christopher Catling** completed the proof-reading and indexing and **Jill Anderson** guided the text through a variety of Macintosh computers.

Gormsen

Schumacher

Seger

Franz

Diechtl

History and People

Places

A MEGALOPOLIS OF EXTREMES

What would Montezuma II say if he could see what has become of the former Aztec metropolis of Tenochtitlán? From its ruins rose the capital of the colonial empire, New Spain, named Mexico after the Mexica (Aztecs). Today what is now Mexico City breaks all records as the largest city in the world. But is that anything to be proud of?

The agglomeration of 19 million people living in a valley 2,200 meters (7,220 ft) high can only be appreciated when approaching from the air. Twenty percent of the population and 50 percent of Mexico's industry is concentrated in one percent of the country's area. The megalopolis not only manufactures most of the country's goods, but also produces air one can cut with a knife and 10,000 tonnes of rubbish per day. At the same time, the monster is quickly depleting its water resources. Moreover, the city still continues to draw people from the provinces like a magnet. Experts paint a nightmare picture of 25 million inhabitants by the year 2000 and warn of the imminent "Calcutta-isation" of the city.

Mexico City cannot be compared with any other city in the world. It is a city of miracles. The first miracle that the Indians who survived the Spanish conquest experienced was the manifestation of the Virgin of Guadalupe on the hill of Tepeyac. It is no doubt due to the Virgin, now the country's patron saint who is called upon in all cases of need, that the population tolerates the discomforts of urban life with such stoic patience.

It is also a miracle that so much in this city functions at all: the public transport system with its modern underground network, the telephone system and food distribution all continue to cope despite the pressures on them. Residents often demonstrate a readiness to organize themselves and to overcome urban problems which the city fathers cannot, or will not, do anything about. It was through their resilience and strength of character that the people mastered the disastrous results of the earthquake of 1985.

"Nevertheless" is the key word for Mexico City. Despite the disadvantages, many Mexicans would not want to live anywhere else. There are numerous beautiful and interesting aspects of the city worth exploring: the excavations of Aztec temples, the old city with its baroque churches and palaces from the colonial period, the idyllic districts of Coyoacán and San Angel, the Chapultepec Park with its colorful weekend life, the canals of Xochimilco and the outstanding museums.

Preceding pages: polluted haze at midday; the Zócalo at night; pilgrimage to the patron saint of Mexico, the Virgin of Guadalupe; patio of the Hotel de Cortéz. **Left**, Conchero dancer in the Zócalo.

TENOCHTITLAN – VENICE OF THE AZTECS

"This city is so great and so beautiful that I can hardly say half of what I could say about it. And this bit alone is practically unbelievable. It is even more beautiful than Granada." With these words, the Spanish conquistador Hernán Cortéz described Mexico-Tenochtitlán, the capital of the Aztecs, in a letter to Charles V.

On that November 8, 1519, the resplendent city lay before the amazed Europeans as they crossed the pass between the two high volcanoes, Popocatépetl and Iztaccíhuatl. The Spaniards looked out over the expanse of Lake Texcoco which partly covered the high plateau of Anáhuac.

The lake was full of barges and canoes. Located in the middle of a subsidiary lagoon, with paths across dikes joining the city to the banks, Tenochtitlán must have seemed to the European soldiers like an Indian Venice – a magical mirage after all their fighting and deprivation on the march. In the middle of the canal-riddled city, they could make out an imposing central plaza with pyramids crowned by temples.

One and a half years after this first glimpse, Cortéz had achieved his objective and the empire of the mighty Aztecs was under his control. Tenochtitlán, the economic, political and cultural center of the empire was robbed of its treasures. The European Renaissance's lust for gold and conquest had put to the sword the heart of Mexico, indeed the heart of all of what was ancient America.

Bernal Díaz del Castillo, an ordinary soldier in the service of Cortéz, is considered the most reliable eye witness and vivid chronicler of the conquest. He described the end of the Tenochtitláns thus: "The streets, plazas, houses and courtyards were so filled with corpses that it was nearly impossible to get through. Cortéz himself was nauseous from the stench."

The mighty state: Less than 200 years had passed between the founding of the city and its conquest by the Spanish, in the year of 1521. With unparalleled speed, Mexico-Tenochtitlán had developed from a shabby hamlet into an Indian metropolis of breathtaking beauty and almost Prussian sense of order. When Cortéz and Montezuma met for the first time on the dam path to Tenochtitlán in 1519, the Aztecs were at the absolute pinnacle of their power (the Aztecs, in fact, called themselves Mexica, a name derived from that of their patron god or possibly a corruption of *metzli* (moon) and *xictli* (center), meaning the town in middle of the lake of the moon; the term Aztec came later and is derived from Aztlan island, the tribe's legendary ancestral home).

The Aztec emperor, who bore the title *tlatoani* (He who speaks), ruled over an enormous territory that extended from Guatemala to the steppes of northern Mexico and from the Atlantic to the Pacific. Between 6 and 7 million people were his subjects and Tenochtitlán lived off their tribute. Nevertheless, a few enemies, such as the Tarascas in the northwest or the powerful Tlaxcaltecs in the east, frustrated the Aztecs' imperialistic appetite. Nor could it be called a tightly controlled empire since other peoples within the Aztec sphere of influence resisted central subjugation. It was more like a patchwork of tribute-paying vassal states which could be torn apart at any moment. Cortéz was an adept politician and he knew how to exploit this by playing the different Indian peoples off against each other and the Aztec state.

The Indians, Cortéz recorded, "live almost as we do in Spain and with quite as much orderliness. It is wonderful to see how much sense they bring to the doing of everything."

A migratory people: According to the widely propagated official state history, the Aztecs believed themselves to have embarked on a mass migration in the year AD 1111. In the course of 200 years, these fighting people wandered from the mythical island of Aztlan, in the high north, to the banks of Lake Texcoco, all the while bringing with them their god Huitzilopochtli for whom they build a temple wherever they settled for any period of time. The god, they believed, spoke to seven priests through this simple temple, his sacred pronouncements then being transmitted to the seven groups which constituted the whole tribe.

In AD 1300, the Aztecs, numbering only a few hundred, came to the hill of Chapultepec, which lies in today's park of the same name in Mexico City. There they stayed for 20 years until they were expelled by their neighbors, whom they had been trying to wear down with constant surprise attacks

ples. Many of them, like the Aztecs, spoke *náhuatl*, which soon became the lingua franca of the highlands.

Although still an insignificant group, the Aztecs seemed even then to be convinced of their future glory. They believed themselves to be the chosen people of Huitzilopochtli, a god of war who had destined his people for greatness, and who had proclaimed that one day they would no longer be anyone's subjects. This all-pervading sense of mission among the Aztecs was seen by other tribes as incredible arrogance.

The eagle on the cactus: At the time of the founding of Tenochtitlán, there was little

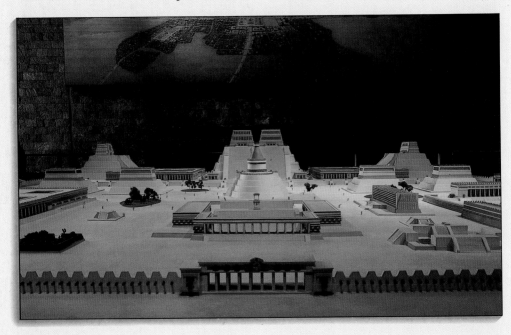

and raids. The Aztecs were treated as barbarians, so-called Chichimecs; no one wanted them as neighbors, and at least according to the Aztecs themselves, they were always being pushed around. At that time the high valley around the Anáhuac lake was controlled by many small and mutually antagonistic states. (The Aztec term *anáhuac*, meaning "on the edge of the water," came to refer to the whole Valley of Mexico.)

After the collapse of the Toltec empire in the 12th century, which preceded that of the Aztecs, these states had formed from Toltecan and Chichimec (barbarian) peo-

reason for such self-confidence. In 1325, the Aztecs passed through an internal crisis having just lost a battle against their rulers, the Colhua. They sought refuge on some reed-covered, swampy, uninhabited islands in Lake Texcoco, and from here they manoeuvered themselves into the no-man's-land that lay between the two powerful states bordering the lake.

On the western side, the Chichimecan Tepanecs lived in their capital, Azcapotzalco. On the eastern side, in Texcoco, the Toltecan Acolhua ruled. The choice was ingenious from a strategic point of view.

Huitzilopochtli also had a hand in the choice: the god commanded the Aztec high priest, Tenoch, to establish the city on a very special point: on a rock (*tetl*) where a pear cactus (*nochtli*) grows on which sits an eagle with a rattlesnake in his beak. From this debateable legend the place supposedly derives its name, Tenochtitlán.

The Mexica duly sighted their eagle and erected a shrine to Huitzilopochtli on the spot. By digging canals and levelling pasture using the earth they had dug out, the initially very poor Aztecs created small plots of arable land, the so-called *chinampas*. Today visitors to the somewhat seedy "floating gardens" of Xochimilco can view this skillful system of land reclamation.

Shortly after Tenochtitlán, a second independent city named Tlatelolco was established on a neighboring island.

Acamapichtli is the first recorded Mexica ruler at this time, governing from 1376–1396 and allegedly descended from old Toltecan (Tula) nobility. The Aztecs regarded everything Toltecan as the pinnacle of cultural superiority. The *tlatoani*, or ruler, had to be a descendant of the kings of Tula, thereby legitimatizing his sovereign authority. Many elements of Aztec architecture are, in fact, copied directly from the Tula. Socially as well as artistically, the Toltecs were admired as the predecessors and the forefathers of the Mexica.

The Triple Alliance: For the first 90 years of Tenochtitlán's existence, the children of Huitzilopochtli served the nearby tribe of Tepanec Azcapotzalcos, primarily as soldiers, helping to create the Tepanecan empire, which finally dominated the whole region around the lake.

In 1426, the powerful Tepanecan lord Tezozómoc died. For many years thereafter, the empire lay in chaos and finally, in 1430, the Aztecs of Tenochtitlán took their chance to free themselves from the Tepanecan yoke. Together with Tlacopán and Texcoco, they conquered Azcapotzalco and destroyed the

Tepanec empire. From then on, the *tlatoani* gave the orders, together with the princes from the other two cities. Thus the so-called Triple Alliance (Tlacopán, Texloco and Tenochtitlán) came into existence and ruled the Aztec empire from then on.

After the *tlatoanis* Huitzilihuitl (1397–1417) and Chimalpopoca (1417–28) came the energetic Itzcoatl (1428–40). His successor was Montezuma I Ilhuicamina (1440–69). His real name in *náhuatl* was *Motecuhzoma* (the "irascible prince"), originally a title of the fire god. The surname Ilhuicamina means "heavenly fire". He was the grandfather of the second ruler of the

same name, Montezuma Xocoyotzin, the "Younger", who would later suffer at the hands of the Spanish.

Montezuma I led the imperial expansion, especially after a famine in Tenochtitlán, in order to acquire the fertile area of the Gulf region (now the Gulf of Mexico). During his rule, Tenochtitlán was fundamentally renovated. An aqueduct was laid to provide drinking water from the Chapultepec hill to supply the growing metropolis and a dam was built across the lake. This project was directed by the ingenious prince, master builder and poet Nezahualcoyotl of

<u>Left</u>, model of the Aztec temple district. <u>Right</u>, maize planting on the *chinampas* and the preparation of tortillas as depicted by Mexican artist Diego Rivera.

Texcoco. The dam was intended not only to stop the floods which had regularly afflicted and laid waste to the city, but also to separate the salt water of the main lake from the freshwater lagoon in the capital.

During the reigns of the Aztec emperor Montezuma, in the 15th century, and that of his neighbor Tlacaetel in the Valley of Puebla the need for human sacrifices to appease the gods was so great that the two emperors forged a macabre pact. At designated intervals at a particular place and time battles would be fought between the two armies to provide prisoners that each side could sacrifice on its altars. These ritual contests (wrote Nigel Davies in *The Aztecs*) came to be known as the Wars of Flowers. The seventh Tlatoani Axayácatl (1469–1481) as well as his successors Tizoc (1481–1486 and Ahuitzotl (1486–1502) expanded the Aztec empire, with the changing fortunes of war, to its final size. In 1473, the neighboring city of Tlatelolco was annexed with its important market and, in 1502, the 34-year-old Montezuma Xocoyotzin (Montezuma II) was elected supreme chief of the empire.

The largest city in the New World: The population of Mexico-Tenochtitlán with all of its suburbs, and of Tlatelolco is generally accepted by historians to have reached 400,000 during the reign of Montezuma. That would have made it the largest city in the New World with an area of between 12 and 15 sq. km (5 and 6 sq. miles). When the population of all the rest of the valley was added, the total probably exceeded one million. The inhabitants were primarily *nahuátl*-speaking, but Mixtec, Otomí, Zapotec and other Indian languages of the empire were also spoken. The Aztecs forced many craftsmen from throughout the conquered territories to resettle in the capital.

Tenochtitlán was organized into four *barrios* or districts which were then subdivided into 80 wards. Each administrative unit, the smallest being the clan-sized *calpullí*, was headed by a council leader and had its own assembly rooms. The life of the normal inhabitant was tightly regulated by strict customs and laws and everyday life was determined by trade, war, and religious practices. The State was ubiquitous. The Aztecs took compulsory education, cleanliness regulations, taxes, military service and many other things totally for granted in their urban society.

Physically the city was like a checkerboard, intersected by canals, which carried all the freight traffic. The causeway, with a width of up to 5 meters (16 ft), that connected Tenochtitlán with the mainland could be raised by a system of drawbridges to allow the passage of ships or to defend the city.

The accommodations of the residents were flat roofed, single-storied and built from stone or clay bricks. The *chinampas*, or

areas of arable land, belonged to everyone although at best they yielded only enough crops for bare subsistence.

An aggressive empire: In this highly stratified society, the *tlatoani* was practically a god-like figure at the pinnacle. He was like an emperor, pope and commander-in-chief all rolled into one. Montezuma's court was extremely luxurious and he was naturally polygamous. In many ways the Aztec imperial household resembled that of an ancient Japanese emperor or oriental potentate, and it has many counterparts in history. The ruling elite came almost exclusively from the Aztec upper nobility. The sacerdotal class of priests exercised special powers, and the "orders" of eagle and jaguar warriors enjoyed special prestige and possessed great personal influence.

The broad mass of the people consisted of free craftsmen and peasants. The lowest class in this society were the slaves who, in contrast to those of the old world, possessed well-established rights.

The Aztec empire based its power on war and intimidation through the use of its highly efficient and splendidly organized army. The Aztecs considered their battles as a kind of divine service or holy act. Subjugated

imperial borders and served the State as spies. They brought back the most astonishing imports to Tlatelolco.

The respected Spanish historian Bernal Díaz del Castillo wrote of this flourishing trade: "Every sort of commodity had its place. There were gold and silver wares, jewels, cloth of all kinds, feathers, cotton and slaves... Then came the stands with simpler products, such as twine and cocao... There was sisal cloth, rope, and knitted shoes... There were raw and tanned hides from... wild cats and other beasts of prey. We also found stands where beans, sage, and many other vegetables and spices were sold. There

vassals regularly had to supply the capital with luxury goods, clothing, labor and, above all, food. Without this tribute, the enormous population of Tenochtitlán was practically incapable of surviving.

The central market: The majority of these goods were traded at the central market in the second city of Tlatelolco, which formed the commercial heart of the empire. There the trading castes predominated, highly privileged people who journeyed far beyond the

was a special poultry and game market; one for the cake bakers and one for the sausage dealers. In the pottery stands we found everything from the largest vase to the smallest nightpots.

"We passed sellers of honey, honey cakes, and other delicacies; past furniture, wood and coal dealers … And I nearly forgot the craftsmen that make flint knives, the salt, the fish market and the breads which are made from dried silt fished from the lakes. It tastes like cheese. Finally there were instruments made of brass, copper, and tin, hand-painted cups and pitchers made out of wood. In short,

Left, Montezuma II by an unknown artist. **Above**, Rivera's mural *Tenochtitlán*.

there were so many goods that I would run out of paper to list them all."

Human sacrifices: Along with the high taxes, those tribes subject to the Aztecs were angered by Tenochtitlán's constantly growing demand for human sacrifices. Not only were prisoners of war sacrificed, but the Aztecs expected regular supplies of "high value", that is to say, younger, stronger men and women, for their rituals. Bodies, blood, and human hearts were the sustenance of the gods. According to Aztec beliefs, without these the world would come to an end, and with the expansion of their domain, the Aztecs intensified their sacrificial activities. Although the Spanish chroniclers greatly exaggerated the numbers of victims, the sacrificial cult bordered on decadent excess by the time of the conquest.

Tenochtitlán's sacred precinct, Teocalli, was the site of these rituals (Tlatelolco had its own place adjacent to the market). The Teocalli was a monumental plaza of anything up to 440 meters (1,440 ft) wide, depending on the source cited. A battlement ornamented with carvings of snakes surrounded the quadrangle. Four gates led into the plaza, which was orientated toward the west. Through three of these gates ran causeways to Ixtapalapa, Tacuba, and Tepeyac respectively.

Out of a total of 78 shrines in Tenochtitlán, the most important temples, pyramids, and platforms were to be found on the Teocalli. Among these were included shrines to non-Aztec gods which had been integrated into the state religion after the conquest of their followers. Montezuma's palace complex (which covered around 2.5 hectares/6 acres) adjoined the Teocalli where today the National Palace, on the Zócalo, is situated. The two-storey residence, with its pleasure gardens, game preserve, fountains, and grand rooms from which Montezuma managed his affairs of state, greatly impressed the conquering Spaniards.

Surrounding the plaza were the school for the nobility (Calmecac), assembly halls, and manor houses as well as the palace of Montezuma's father, Axayacatl, where in 1519, the conquering Cortéz was billeted.

The temple district: Recently the Templo Mayor, the double pyramid of the main temple, has been unearthed; the ruins lie northeast of the Cathedral. This temple was by far the most important building of the Aztec empire, almost its sacred heart.

For more than 200 years, the Templo Mayor was under continuous construction, being constantly enlarged and encased in new constructions. Such over-building of sacred buildings had a 1,000-year-long tradition in Central America, and it involved the preservation and at the same time the enlargement of the decayed walls. The expansion of the Aztec empire was expressed in ever more gigantic building projects around the Aztecs' main temple, where the pyramids and the temple itself not only honored the gods but also served to promote the self-image of a powerful kingdom, reflecting it in all its glory.

The Templo Mayor was, like all other sacred and government buildings, built with stucco-covered walls, ornamented and, presumably, colorfully painted. It must have been an awe-inspiring sight: a ramp with double staircases, orientated westward, led up the approximately 30-meter (100-ft) high pyramid, which was crowned with two imposing, high-roofed temples.

On the northern side of the platform stood the temple dedicated to the rain god Tlaloc while next to it, on the southern side, was the temple to the tribal god, Huitzilopochtli, who was not only the lord of war but also the god of the morning sun. When victims were about to be sacrificed they were first painted, and then covered with feathers and led up the great staircase before being forced to dance in front of the god's image.

Looking to the west from atop the pyramid, the Huitzilopochtli temple stood on the southern half of the pyramid facing the midday sun. When an Aztec warrior fell in battle, he was thought to accompany his war god, the young sun, as a hummingbird (in *náhuatl, huitzizl*). *Pochtli* means "to the left", hence "hummingbird to the left". In this way the whole building symbolized a religious concept and represented for the Aztecs a piece of petrified heaven on earth.

Also in the Teocalli was the round temple to Ehecatl (a variant of Quetzalcoatl), the shrine of the dark god, Tezcatlipoca, as well as the spring and fertility god Xipe Totec. In March, the latter's priests wore a costume made from the skin removed from a sacrificial victim in order to celebrate spring, nature's rejuvenation.

To the northwest of the holy court the sun god Tonatiuh had his temple. It was there that the famous calendar stone, with its Sun God face surrounded by reliefs representing prior world history and glyphs depicting the 21 days of the ceremonial calendar, was found in 1790. The stone is now the pride of the Anthropological Museum to which it was moved in 1984 from the National Museum which is situated on Calle Moneda.

symbol for the thousands of human sacrifices which were to be offered to the gods in the Teocalli.

The skulls of sacrificial victims were arranged in ranks on the *tzompantli*, a skull scaffold, whose base was also adorned with skulls made of stone. Cutting out the victim's heart with a stone knife, a form of death to which many Spaniards literally fell victim during the conquest, was a deeply religious act, like every other offering of life. This might seem both perverse and savage to modern civilizations, but it should not be forgotten how many deaths have been ordered in the history of European nations for

In front of the Templo Mayor lay the sacrificial stone of the Coyolxauhqui, discovered accidentally by construction workers in 1978 and today adorning the Museum of the Templo Mayor. On it, the moon goddess and sister of Huitzilopochtli is depicted as a naked woman with disjointed limbs after the god had killed her in a battle and subsequently dismembered her. She stands as a

The eagle was the emblem of the founders of the city and later symbol of the "eagle warriors." This example comes from the Templo Mayor.

similarly spurious reasons. The Aztecs remain, through their art and culture, a people animated by mysticism, magic, and divine service to whom our idea of enlightenment was, perforce, even though alien, the Indian lords of the ancient American world, ruled at the time of Leonardo da Vinci, Albrecht Dürer and Martin Luther.

Montezuma taken by surprise: It was into this strange world ruled by magic, unearthly idols and bloody rites, that Cortéz and his men ventured. Coming from Cuba, they landed on the Gulf coast in the Holy Week of 1519 and founded Veracruz.

The army of Cortéz consisted of more than 110 seamen, 553 soldiers, 45 crossbow and longbow marksmen, 200 Cuban Indians, 12 horses and 12 artillery pieces. Initially, the Totonac Indians received him warmly. They sensed the long-awaited possibility of finally casting off – with help from the Spaniards – the hated repression of Aztec supremacy. Cortéz was fortunate that one of the chiefs presented him with a woman who was both well-educated and a fluent linguist. Doña Marina, or the "Malinche" was to become his interpreter and advisor during the entire conquest and proved to be invaluable to him.

With Indian auxiliary troops, he marched up into the highlands to inflict an annihilating defeat on the Tlaxcaltecs, the Aztecs' arch-enemies. By doing so he not only gained thousands of battle-tried prisoners who turned into warriors, but the Tlaxcaltecs also provided him with the strategic expertise for his campaign against Montezuma's empire. Montezuma was certainly taken aback when he heard that these neighbors, who were considered undefeatable, had been beaten in a head-on confrontation by the "White Gods".

Montezuma's best efforts to keep the Spaniards out of Tenochtitlán failed. He had no choice but to receive the mysterious foreigners as hospitably as possible and to quarter them in his capital.

From then on he was obviously overwhelmed by the rapid pace of events. Imagine that the France of 450 years ago had been wiped out by General Eisenhower and several brigades of modern soldiers with tanks and machine guns and that Eisenhower had then marched down through Spain into Seville. Emperor Charles V would certainly have been stunned by the seemingly limitless power of such an invader.

Montezuma was similarly impressed. He was considered unusually pious, which in those days meant inspired with magic, so it should not be surprising that he saw Cortéz as the Toltec culture hero and legendary god-king, Ce Acatl Topiltzin, alias the "feathered serpent" Quetzalcoatl, who had sacrificed himself after his flight from Tula and prophesied that he would return one day from the East. At first this explanation seemed to Montezuma to be the most likely explanation for the phenomenon of Cortéz, an interpretation that subsequently proved to have fatal implications for the Aztec leader.

In the Indian tradition Quetzalcoatl is usually depicted neither as white nor as blond, and the year of his return is nowhere to be found in the ancient sources. To suit their purposes Spanish historians conveniently redefined the god after the conquest. But in some ways the legend matched: Quetzalcoatl is said to have had a beard and to come from the East, as did Cortéz.

Night of sorrow: Shortly after his arrival,

Cortéz found an excuse to imprison Montezuma, and seemed to have the initiative. But when the conqueror left the city to deal with an urgent problem on the coast, catastrophe struck. On May 23, his deputy, Alvarado, caused a dreadful bloodbath among the Aztec nobility during a celebration in the holy district. As a result, the Spaniards were besieged in their billets by the furious Aztecs.

When Cortéz came back to Tenochtitlán, he found the city in a state of chaos and his people in acute danger. He asked Montezuma to speak to the masses in order to calm them down, but as the ruler did so he was stoned to death by the angry mob.

The situation grew even more threatening, and Cortéz decided to retreat on the night of July 30. The Spaniards tried to take with them their stolen gold treasures and escape over the causeway to Tlacopán (Tacuba), but the Aztecs fell upon them mercilessly and Cortéz could only just barely save himself. He lost more than half his troops, all of his artillery and horses and most of his booty in the fray, which went down in history as the "Noche Triste", the night of sorrow.

The decline of Tenochtitlán: The defeated Spaniards retreated to Tlaxcala and the

sistance, was captured while trying to escape over the lake. Cortéz had him executed in 1525. The last decisive battle was in Tlatelolco, the trading city. In the afternoon of August 13, 1521, the Aztec empire and the power of the capital were broken forever. In the end the sword and the Cross of the Spaniards triumphed over the magical world of the Aztecs.

Tenochtitlán lay on the lake, totally devastated. The *chinampas* had been ransacked during the siege by the city's starving inhabitants in their desperate search for anything edible. The Spaniards had torn down the houses to make the canals passable for

safety of their allies. With fresh soldiers and new artillery, that had arrived in the meantime from the coast, Cortéz spent months preparing for a great attack on Tenochtitlán. Using newly built boats and crossing the causeways, the Spaniards and their Indian auxiliaries managed to take the city after a 90-day siege.

The *tlatoani* Cuauhtémoc (1520–25), who had taken over command of the Aztec re-

Above, the stone "tzompantli" or skull scaffold from the days of human sacrifices. **Right**, snakes' heads on the Templo Mayor.

horses and artillery and the streets and waterways were filled with corpses. The stench was atrocious. After the evacuation of all survivors, Cortéz had the city torched and the once gleaming metropolis ended as a smoking pile of debris.

In 1522, one year later, Cortéz began to build what he called New Spain, the new capital of the future viceroyalty, on the ruins of the Aztec capital. New Spain had a population of only 30,000, and not until 1900 would it again have as many inhabitants as Greater Tenochtitlán at the time of *tlatoani* Montezuma.

The decision to establish the new Spanish capital on the ruins of the Aztec Tenochtitlán was a political as well as a symbolic act. Strategic, climatic and practical considerations played a decisive role in the siting of the city, as well as the availability of the necessary labor force and materials.

The Spanish Court received reports of the progress of colonization with great interest, particularly the sketch by Cortéz of the city as it was when conquered in 1520. It was made for Charles V and published in Nuremberg as a woodcut; in it Cortéz emphasized the square-sided structure of the temple precinct in the center, the residential quarters artfully divided by numerous canals and the bridges which joined dams to the mainland. This infrastructure of islands and bridges became the most important factor in the plan for the new city and it inspired the utopian fantasies of the Spanish.

Colonial chessboard: Work began in 1521 when Cortéz appointed Alonso Garcia Bravo to draw up the ground plan. The first city architect and the conqueror faced a difficult problem. They could draw on their experience in redesigning the Moorish cities of Spain, but the topographical characteristics of Mexico were infinitely more complicated. Neither Renaissance concepts of city planning, nor the styles developed by the conquistadors for their Caribbean cities could be applied except with difficulty. Accordingly, Mexico became the most important Spanish experiment in urban planning on the continent.

The Spanish liked the geometric layout of the Aztec ceremonial center and Garcia Bravo retained the ground plan of the main temple plaza for the new center as well as the north-south and east-west axes. In the resulting chessboard form, more space was earmarked for plazas. The streets mainly followed the pre-Spanish waterways, thereby preventing absolute regularity.

Left, Cortéz enters Tenochtitlán (detail of a painted screen from the colonial period).

The services of the conquistadors were rewarded with land and the interests of Church and Crown were taken into account when the city was divided. Since the new capital was to serve as a base for the consolidation of Spanish power in the New World, it had to be built as quickly as possible, or else the Spanish would miss the best opportunities. The ambitious plan for the new city, however, could only succeed if the subjugated Aztecs were made to work as labourers for the Spanish.

This was accomplished with massive force. The Franciscan Motolinia, who came to Mexico in 1524, compared the sight that greeted him to the construction of Solomon's temple. A "seventh plague" broke out among the subjugated Indians. In order to protect themselves and the Indians, the Crown ordered the separation of the Spanish city from the Indian districts. But that only worked for a short while, and then the Indian settlements and the Spanish areas were reintegrated again.

The new city rapidly grew to 100 blocks and it had to be broadened as early as 1527. Some useful elements of the pre-Spanish infrastructure were taken over by the Spaniards. For example, Cortéz had the water lines from Chaputepec repaired, and the city continued to be connected with its surrounding areas by canals and dams, based around four great canals from which dozens of others flowed in a co-ordinated system. The Canal de la Viga, paved over long ago, led past the west side of the National Palace to the city hall. It was used by the Indians to transport their goods to market and by the Spanish to ship building materials.

Center of power: The colonial Plaza Mayor (Zócalo) is the result of a long process of development. Cortéz, anxious to secure lasting influence, acquired two large plots of land. He had his residence, the Casas Viejas, built over the ruins of the Axayácatl palace on the south side of the Plaza. The Monte de Piedad, or National Pawnshop, was built on this site in the 18th century. On the north side of the Plaza, the former site of Montezuma's palace, the Casas Nuevas was erected.

Cortéz' desire for riches and power soon led to conflict with the Crown which wanted to assure its decision-making power in all important questions and Cortéz lost the governor's title in 1527. A five-man Audiencia assumed power until 1535 when Antonio de Mendoza was made the first viceroy. This made efficient administration and city planning possible.

To the chronicler Francesco Cervantes de Salazar the magnificent houses built by the Spanish in the city center seemed like fortresses, an impression which was created by the battlements on the towers and upper storeys which were reminiscent of the buildings of Extremadura, the homeland of many of the conquistadors. The arcaded buildings also resembled those found in Cáceres on mainland Spain. There were, in addition, some noticeable topographical innovations. De Salazar pointed out that the broad streets provided room for two coaches, a feature uncommon in Spanish urban planning.

The first cathedral, built in 1525, was a very small church. In 1552 Philip II ordered a new cathedral to be built that would express the significance and wealth of New Spain. It took the Spanish many many years just to build a solid foundation on the swampy ground. Claudio Arciniega of Burgos designed the layout for the five-naved basilican structure and work commenced in 1616.

The overall concept meets the requirements of a processional church with the outer naves housing numerous chapels, but during the cathedral's long process of construction there were many changes to the aesthetic detailing of the building. While some chapels have Gothic vaults, the vaults in the naves are in Renaissance style and the entrances to the transept have columns in the classical style of the 17th century. The main facade (1681) with its dominating twin spires (1788) is baroque in style and the dome over the transept was not completed until 1813.

The city administration was one of the metropolis' most important new institutions. The mayor held wide-ranging authority in disputes while the city councillors enjoyed a form of diplomatic immunity. The viceroy was not allowed to interfere in the internal affairs of the city. The permanent city hall was built in 1532, fundamentally renovated between 1692 and 1724 and rebuilt in 1948 in neo-colonial style.

The *portales*, arcades and colonnades, which provided protection from the sun and rain, were an important architectural element of the Plaza Mayor and beneath their shelter silk merchants conducted trade. At the same time, the *portales* gave the plaza a uniform character.

Only a representative seat of government was missing. In 1562, the Spanish king acquired the palace on the north side of the plaza from the Cortéz family and had it reconstructed at great expense in 1693. Its three portals served different functions. The law courts, prison, mint, revenue office, chapel and audience hall could be reached from the main courtyard. The apartments of the viceroy were in the courtyard to the left and opened into the garden. The palace was also planned with enough room to accommodate a complete garrison of soldiers. Here was the center of power, the focus of the political rituals by which the viceroy and president, after mass in the cathedral, demonstrated their supremacy in processions through the capital.

The plaza served as a festival stage for these occasions as well as for religious holidays. Along with its structural features, it was furnished with mock-facades of wood and cloth and decorated with carpets, flags, flowers and artful triumphal arches especially for the *fiestas reales*. Although it is empty today, during the colonial epoch the plaza was the belly of the city. In it was a permanent market hall for the sale of precious commodities, the *parián*. Next to it were the countless stands of the *tianguis*, the Indian market for fruit, vegetables and handicrafts.

The plaza was New Spain's most important commercial center. Here goods from Spain or from the Far East and the Philippines were traded. The abundance of products, many of them new to the Europeans, was constantly augmented by the cargo boats traveling between New Spain and

Manila in the Philippines. As a result of their control of this international trade the Mexican merchants became a respected and influential class in the 17th century.

City of cloisters: The new dioceses formed by the Spanish in the conquered territories further propagated the Catholic faith. In 1527, Mexico was designated an episcopal see. All the major religious orders established missionary activities in the metropolis and in the regions which were specifically allocated to each order. There were 41 cloisters in the capital as the colonial epoch came to an end. They each consisted of a church, an atrium, the cloister itself with its several

influence led to conflict with the secular powers, until in 1644, the city council petitioned King Philip IV to forbid the founding of further cloisters.

Whoever makes the effort to follow the cloisters' history is sure to discover some fascinating gems. The Franciscan cloister (1525) was among the largest of its day and covered an entire ward. A part of the two-storey court, dating from 1649, is still intact and has served as a Methodist church since 1873. The Church of San Francisco (1716) has also survived.

The San Jerónimo cloister was founded in 1585 and its church was consecrated in 1623.

courtyards, living quarters, study rooms, offices, workshops, schools, dispensaries and gardens.

Together these formed complex islands of spiritual life, because each cloister exerted a tremendous influence on its surrounding neighborhood. The wealth of the Church was based on its earnings from tithes and charitable foundations and was invested in real estate; in addition the clergy had a thriving banking business. This enormous

Above, at the beginning of the 18th century Mexico City was still surrounded by its lake.

It was here that the religious poetess Sor Juana Inés de la Cruz worked. The Claustro La Merced, whose court is ornamented with simple pillars, makes an elegant picture. The rich botanical ornamentation creates a vivid three-dimensional effect – a vibrant play of light and shadow.

Mexican cloister architecture produced a number of innovations such as the twin portals that were developed for the church of La Concepción in 1655, designed to cope with enormous crowds of the faithful during processions. The church was built as part of the oldest nunnery in Mexico, which was founded by the first archbishop Juan de Zumárraga (1540), a student of Erasmus.

Soon the twin portal motif was further developed in more elaborate versions at the Church of Santa Teresa la Antigua (1678–84) and San Agustín (1691). Here, we find the twisted "Solomon" columns, made famous by the Italian architect Bernini in the first third of the 17th century.

Building fever of the baroque: In the course of the 16th century, Mexico became the capital of an enormous land area and by the middle of the 17th century, a real building boom took hold of the city. Trade, the prosperous mining industry, and successful ag-

The staggering of the *estípites*, pilasters tapering toward the base to resemble an inverted pyramid, creates an impressive spacial effect. One finds similar *estípites* especially on palaces and churches. The Churrigueresco-style facades, for example at La Santissima (1783), add a dramatic touch to the urban landscape.

The facade of the three-nave Jesuit church of San Felipe Neri (1751) is very impressive even though a mere fragment its former glory. After the order's expulsion, the church served as a theater, and today it is a library. The church of the Regina Coeli also conveys the range of expression achieved by

riculture and livestock farming formed the basis of an economic and cultural golden age. This wealth was reflected in the overwhelming demand for decorative ornaments with which to display the owner's prosperity. The metropolis played a key role in the propagation of the Churrigueresco style, a variation of Spanish high baroque.

With its tendency toward luxurious, ostentatious decoration, Churrigueresco became the preferred style for stately buildings. A pioneer work is architect Lorenzo Rodríguez's sacramental church, the Sagrario, next to the cathedral (1749–60).

the Churrigueresco. New spacial conceptions emerged, such as those exemplified in the churches of El Pocito and Nuestra Señora de la Enseñanza. Regina Coeli's narrow facade (1772–78), flanked by two former religious seminaries (1754), conceals a treasure: the bright, dome-ceilinged space has an octagonal, practically an oval, layout. Despite its small dimensions, the architecture, sculpture, painting, light, and color combine to produce a baroque masterpiece of the highest order.

Life in the palaces: The viceregal elite was concentrated in the metropolis. The nobility of the 18th century formed a plutocracy and much-desired titles were expensive. Access to the select circle of the oligarchy, as well as the pleasure of a title, cost a fortune. The Crown earned extra money from this system, but it led to a sharpening of social contradictions. Nonetheless, it also favored the arts.

The aristocracy also had to pay high taxes. Charitable foundations and the support of church construction were *de rigueur*. Building a palace was one way of securing a part of one's personal wealth for the family's benefit; its furnishings and size were matters of prestige and a testimony to the social rank and business success of the owner. Such

houses were naturally very expensive to maintain and an aristocratic household usually employed between 10 and 20 servants.

Sites along the route which the viceroy used for his procession into the city were favored by the aristocrats. For this reason, a whole series of elegant palaces were built on the Calle de San Francisco (today Madero). For example the Palacio de Iturbide, an 18th-century masterpiece designed by Francisco

Left, colonial patios form tranquil oases (Museo Franz Mayer). Above, Mexican baroque in the facade of the church of Santa Veracruz.

Guerrero y Torres, was the residence of the family of Juan de la Moncada, Count of Jaral de Berrio. The facade is covered with medallions with pastoral iconography and furnished with rich ornaments and figures of Hercules. Balconies and an arcaded upper storey flanked by two turrets emphasize the owner's importance. The courtyard itself, following an Italian motif, is framed by elegant columns.

The Casa de los Azulejos, built as a residence for the Count of Tales de Orizaba at Ares Madero and Lazaro Cárdenas is decorated in the Pobla tradition with *azulejos* or colored tiles on the outer walls. The courtyard with its stone pillars has survived and is now Sanborn's Restaurant.

Buildings of more modest dimensions were by no means less extravagantly designed. The house of Don Hernando de Avila and Doña Gerónima de Sandoval, dating from the second half of the 18th century, is remarkable for its harmonious proportions. The interior is embellished with *azulejo* ornaments depicting a cycle of popular characters of the period, preserving a picture of what everyday life in the colony. The baroque buildings of religious, public, and private institutions were also characterized by palace-like edifices. For example the complex of the Colegio de las Vizcaínas in Coyoacán, a girls' school founded in 1734, filled a whole block and features more than seven courtyards.

Patios, streets, and plazas: In the 19th century, the Englishman Latrobe raved over the "city of palaces", an impression which was based on the uniformity of the colonial ensemble. The basic elements of the palace are still to be found in miniature in the bourgeois patio house which has proven its suitability to the climate of the Mexico valley. The patio house, in turn, served as the model for the aristocratic versions. Through the use of similar materials, lattices, ornaments and proportions, a townscape developed in which each element corresponded with the others surrounding it.

Many streets do not intersect at right angles. Slight bends and curves, according to the terrain, lead to amazing views. Entrances, windows, cornices and recesses on the facades echo each other down the streets. These architectural characteristics, developed over centuries, were never abandoned, only modified in the 19th century. It was progress-obsessed Modernism which finally posed the first real threat but today Mexico's colonial heritage and architecture is recognized as a part of the country's modern cultural identity.

In the old city there are still charming colonial streets such as the Calle Moneda. In the enclaves of Coyoacán and San Angel, complete ensembles have survived – reminiscent of an epoch of amazing beauty, now long gone. The Irishman Thomas Gage

summed up the impressions of his contemporaries when, in 1625, he called Mexico the "Venice of the Americas". The waterways which divide so many streets, the effect of their reflections, the changing perspectives offered from the boats, they all shaped the way the city presented itself to those early visitors. As in Venice, for a long time the canals formed the most important transport arteries, but they were gradually displaced as the city grew. Land reclamation has altered the natural environment with enormous consequences, destroying the island character as well as the lake landscape.

In the colonial city the road network was interconnected through 78 plazas, most of which had some commemorative purpose. With their various functions, these plazas were a mirror of urban life. Among them were smaller plazas, such as the Plaza de Santa Catalina with its church of the same name (1740) which was originally a hospital founded in 1537.

The impressive Plaza de Santo Domingo, two blocks north of the cathedral, was built on the site of the Dominican cloister founded in 1537 and assumed its present form in 1628. The baroque facade and bell tower of the church of Santo Domingo (1716–36) dominates the plaza.

The former palace of the Inquisition (1736), now the School of Medicine, on the same square is reminiscent of the character of this influential colonial institution. The Inquisition was formally introduced in 1571 in order to defend the faith and morals of the Spanish, but the Indians were exempted from its jurisdiction. The Alameda Park and a small plaza near the cathedral served as execution sites.

Alameda Park, one of the most important urban projects of the baroque era, was laid out when it became clear that the city was going to outgrow its old boundaries. Expanded in 1717 and completed with diagonal paths, it has been complemented with monuments and sculptures right up to the present. The Alameda, with its fountains and *portales*, was an important crystallization point for city life, a favorite place for meeting and relaxation. It also marked a counterpoint to the Zócalo and became a new axis of expansion. Soon new neighborhoods sprang up around the park, as did the Plaza de la Santa Veracruz. This small space, opening onto the Alameda, grew out of a simple but effectively realized idea, namely the combination of the forecourts between the churches of Santa Veracruz and San Juan de Dios. From the steps of the church of San Juan de Díos (1764), whose niche facade with triumphant images resembles an altar piece moved outdoors, the double-towered facade of the church of Santa Veracruz (1765–76) fills the view.

From baroque to classicism: The last phase

of colonial culture was shaped by the Bourbon reforms which were intended to reorganize the administration and economy to the Crown's advantage. New institutions were founded in the spirit of the Enlightenment, among them the Academy of San Carlos, started in 1785 whose master craftsmen were oriented toward classical ideals. The Academy's royal charter practically guaranteed a monopoly role in controlling building activity in the colony.

As director of the architecture division, the Valencian Manuel Tolsá was responsible for setting the tone for the first generation of young artists. The Palacio de Minería

gether had extracted silver and gold then worth more than US$650 million in the previous two and a half centuries.

Another great project, the tobacco factory Real Fábrica de Tabacos, a textbook example of early industrial architecture erected between 1792 and 1807, was in line with Bourbon financial policies. Its significance lay in its functional character, generous lighting and ventilation and new stylistic expression together with a clear division of the interior spaces. These new constructions, as well as the growing destruction of the baroque buildings, were symptomatic of a shift in the dominant taste.

(1797–1813) on Calle Tacuba, the first mining school in the Americas, was built under his supervision. It was a palace-like building with a monumental courtyard lined with pairs of classical pillars, a chapel, staircase, lecture hall and adjoining courtyards. When Alexander von Humboldt, the renowned Prussian scientist and explorer, visited in 1803 he estimated that there were then about 3,000 mines in the viceroyalty which to-

While in 1803 Alexander von Humboldt compared Mexico City with Berlin and St Petersburg, the signs of decadence in some precincts were unmistakable. It was mainly the city center which benefitted from improved infrastructure with lighting, road-paving and urban planning measures. In 1803, the Plaza Mayor acquired a new focal point with the erection of Manuel Tolsás' equestrian statue of Charles IV. Although it praised the new enlightened monarch depicted in classical garb, the Bourbon reforms could not stop the crisis which would lead to Mexico's political independence.

Left, Royal fiesta in Chapultepec (18th century). **Above**, *San Rafael and Tobias* by Miguel Cabrera and painted tile from the Casa Sandoval.

In the 18th century Mexico made enormous economic progress, a development which above all benefitted the *gachupines*, members of the colonial administration sent from Spain, and the increasingly wealthy *creollos*. The latter, the Mexican descendants of Spaniards, saw themselves as being more and more restricted by Spain. Through economic and political restrictions, Madrid held the country on a tight rein. The higher posts in the administration, the military, and in the Church were reserved for the *gachupines*, while the *creollos* were represented only in the city councils. Needless to say, the Indians and landless peasants had no political voice whatsoever.

Exports and imports were subject to state monopolies and industrial goods had to be imported from Spain. The development of a national industry was almost completely obstructed and only in the large cities were there wool and cotton industries.

Spain's pains: It was under these conditions that events in mainland Spain provoked the revolt of 1810 which brought with it an 11-year war of independence and 600,000 dead. After Spain's defeat by the British at the battle of Trafalgar, the decadent Charles IV of Spain was unable to bring his heavily indebted country out of a recession.

His wife's favorite, Manuel Godoy, opened Spain to Napoleon, who marched in and occupied the country, interned the king's son Ferdinand and put his brother Joseph on the Spanish throne. In the eyes of the *creollos* in Mexico, this usurpation threw the Crown's legitimacy as their colonial ruler into question.

The *creollo*-dominated city councils of Mexico City forced the viceroy Iturrigaray to summon a municipal assembly which was to obey only the orders of the imprisoned Ferdinand. Naturally the Audiencia (the highest Spanish authority in the colony) felt its power threatened. The viceroy was quickly dismissed, but this only served to infuriate a small group of *mestizos* and whites who were followers of the ideals of the French Revolution and the American War of Independence.

Captain Ignacio Allende from San Miguel planned the first conspiracy against colonial government and won the support of Father Miguel Hidalgo, the parish priest of the poor village of Dolores. Since his transfer to this primarily Indian parish, Hidalgo had developed a rather unusual understanding of his pastoral duties: he dedicated himself almost exclusively to the practical instruction of his flock and taught them nearly everything which was forbidden under Spanish law – wine and olive farming, leather-tanning and weaving. He had nothing but contempt for the *gachupines* who drained the land of everything and for whom the fate of the Indians and peasants was irrelevant.

On the evening of September 16, 1810, Hidalgo stirred up the peasants and Indians assembled in his church with the words "Viva Mexico! Long live Our Lady of Guadalupe! Down with the terrible government! Death to the *gachupines*!" and bid them to follow him. Even today on Independence Day one hears the "Cry of Dolores" – although today's version does not include an incitement to bring down the government! – from the balcony of the government palace in the capital and from numerous city halls in the provinces.

The army of the *insurgentes*, which was made up of peasants and barefooted Indians, scored amazing victories. In rapid succession, they seized San Miguel, Celaya and Valladolid (Morélia). Hidalgo proclaimed a new constitution that provided for the redistribution of land and the abolition of castes and privileges. As he began his march on Mexico City, he already had 80,000 men following him.

However, the viceroy gathered his troops north of the city and forced Hidalgo to retreat. The priest retaliated, took Spanish pris-

Preceding pages: the Independence, from a mural by Juan O'Gorman. **Left,** the Palacio de Iturbide (engraving by C. Castro, 1874).

oners and put them to death, but then was captured and executed himself. The revolt was suppressed, but in 1813, one of Hidalgo's students, Father Morelos, summoned a national assembly which proclaimed Mexico's independence. The new constitution called for the expropriation of the *latifundia* (aristocratic estates), the abolition of Church tithes, universal equality, and the dissolution of the state monopolies. The Spanish were to leave the country for good. The *creollos*, the descendants of Spaniards, however, refused to support this plan since the aim of the revolutionaries – a fundamental agrarian reform – far exceeded

this plan failed, they decided their only hope lay in separation from the motherland.

In order to achieve independence they needed a strong leader, which they found in the man who was supposed to lead the southern army against the last remaining guerilla troops – the creole General Augustín Iturbide. He was able to win the rebels over.

On February 24, 1821, the Iguala Plan was announced: Mexico was declared independent; Spaniards and *creollos* were granted the same rights; Roman Catholicism was made the state religion and the new state was to be a constitutional monarchy. The proclamation was nowhere near what Hidalgo and

their own wishes and their own interests.

Independence: Morelos was shot dead in 1815, but things were changing in Spain. Upon Ferdinand's release from prison and restoration to the Spanish throne, the central junta in Cadiz, which had agreed a new revolutionary liberal constitution, threatened a military revolt if the king did not accede to their wishes.

In Mexico, the *creollos* now feared they would lose their privileges over the *mestizos*. They allied themselves with the Spanish upper classes and encouraged the viceroy to ignore the new liberal constitution; when

Morelos had advocated. A conservative alliance, which included the Catholic Church, had pushed itself into the forefront of the independence movement.

But when one province after another, as well as the majority of the Spanish officers, announced their support for the plan, the new viceroy O'Donojú saw no way out. On his way to Mexico City from Veracruz, he met Iturbide. The upshot of their meeting was that he was given a seat in the ruling junta and in turn ordered the Spanish troops to leave the capital. Shortly afterwards the treaty of Córdoba/Mexico was signed, but mainland

Spain did not officially recognize Mexico as independent until as late as 1836.

Soon the flags of the *Trigarantes*, the symbol of independence, religion, and equality, were flying everywhere. On September 27, 1821, Iturbide rode into the capital at the head of his army. O'Donojú received him in the viceroy's palace and the archbishop honored him with a *Te Deum* celebrated in the cathedral. The next day a regency council was formed and the colony of New Spain had ceased to exist.

The young nation: Immediately conflict broke out within the coalition over whether the new state should be central or federal in

Iturbide was only to enjoy being emperor for 10 months before falling victim to a revolt.

Many of the former rebels, disenchanted with Iturbide, joined the republican captain Santa Anna. Eventually the latter had so many followers that Iturbide voluntarily relinquished the throne and retired to exile in Europe with a fat pension, allowing Santa Anna's rebel army to march into the capital without meeting any resistance.

This time the deputies did not compromise, but adopted a constitution along the lines of their North American neighbor in which every prerogative of birth and property was abolished and all citizens were

form. The Congress itself could not agree on a head of state until a cry from the ranks of the Iturbide supporters broke out "Long live Augustín I, Emperor of Mexico!" The capital was suddenly full of frantic activity. A throne was erected; flags were hung from the church steeples, and peasants filled the streets. A spectacle was prepared the likes of which the inhabitants had never seen, to celebrate the new monarch. In the event

declared fundamentally equal. The remains of Hidalgo and Morelos were brought to the capital and were honored as the founders of the independence movement. Guadalupe Victoria was declared the first president of the new republic. The last Spaniard embarked at Veracruz for Spain in 1825.

Proud city: At the time when the republic was proclaimed, the city was the center of culture and administration, and whoever approached it for the first time saw it as if it were surrounded by a mystical aura.

The city boasted 60 churches. From the Chapultepec hill one could see the surround-

Left, Emperor Augustín (artist unknown) and Emperor Maximilian (bronze by Felipe Sojo). <u>Above</u>, by the Salto del Agua fountain (C. Castro).

ing villages which supplied the city with fruit, vegetables, laborers and domestic servants. Five *calzadas* (avenues) led across the lakes into the city center. Next to the Paseo de las Vigas ran a canal along which Indian canoes brought goods from throughout the vicinity directly to the Zócalo. Here, next to offices and vendors' stands, were the presidential residence, the Senate and the House of Representatives. In the cathedral, Mass was celebrated every half hour. The city hall stood on the south side of the Zócalo and the great trading houses on the west side. The finest homes were to be found in the Traza, the Spaniards' enclave to the south

and southwest of the central Zócalo.

Water was brought to the city's residents in huge clay containers. Twenty-nine public and 505 private fountains were fed through a conduit system. On feast days and holidays, municipal employees and water sellers worked together to obstruct the water supply in order to push the price up.

Waste water drained into sewers which led through the middle of the city into Lake Texcoco. There was no escape from these overflowing sewers when the heavy rains came. The overflow was the result of years of neglect, since no money had been invested in

the sewer system since the beginning of the century and, in the eastern quarters of the city, the water often rose knee-high. Wherever the streets were too narrow for wagons, porters had to carry the heavy loads out to the merchants. In these streets robbery and assault were a daily affair and whoever went out at night did so armed – not only against men but against the many stray dogs.

The dictator Santa Anna: But despite its supposed integrity the new constitution was for the most part a mere facade. The colonial political and economic structures remained essentially intact, along with the domestic difficulties which had preceded independence. The Indios were again the victims and were often forced to leave their communal lands on account of enormous accumulated debt. The central government in Mexico City was too weak, and numerous conflicts and power struggles continued among the people of the provinces. The few laws which had been passed in the capital to protect the Indios were also as a rule ignored. Mexico came under more and more pressure from foreign creditors who, on account of the country's enormous debts, attempted to interfere in its internal affairs.

In the first 30 years of the young republic, 50 different governments occupied the Palacio Nacional, of which 11 were led by Santa Anna. Despite his dictatorial manner, the Congress elected him time and again as the head of state. Many construction projects in the capital had their roots in Santa Anna's vanity: the Gran Teatro de Santa Anna, a new market, and the paving of the streets. The year 1842 marked the pinnacle of his dictatorship – the capital was wrapped in constant celebrations: Santa Anna's birthday, Independence Day, parades, pompous Mass in the cathedral. His Majesty had to be entertained. All of this cost money which the dictator raised with a 20 percent import duty and "voluntary" contributions from the capital's residents. Understandably this extravagance made him increasingly hated among the population, until finally his short-sighted policies in the conflict over Texas led to his downfall.

Loss of territory: The Anglo-Saxon settlers of Texas, until then a part of Mexico, were in no way prepared to pay the taxes demanded by Santa Anna. Instead, they declared their state a free republic. In response, Santa Anna personally led a 6,000-man army against the rebels in Texas. His soldiers brutally slaughtered hundreds of settlers at the mission station of El Alamo, providing the US with the opportunity and justification of attacking and defeating Santa Anna's forces. To save his life, the dictator was forced to recognize Texan independence. He returned humiliated to Veracruz where he then abdicated.

The North American Congress subsequently annexed Texas provoking the Mexican generals to declare war once again. The lives resisting the invading Yankees. For a mere 15 million dollars, the Mexican government was forced to cede Texas, California, Arizona and New Mexico to the US. The whole nation had been humiliated, producing a "Yankeephobia" or hatred of the Americans, traces of which remain in the Mexican outlook to this day.

Meanwhile intolerable economic and political conditions led to a sharpening of the conflicts between the Liberals (the leaders of the middle class with their preference for an North American constitutional system) and the Conservatives, who represented the *latifundia* (estate owners) and who were

Americans were only too happy as it gave them the chance to seize other northern provinces from Mexico, which they did with ease. In February 1847, General Winfield Scott grouped his troops ready to storm the Mexican capital. By September of the same year, the American flag flew over the National Palace. At the foot of the Chapultepec hill stands a monument to the Niños Héros, the young military cadets who gave their

Left, Lizard's realistic portrait of Benito Juárez. **Above**, the puppet regime of the long-time dictator General Porfirio Díaz.

supported by the Roman Catholic and military hierarchies, who wanted a European-supported dictatorship. Again the command was given over to Santa Anna who proceeded to suppress the Liberals. The result was a revolt in 1855 which finally forced Santa Anna out of power permanently.

The Juárez Reforms: Comonfort became President and an Indian attorney from Oaxaca, Benito Juárez, Vice President. In 1861, the latter became President and soon enacted the so-called Reform Laws, the central effect of which was to neutralize the clergy. The property of the Church was expropriated and the legal and education systems were secularized.

However, the years of war and internal turmoil had left the country so deeply in debt that Juárez had no choice but to suspend payments to Mexico's creditors. Using this as an excuse, Spain, France, and Great Britain seized the chance to come to the aid of the Conservatives. They landed at Veracruz on the pretense of forcibly collecting the money from the Mexican government and with grandiose designs of helping the "regeneration of Mexico".

After friction developed between the trio of invaders, Britain and Spain quickly with-

drew, but Napoleon III took advantage of the invasion to extend his dominion in the New World. The French army was eventually defeated near Puebla on May 5, 1862. Nonetheless, they were able to occupy the capital for a short time through the massive support of the Conservatives.

Imperial intermezzo: The National Assembly set up by the French offered the Mexican crown to Maximilian von Habsburg, the brother of the Austrian emperor. Shortly afterward he and his wife, Archduchess Charlotte, arrived in Mexico and took up residence in the Chapultepec Palace where they were to live most of the time. Maximilian and "Carlota" were very much impressed by Mexico, spoke Spanish whenever possible and frequently traveled through the provinces. They were also great patrons of literature, the arts and sciences. The emperor, however, followed a liberal line in politics and since he refused to restore the Church to its property, he lost the support of the Conservatives.

In the meantime, the North American Civil War had come to an end enabling the US Federal government to return its attention to Latin America. In pursuance of the Monroe Doctrine, the US placed its backing behind the Liberals in order to force the French to withdraw.

It wasn't hard to get rid of them. Napoleon had not only lost interest in the devastated country, he also needed his valuable troops more urgently for the war against Prussia. Maximilian, whose intentions were apparently honorable and who had been misinformed about his approval by the Mexican people, wanted to abdicate but, according to legend, hesitated at the insistence of his mother who declared "We Habsburgs never abdicate!" On June 19, 1867, the unfortunate emperor was set before a firing squad. It was Benito Juárez, having resumed the Presidency, who actually gave the emperor's execution order.

For a further decade calm prevailed in the republic although continuing economic problems left the government too weak to exercise much power outside the capital. Juárez reformed the education system and had the railway line to Veracruz completed. Surprisingly he also privatized the Indian communal lands, with the result that they fell into the hands of the *latifundia*, the former estate owners. The Indians were again forced to sell themselves into semi-slavery.

Juárez defeated his opponent Porfirio Díaz a second time in the 1871 national elections, only to die a year later of a heart attack, and to be succeeded by Sebastian Lerdo de Tejada.

Left, Don Porfirio, portrait by G. Morales. Right, the elegance of the turn-of-the-century Palacio de Comunicaciones, built as a ministry.

Don Porfirio had every reason to be proud as he solemnly dedicated the "Angel", the monument on the Paseo de la Reforma, to the memory of liberty. It was exactly 100 years since Father Hidalgo had called on his compatriots to take up the struggle against the Spanish on September 16, 1810. The dictator Porfirio Díaz had invited the whole world to Mexico City as guests for the pompous centenary celebrations which were being held in honor of Mexican independence.

There was reason enough to celebrate. Díaz had himself just been elected head of state for the seventh time and he had just reached his 80th birthday. For more than 30 years, all but for one brief break in 1880–1884, he had held Mexico in his iron grip. Since coming to power in 1876, he had fought relentlessly for the maintenance of order after decades of chaos. Through the centenary celebrations of 1910 he managed to present his epoch, the Porfiriat, as a series of economic successes to the world at large.

Decline of the Porfiriat: Díaz had expanded the railway network to over 20,000 km (12,500 miles). He had brought foreign capital into the country. The oil and mining industries were flourishing. The enormous *haciendas* were producing fabulous surpluses. The export balance looked splendid. Eighty percent of the exports went to the US, to which the regime was so closely tied that Diaz was said to have uttered the classic sigh "Poor Mexico, so far from God and so near to the USA". None of the foreign guests for the celebrations of 1910 could imagine that within a few months, Mexico, the "paradise of progress" would mourn nearly a million victims in the first great social revolution of the 20th century.

Certainly the Porfiriat was heading for trouble. The price which had been paid by Mexico's 15 million people for the ambitious policies of the career president was too high. After the turn of the century, inflation rose, prices increased rapidly, illegal strikes paralyzed mines and industry. Riots resulting from the social tensions were bloodily suppressed by the dictator. Even the bourgeoisie began to grumble.

Díaz had surrounded himself with a geriatric clique of advisors, the *Cientificos*. "Much administration, little politics" had been their motto. Foreign capital and a few Mexican career bureaucrats were the real beneficiaries of the ossified and corrupt adminstration. In 1910, one percent of the Mexican population owned 90 percent of the land while 97 percent of the peasants owned no land whatever. Their communal lands, the *ejidos*, had been lost to the *latifundia* which had swollen to take over the traditional village commons. The peasants were reduced to serfs, slaving on plantations for subsistence wages.

The Madero revolt: By 1908, the stubborn potentate Díaz had accelerated his own end. In a famous interview with an American journalist, John Creelmann, he declared that he would welcome an opposition candidate in the coming elections. Francisco Madero, a landowner from the state of Coahuila, took him at his word with the motto "No re-election". His quickly organized Partido Anti-Reeleccionista enjoyed astounding success in 1910. Díaz showed that he had not been so earnest about having serious opposition. Shortly before the election he had Madero arrested, and the ballot was rigged.

Madero escaped from prison and sought exile in Texas. There he proclaimed the Plan de San Luis Potosi, in which he called for armed struggle against the dictator. After initial failures, in February 1911, the Madero revolt gained ground. The peasant leader, Emiliano Zapata, joined the revolution along with the charismatic bandit leader from Chihuahua, "Pancho" Francisco Villa. By April,

into the capital, accompanied by his victorious revolutionaries. On the same morning the city was shaken by an intense earthquake – a bad omen.

Out of the frying pan: Now it was Madero's turn. He discharged his revolutionaries. For him, the struggle was won with his election to the presidency. He planned to build a new Mexico through the implementation of far-reaching reforms. But Zapata refused to cease fighting as long as the estates of the *latifundia* were not radically redistributed. In his opinion Madero was too hesitant, an enemy of the revolution. Zapata proposed in his Plan de Ayala the partial breakup of the

18 Mexican states had rebelled against the decaying Porfiriat. The army leaders, Orozco, Villa and Obregón defeated the governments' troops (Federales) in the north. Zapata advanced on the capital from the south. The border city of Juarez and the railway junction at Torreon were captured. In May 1911, Díaz gave up. In the ensuing confusion he resigned and fled to Paris. On June 7, 1911, Madero marched triumphantly

Left, Francisco Madero started the Revolution. **Above**, Revolution is the subject of many murals, including this one in the castle of Chapultepec.

haciendas and the return of all communal lands to the villages. Madero rejected such ideas; as the "apostle of democracy" he shied away from dictatorship and radicalism. He hoped that the "Mexicans would use their newly won liberty within a responsible democracy". He hoped in vain.

The big landowners and conservatives in his cabinet felt threatened by the liberal reforms and it was only with great effort that Madero was able to quash the revolt led by Orozco, Villa and Obregón in Chihuahua. Mexico was seething with dissatisfaction.

The US began to fear for its enormous

investments in Mexico. The US ambassador, Henry Lane Wilson, openly declared the idealistic Madero a dangerous dreamer. Uncertainty grew. The threatening clouds of an imminent civil war gathered over Mexico City. Then, in February, 1913, came what was to be called the "ten days of tragedy".

On February 9, Don Porfirio's nephew, the arch-conservative Félix Díaz, staged a coup. Madero and his cabinet entrenched themselves in the National Palace, surrounded by intense fighting. Madero gave the responsibility for the defense of his government to his Interior Minister, General Victoriano ("the Jackal") Huerta. The rebels

the residence of Ambassador Wilson, who had orchestrated the collaboration – Huerta was to take over. On February 22, 1913, Madero and Pino Suárez were clandestinely led out of the palace, and were later found lying shot dead against a prison wall.

To the relief of the conservatives, Victoriano Huerta now took over the presidency. His dictatorship proved to be one of unprecedented horror. Terror reigned in the cities and the country as a whole. All reforms were made null and void and the status quo of an earlier era was restored. In the north, a follower of the murdered Madero, the Governor of Coahuilas, Venustiano Carranza,

had meanwhile occupied the Citadel (Ciudadela), and were well equipped for a long battle. The struggle in the streets of Mexico City lasted for days, during which hundreds were killed.

Treacherous pact: The US Ambassador Henry Lane Wilson supported Díaz and his fellow plotters but also made contact with General Huerta. On February 18, the National Palace fell into the hands of the rebels as a result of Huerta's betrayal. Madero and his vice president, Pino Suárez, were arrested. That same evening, Félix Díaz and Huerta concluded their treacherous pact in

rose up against the new dictator and tyrant. As commander-in-chief of the newly mobilized revolutionary troops, Carranza challenged Huerta's claim to the presidency. On March 26, 1913 his Plan of Guadalupe proclaimed a national uprising and demanded re-establishment of the 1857 Constitution. At the same time, US President Woodrow Wilson occupied Veracruz under a flimsy pretense and refused to recognize the Huerta regime. In the south, Zapata led a guerrilla war while in the north Generals Villa and Obregón again took up the fight – this time against Huerta. In fierce battles with tens of thousands of soldiers, cavalry and heavy artillery, Torreón, Chihuahua, Ciudad Juárez and other cities were captured.

For Pancho Villa, it proved to be his most successful year. However, the obstinate leader fell out with his *Jefe* (chief) Carranza on account of insubordination during his glorious conquest of Zacatecas. The defeated "Jackal" Huerta resigned on June 17, 1914 and fled to Texas. The victorious leader of the revolution, Carranza, marched into Mexico City. Despite not being officially president, he managed to persuade the US to make a discreet withdrawal from Veracruz.

Revolutionary chaos: At this point Pancho Villa began to cause problems. The eccentric and unpredictable popular hero resisted Carranza. He, with the support of Zapata and other generals who were disappointed in Carranza, began to take revolutionary matters into their own hands. A conference in the town of Aguacalientes was intended to reconcile the quarreling revolutionary leaders, but the result was further strife. The radicals around Zapata and Villa opposed the more moderate generals grouped around Carranza, and the revolutionary movement was split with the various factions fighting against each other. Ultimately Mexico sank into anarchy.

As the advancing armies of the Villa-Zapata alliance approached Mexico City, Carranza evacuated the presidential palace and moved the government to Veracruz. The alliance quickly appointed their own president, the bland Gutiérrez and, at the beginning of December 1914, marched with thousands of troops into the devastated capital. The inhabitants of Mexico City, then around half a million, trembled before the hordes of revolutionaries. Initially, it was possible to keep the wild boys in line. In the capital's famous "House of Tiles," at that time already Sanborn's Restaurant, it was possible to photograph the Zapatistas displaying impeccable table manners, but Villa was less predictable. A hero of the masses due to his charisma and military prowess his deeds were already almost mythical.

It was at that point that Zapata and Villa met for the first time. They concluded a mutual assistance pact which had no practical results. After the withdrawal of the alliance in January 1915, Obregón marched into the city with his army. Mexico City was terrorized by plundering, raping, and murderous soldiers, on top of which food became scarce and epidemics broke out.

Fight for the north: After some months, Obregón finally left the shaken capital. He set out for the north after Pancho Villa with fresh troops and reinforcements from the "Red Workers Battalions". In the north, Pancho Villa, the Governor of Chihuahua, was at the height of his popularity, ruling like a feudal prince. Even today he is regarded as the prototype of the North Mexican, the *Norteño*, without old Indian traditions; a daredevil and adventurer, who cared little for the ideological delicacies of quibbling revolutionary theorists, at the head of his *División del Norte*.

It is no coincidence that most of the leading revolutionary figures except Zapata – Calles, Orozco, Madero, Carranza, Obregón and Pancho Villa – came from the north. Zapata respected the interests of the US, which was, after all, his neighbor, but beyond that the "Centaur of the North" feared nothing and no one.

Obregón was to teach him that fear. He knew that he who controlled the north, controlled the country. Clandestinely, the US channelled weapons across the border. Only with the railways could the convoys of men, material and horses get through. Torreón, Ciudad Juárez and Chihuahua were cities of decisive strategic importance.

Obregón commanded 11,000 soldiers. Villa, with his *División del Norte* and his *Dorados* had 20,000, but numerical superiority didn't help him. Obregón was the better strategist and Villa was repeatedly routed. In the Battle of Celaya, the famous Villista cavalry was mowed down by Carranzista machine gun fire. In the end, General Villa was left with only 3,000 *Dorados*.

Carranza exulted in his triumph and reestablished his government in Mexico City. Washington, which had shortly before honored Pancho Villa as the "greatest Mexican of the century", abandoned him perfunctorily and immediately recognized the Carranza regime. The fallen hero, embittered over his betrayal by the treacherous *gringos*, sought revenge.

Carranza government: No sooner was Villa defeated in 1916 than the Carranzistas marched with 30,000 soldiers against Zapata's revolutionaries who had been enjoying a certain period of peace because Obregón needed all his strength to combat Villa. After the *hacienda* owners had been executed or driven away, Zapata had actually implemented his land redistribution program. But that was over now. Carranza's

seek out Villa who cunningly managed to elude them for 10 months, all the while stirring up anti-American feeling. The outbreak of World War I forced the Americans to withdraw Pershing's expeditionary force which had accomplished nothing.

Carranza, the moderate reformer, now had the country more or less under his control. On February 5, 1917, his government adopted the new Mexican Constitution. It improved the situation of the workers, reformed the education system and introduced a truly revolutionary land reform. Officially, this constitution re-established order in Mexico. But Zapata was not satisfied that the

troops brought Cuernavaca and a large part of the state under their control, forcing Zapata's armed peasants to go underground. Then, in March 1916, the avenging Villa struck again. He and his *Dorados* torched the US border town of Columbus, causing hundreds of casualties.

By burning Columbus Villa had hoped to provoke the Americans into invading Mexico and overthrowing Carranza, but the invasion did not materialize. Instead Washington, with the consent of the Mexican government, sent a punitive expedition under General John "Black Jack" Pershing to

reforms had gone far enough and continued to fight. In Chihuahua, the eccentric Pancho Villa also continued the war against the legal government of Carranza.

In 1917, Mexico found itself in a desperate state. Foreign investors, occupied with the war, hesitated to invest in Europe, put off by the socialist constitution. Carranza, who had in the meantime been elected president, rapidly lost popularity because of the economic crisis. Strikes and workers' uprisings increased the enormous pressure on him.

The Revolution devours its own children: Carranzista officers assassinated Zapata in

April 1919. But Carranza's time was also running out. When it became clear that he had no intention of retiring at the end of his term in 1920, his former supporter, General Obregón, reacted immediately. In Sonora, to which Obregón had retired, he organized a new fighting force with the support of the labor movement and marched against Carranza. The president fled from Mexico City by rail, heading toward Veracruz. Because the convoy was blocked, the fleeing party continued on horseback. On May 21, 1920, during a night attack in the mountains, Venustiano Carranza was shot dead and Alvaro Obregón became the new president.

sination which was believed to have been instigated by Obregón. In 1928, Alvaro Obregón was himself murdered in Mexico City's "La Bombilla" restaurant.

No event in this century has so influenced the identity of Mexico as has the Revolution, which still prompts plenty of argument. Some still dispute whether the end of the Revolution was marked by the 1917 Constitution, the presidency of Obregón or whether, in fact, it has not continued on right up to this day.

The great deeds of the heroes and the evils of the traitors survive in the *corridos*, the ballads of the revolutionary troubadours

Obregón himself had to contend with numerous coup attempts and unrest as did his successor, Calles, but the era of the guerrilla and of great battles was finally over. The constitution was no longer threatened. Under Obregón, a moneyed elite emerged, consisting of all-powerful, highly unrevolutionary politicians – the so-called *politicos*. In 1920, Pancho Villa also surrendered his weapons. In 1923, he fell victim to an assas-

(Zapata had several of these extemporisers among his followers). The anthem of Pancho Villa's powerful *División del Norte* was *La Cucaracha*. *La Valentina* praised the brave *soldaderas*, the women in the train of the revolutionaries who cooked, made love, bandaged, buried and not infrequently died with them.

Nearly every tenth Mexican lost his life in the Revolution. Nearly all of the *caudillos* or leaders of the Revolution died through betrayal, fundamentally as losers. The only winners have been the Mexican people. It is they who have survived.

Left, **Villa and Zapata in the President's palace.**
Above, **locomotive near the Revolution Museum, a reminder of troop transport by rail.**

Viva Zapata!
Viva Pancho Villa!

A vintage photograph! Pancho Villa sits in the presidential chair, grinning into the camera. Next to the cheerful General sits the restrained and wary Emiliano Zapata. In his left hand, the inevitable cigar and on his lap, the legendary sombrero. Two revolutionaries at the pinnacle of their success. They had met for the first time some days before in Xochimilco, from where they had marched into the anxious capital city and on to the National Palace with their combined armies of 50,000 Zapatistas and Villistas. It was there, on the November 6, 1914, that the photographer of the revolution, Casasola, took the classic photo of the two caudillos described above.

While Zapata stayed in a modest hotel on the edge of the city, Villa made himself conspicuous by his raucousness downtown. According to legend, Villa stormed the distinguished Café Tacuba with his horse. In addition, he seized the opportunity to settle a few old debts in the city. He shed tears of mourning at the grave of his murdered idol Madero and then personally renamed the Calle de Plateros Calle de Madero. Brazen appearances – that was Pancho Villa's style. In 1914, he was 36 years old and weighed over 90 kg (200 lb). He spoke loudly, with the distinct accent of the north. He could be charming, but frightful when he lost his temper. Shrewdness and cunning shone from his eyes. His skin was white; his face flushed. He was the Centaur of the North.

The smaller, dark-skinned Zapata was completely different. He avoided calling attention to himself, sensed every danger, and spoke with a soft voice. He valued fine food and savoured French cognac. There is hardly a picture of him smiling but he used to let himself go during a cock fight or village fiesta. Emiliano Zapata was undoubtedly the best-dressed guerrillero of his day. He was called admiringly "Charro entre Charros"

(horseman among horseman, i.e. tops in his field). He loved riding sports and, just like Villa, was a horse fanatic. Also, like Villa, he competed in riding, shooting and bullfighting competitions with the best of them. Both hated bureaucrats and loved dozens of women. Both left behind only one widow. Both feared betrayal and died in the treacherous gunfire of traitors. By comparison, their popularity in Mexico makes all other revolutionary heroes seem like mere stand-ins. Zapata and Villa were born leaders of legendary charisma and their soldiers followed them unconditionally.

Despite all their similarities, they came from two opposing worlds. Both were orphaned at an early age. Villa, a Norteño, came from a part of Mexico where the cattle ranches were the size of an average European duchy, a region of outlaws and the landless; the breeding ground of tough guys, all-powerful cattle barons, and the leaders of marauding bandits. During the Revolution, Villa intermittently controlled up to half of Mexico.

For Zapata, the nation was an abstract concept. His army of the south, peasant guerrilleros in sandals and straw hats, operated practically only in the State of Morelos. It was there, in the village of Anenecuilco that Emiliano Zapata was born. Early on, the small entrepreneur was elected head of his village. In 1911, he took up the armed struggle and with his peasants occupied the Hacienda Chinameca, where he had worked as stable master. The owner was killed in the fighting. On April 10, 1919, his Carranzista political opponents lured him back to this farm where they shot him. To the end of his life, Zapata neither served in a government nor did he recognize any president. He was an anarchist with fundamentalist, peasant ideals.

For generations, the powerful sugar haciendas (estates) of Morelos ruthlessly annexed the so-called ejidos, the village common lands. They made the peasants into peons. Like all Mexican peasants, Zapata shared a religious bond with the sacred "Mother Earth" from which their Indian forebears had lived down through the millennia.

The latifundia (landed aristocrats) were his natural enemies. The Zapatistas always carried the Virgin of Guadalupe as their battle standard. She and Zapata stood for the Land, respectively Earth and Freedom – "Tierra y Libertad!" A journalist once asked him what he fought for, and Zapata pointed to a dusty tin box, containing the ancient title deeds of his village, Anenecuilco. "That's what I fight for", was his reply. His manifesto from November 25, 1911, the Plan of Ayala, declared that all communal lands must be returned by the haciendas and a third of the remaining land divided among the peasants.

In contrast, Pancho Villa was a warrior without a program who fought for the sake of fighting. Doroteo Arango (his real name) was born into bitter poverty on July 5, 1878, in the State of Durango. After the death of his father, he assumed responsibility for the care of the family. As an adolescent, he shot his landlord after the latter had tried to rape his sister. He then fled to the mountains and led an adventurous life as a cattle thief and killer, adopting the name "Pancho" (a Spanish diminutive form of Francisco) Villa. As a gang leader, he terrorized the State of Chihuahua. With the help of gangs of cattle rustlers to organize the meat supply, he finally established himself as a prosperous butcher in Chihuahua state. In 1910, Villa joined the Madero revolution against the despised Díaz regime.

Villa's charismatic personality drew thousands of adventurers, landless people and pistoleros (gunfighters). From these people, he formed his elite troops, the Dorados – the Golden. As caudillo of the Revolution, he took revenge against the rich and powerful in the name of those deprived of their rights, ending up in prison many times. Under Huerta he was forced into exile in the US – he had always been popular with the Norteamericanos.

Initially he fought with Obregón in support of Madero. Then he fought with Carranza against Huerta and in the end against both Carranza and Obregón.

In 1920, Villa and the last 759 of his Dorados surrendered. In Canutillo, Durango, he and his veterans built up a model farm. But in 1923, he entered politics once again, this time in opposition to President Obregón. On July 20, 1923, while driving his Dodge through Parral, Chihuahua, he was ambushed and his body was riddled with bullets.

In his book Insurgent Mexico, author John Reed drew an animated picture of the Robin Hood of the poor and disinherited. He reported Villa's vision of a new Mexico. "We will put the army to work. In all parts of the Republic we will establish military colonies composed of the veterans of the Revolution... Three days a week they will work and work hard, because honest work is more important than fighting, and only honest work makes good citizens. And the other three days they will receive military instruction and go out and teach the people how to fight."

The course of Pancho Villa's life was littered with corpses. He was dictatorial in his rule as governor of Chihuahua. As general of the renowned División del Norte (Northern Division), he was feared. After his victory over the "Jackal," Huerta, he was celebrated in the US as a geniusof a strategist and the "Liberator of Mexico" A born showman, Villa granted Mutual Film the exclusive film rights of his military actions for use in a feature. Pancho Villa, superstar. But when, in 1919, he marched into Mexico City with Zapata, the latter dreamed only of land reform.

Pointing to the presidential seat, Villa said, "and for this we are busily killing each other." Laughing, he offered the chair to Zapata who turned it down. Villa then threw himself gleefully into the symbol-laden throne, while Zapata sat next to him briefly for a photograph. Later Zapata, the peasant guerrillero from Morelos, hissed: "We ought to burn the thing and put an end to that false ambition."

Left, the legendary Emiliano Zapata and, above, cardboard cut-out of Pancho Villa in the Museo Nacional de la Revolucion.

Even today the question of whether Mexico's Revolution was successful, incomplete or even still going on is heavily debated. In any event, the Revolution was like an overpowering earthquake which shook the entire country, bringing traditional political and economic structures to the point of collapse.

However, just as the debris from the pyramids was used to build the palaces and churches that followed the Spanish conquest, modern Mexico stands on its own pre-Revolutionary foundations. This is true even if the facade presents a new image – the facade of a democratic republic. This facade in fact conceals the ancient pyramid of authoritarian centralism, still there after all these years. Mexico is sometimes mockingly referred to as a "democratorship".

Mexico City is the seat of the central power which today is exercised by a seemingly omnipotent president. The rules of the power game, set by the regime in the 1920s and 1930s, have assured that no post-Revolutionary president can actually become a despotic dictator even if the reality is not so far off that. This centralized power, however, has also helped to establish a certain amount of political stability.

Heir to the Revolution: It was President Plutarco Elias Calles (1924–28) who first managed to tame and channel the political powers that were unleashed by the Revolution. During his presidency, however, a policy of uncompromising persecution of the Church led to a great public uproar largely because the president sought out and succeeded in radically curtailing every means of public influence which had been embedded in the 1917 Constitution inspired by the revolutionary cleric Hidalgo. The clergy were forbidden to wear their cassocks outside the church and to vote or carry on political agitation. Furthermore, they were forbidden to own property or to interfere in

primary or secondary education. The fanatical religious battles that ensued yielded a period of unrest that lasted into the 1930s.

The Roman Catholic church finally had to admit defeat and withdraw from the political stage as the revolutionary leadership and its centralized bureaucracy gained ground. Calles' founding of the National Revolution Party (PNR) was an ingenious strategic decision. In the years that followed 1929, the party succeeded in absorbing all the significant social groups like a sponge. It took over the national colors – green, white and red – as its own colors and became identical with the State. Even the increasingly grandiose names which the party successively adopted show how the energy of the national revolution was gradually molded into a bureaucratic apparatus: Partido Nacional Revolucionario, Partido de la Revolución Mexicana, Partido Revolucionario Institucional (PRI).

The PRI structure of today consists of three overlapping membership divisions: the *sector obrero* (workers' section) which includes the labor unions; the *sector campesino* (peasant section) recruited in large part from those working in agriculture; and the *sector popular* which absorbs practically everyone who doesn't belong to the other groups.

The latter division brings together such diverse people as civil servants, businessmen, intellectuals and slum dwellers. Some are not even aware of their party membership, since prsonal membership is not the norm. As a member of one of the professional associations of farmers, urban industrial workers, or the middle class, one is quasi-automatically a part of the PRI. In return for absolute loyalty, party activists are rewarded with political as well as social advancement. Organizers in the professional associations get perks for their support.

Over several decades, the PRI swallowed up all the other parties and, over the same period it has supplied all the state presidents, governors, nearly all the senators, the vast majority in the House of Representatives and virtually all the mayors. Nevertheless one cannot call Mexico a one-party state. In contrast to previous practice in socialist countries, the party in Mexico is more or less the long arm of the government, functioning like a civil service. The president designates his successor with the so-called *dedazo* (a "hint") shortly before the expiry of his *sexenio* (the one-time six-year term of office). He doesn't make this decision alone but is assisted by the inner circle of the revolutionary family – an elite "club" of some 100 persons from the spheres of politics, business, culture and administration.

positions only become well paid towards the end of the six-year cycle, many hope for an administrative position that offers at least some material security through the spoils of corruption. It is not so much the individuals as the corporate structure of Mexico's political life that is to blame for this abuse of power and privilege in return for favors from petitioners; just occasionally the Mexican public pounces on a particularly outrageous scapegoat in order to get even with the whole structure at the end of a *sexenio*. The size of the morsel which a partaker (interestingly enough, a bribe is called *mordida*, "a bite") gets from the cake depends very much on the

The exact composition of this group is hard to pin down. Almost none of the wheeling and dealing emerges into the open before the *destape*, the disclosure of the candidate.

The six-year cycle: Despite the enormous energy devoted to the election campaign, during which the PRI presidential candidate travels far and wide throughout the country, the election itself has been little more than a charade until very recently. Every six years the elections bring the ossified system back to life. With the change in presidents comes a substantial shuffling of personnel in the government services. Although government

status of his administrative position.

This corruption is an inbuilt and apparently ineradicable part of the political system. The American journalist Alan Riding (*Eighteen Times Mexico*) wrote that corruption "makes the system function, providing the 'oil' which keeps the wheels of the bureaucratic apparatus turning and the 'glue' which holds political alliances together." The Mexican author Octavio Paz sees corruption as a "sign of Mexico's dubious modernity" (*The Philanthropic Cannibal*).

Dubious modernity: In many respects, the 1910 Revolution marked Mexico's entry into the modern era, above all in the business sector. President Calles began to modernize the economy. A decade and a half later President Lázaro Cárdenas (1934–40) displayed an especially reformist zeal in the spirit of the Revolution. The latter will be remembered by the Mexican people as the man who undertook great land reform in favor of the poor peasants and nationalized the petroleum companies, most of which had been foreign-owned. Under his successor, Avila Camacho, the agrarian revolution was cinpleted and the industrial revolution gained momentum.

During World War II, Mexican exports, over six percent – a sort of *milagro mexicano* (a "Mexican miracle"). Mexico became integrated in to the world economy as a "boom country", albeit with a tendency to slide into crises. Economic growth accelerated from the top down but it had no mechanisms for broadening its base; success was absorbed by the rich getting richer and there were no adequate structures for distributing the wealth through the lower classes.

Crisis of confidence: Industry was concentrated above all in the greater Mexico City area, turning the metropolis into the country's swollen head. Very few industrial centers developed outside Mexico City

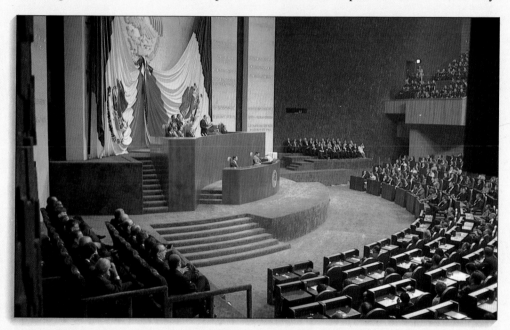

such as oil and agricultural products, were in high demand while the warring countries exported to Mexico very little in the way of finished goods. This lack of overseas competition enabled the local industry to expand and to produce goods for domestic consumption. Mexico's movie industry enjoyed an astonishing boom period during which the country became the major producer of Spanish-language films. Under President Miguel Alemán annual economic growth reached

Left, politics on the street. **Above**, politics in the dignified parliament (Palacio Legislativo).

while the peasant population received hardly any benefit from the headlong pace of development. Those in the city raised their incomes substantially and a broader middle class demonstrated how to spend it.

By contrast, living conditions in the rural areas continued to deteriorate, so that many former agricultural workers moved to the city just in order to hang on to the tail of this prosperity. But without the necessary professional qualifications the rural migrants who came to Mexico City more often than not joined the masses of underemployed slumdwellers living in abject poverty in dirty and ramshackle cardboard shanty towns.

Countrywide tension also increased as a result of the high rate (3.5 percent), of population growth but the situation did not become explosive until shortly before the 1968 Olympic Games. At the time when the eyes of the world were on Mexico, and on the massive international spectacle which the country had prepared, spontaneous protests began among students in Mexico City. Unwisely the Díaz Ordáz government sent police and the military against the students as they marched toward the Palacio Nacional; the outrage over the clash only served to spread the rebellion, which was even joined

President Luís Echeverría (1970–76) confronted this legitimacy crisis (as Interior Minister, he had participated in the decision to suppress the conflicts by force) with a program of "democratic opening" designed to broaden the political landscape. Along with the three small opposition parties that had merely vegetated in the shadow of the PRI, other political groups were permitted to organize as parties. This more liberal policy was continued as "political reform" under President José López Portillo.

The ever-deepening economic crisis of the 1980s brought Mexico's system of "institutionalized revolution" further into chaos.

by a part of the middle class. Huge numbers of demonstrators marched repeatedly down the Paseo de la Reforma to the Zócalo.

Ten days before the lighting of the Olympic flame, the government, afraid of losing international prestige, used armed force to suppress a protest meeting in Tlatelolco's Plaza de Tres Culturas. The massacre of many students coupled with more than 1,000 arrests resulted in the required effect: a Mexico as quiet as a graveyard for the period when it was in the world spotlight. But the Mexicans' own faith in their post-Revolutionary state had been shattered.

Enormous oil discoveries started an oil rush in Mexico and the Mexican state took out huge foreign loans in anticipation of the future wealth which the oil would bring. In 1981, the drastic decline in oil demand and the resulting fall in price led to an economic collapse which only exacerbated prevailing social injustices. Above all the price of basic foodstuffs soared while real wage levels fell to those of the 1960s.

During the Miguel de la Madrid administration (1982–88) the peso dropped drastically in value against the US dollar. The dollar which had bought about 12 pesos in the 1960s was now worth more than 2,000. In 1985, Mexico City suffered a devastating earthquake which measured 8.1 on the Richter scale, the worst in recent memory.

Political collapse: The general loss of confidence in the PRI system became painfully obvious in the 1988 elections. The son of reform president Lázaro Cárdenas, Cuauhtémoc, carried the banner of the left-oriented party alliance "Frente Democrático / Nacional" against PRI candidate Carlos Salinas de Gortari in the presidential race. The official result was the closest majority a president had received since Independence: with 50.4 percent, Salinas just reached the

had not been rebuilt since the disaster.

However the 40-year-old new president Carlos Salinas, who assumed office despite protests in the streets and in parliament, surprised everyone with his campaign against corruption and his energetic economic reforms. One of his first moves was to strike down the power of the unions, some of whose bosses had become virtual dictators of their own particular fiefdoms. Salinas promised stricter control of taxation to assure national revenues. Moribund state industries were privatized with the proceeds going toward a solidarity programme for the poorest of the poor. Restrictive regulations

necessary absolute majority. Not surprisingly, the opposition found the result highly suspect. The challenger Cárdenas won 31 percent of the votes and the conservative opposition party, PAN, got 17 percent. The PRI regime lost, above all, the support of the capital's residents. They felt they had been abandoned by the government since the 1985 earthquake, which destroyed a disproportionate number of lower-class homes that

which hindered the activity of foreign investors were swept away.

President Carlos Salinas set out to cover the country, province by province, to win support for his modernization plans. His foreign policy was aimed at reducing the giant external debt and the financial community reacted positively to his efforts, granting Mexico a generous debt restructuring agreement. Whether or not "baldy", as Salinas is known to his countrymen, can also regain the Mexican's trust in the PRI as a ruling party will have to wait until the end of his *sexenio*, and the new elections.

Left, President Carlos Salinas talking with the people. Above, his opponent Cuauhtémoc Cárdenas during the election campaign.

From the window of an airplane, Mexico City looks like an endless, amorphous sea of houses. Despite numerous attempts to plan the city, the growth of this gigantic metropolis has left its indelible mark on a previously harmonious landscape.

The landscape: The Aztecs reached the central Mexican basin in the 13th century, traveling south from the dry planes of the north. Five lakes glittered between huge, snow-capped volcanoes, mountain ridges densely covered with firs and pine-trees, petrified streams of lava and the cones of innumerable small volcanoes. The lake in the middle, Texcoco, was stagnant and filled with salty water, the result of a meagre inflow during the dry period combined with a high rate of evaporation. On the shores several Nashua peoples had created a blossoming paradise of gardens and fields. The *chinampas* – arable lands – were artfully extended by maize and beanfields (*milpas*) while the "floating gardens" were nothing but beds of mud, layered between wattle and poplars in lake Xochimilco.

A system of canals, partly visible even today, connected the lakes. Pyramids, temples and ballfields were devoted to the worship of the gods. The principal places of worship, Teotihuacán and Tula, had however already been abandoned and fallen into decay. The famous ball game, *hachtli* had been played since ancient times and had both mythological and religious significance, although it was also the pretext for heavy gambling. Splendid ball courts still exist in the Mayan temples of Tula and Chichen Itza. It was a game reserved for upper-class players who were heavily padded and were only allowed to manipulate the ball with their knees or hips.

Aztec planning problems: According to legend the Aztecs founded the city of Tenochtitlán around 1370 on a flat island in lake Texcoco, on the very place where an eagle sat on an cactus devouring a snake – an image that was later to become the national emblem of Mexico. From this base they proceeded to subjugate major parts of the present Mexico. The tributes from these vassal peoples alone enabled them to expand their capital in to the gleaming metropolis that so impressed the Spanish conqueror Hernán Cortéz within 150 years.

The Aztecs achieved miracles of hydraulic engineering to prevent the shallow lake from rising and flooding the city during the summer rainy season. A protective dam, 16 km (10 miles) long, was built to separate the city and the western part of the lake from the larger eastern part. Further dams, as well as aqueducts to supply water, connected Tenochtitlán with the older cities on the shore (Azcapotzalco, Tacubaya, Coyoacán), which have since become incorporated into Mexico City. Urban planning, therefore, played a significant role long before the conquistadors set foot on Mexican soil.

Tenochtitlán, which is said to have had between 60,000 and 400,000 inhabitants at the time of the Spanish conquest, was covered by a network of streets and canals. When the Spanish built their new capital Ciudad de Mexico (Mexico City), after the destruction in 1521, they based their design on the existing Aztec patterns. As a symbol of their power, the Spanish erected churches on the sites of destroyed pyramids; the Franciscan cloister on the pyramid of Tlatelolco, for example, and the cathedral next to the former main pyramid of the Templo Mayor. Cortéz had his own palace built on the ruins of Montezuma's palace, also the site of the present seat of government. In the course of the conquest Cortéz decimated the city, toppling most of its buildings and filling the canals with rubble. In a regretful dispatch to Spain he expressed regret for destroying what he termed "the most beautiful city in the world."

The colonial period: Starting from the central square, today called the Zócalo, the

Left, view into a *vecindad* or neighborhood, showing cramped living conditions. Here everyone shares everything, even water taps.

Spanish plan featured a right-angled street-grid with blocks measuring 80 by 160 meters (260 by 525 ft). The wealth culled from the nation's silver mines enabled the bourgeoisie of the capital to build patio houses with artfully designed facades decorated either with reddish *tezontle* stone or *azulejo* colored tile. The many churches and cloisters bear witness to the important position which the Catholic church then enjoyed.

Due to the massive growth of the city and to several floods the Spanish tried to drain the basin by connecting a 25-km (15-mile) canal to the Río Panuco river system in the north. But the first tunnel collapsed in 1627. In 1767, therefore, the Tajo de Nochistengo, the tunnel which today carries the railway line, was dug.

The drainage of the lake: The problem of draining the basins was not finally solved until this century when the large canal (Gran Canal de Desagüe), with its two tunnels, was dug. On the northern end of what remained of Lake Texcoco an evaporation spiral was built to produce salt; from the air this looks like a shell and therefore it is commonly called the *caracol*. The negative consequences of draining the land, however, were not really considered even though, as early as 1807, Alexander von Humboldt had accurately predicted that such treatment would result in disastrous erosion, deforestation and dried out soil.

What actually happened, following the drainage of the substantial sediments and the increased use of the ground water, was that the houses sunk up to 7 meters (23 ft) and cracks appeared in the walls. This is not only evident today in the massive marble building of the Palacio de Bellas Artes, whose front steps are buckled, but also in the Franciscan church in the Calle Madero, whose entrance is now several meters below street level. The 18th-century Capuchin church, right next to the Basilica de Guadalupe, had been leaning ominously eastward until it was recently given solid concrete foundations and straightened hydraulically. But this kind of sophisticated procedure is too costly to be used except in the most exceptional cases. The cathedral, still sinking to different levels, is an even more complicated problem.

The unstable subsoil is also partly responsible for the extensive damage caused by the earthquake of 1985. Due to the geological structure, earthquakes are a common phenomenon in Mexico, as they are all along the Pacific. The upheavals of September 19, 1985 however, produced oscillations of different frequencies in the sand and clay layers and this led to the destruction of over 400 city buildings.

An important factor in the destruction was the quality of the housing stock. Solidly built colonial palaces stood firm as did the technically flawless steel constructions with deep foundations, such as the 181-meter (594-ft) 42-storey Torre Latinoamerica which, when built in the 1950s had been embedded 30 meters (98 ft) into the ground. Under the pressure of the earthquake it was the clay tile houses and the shoddily and densely built skyscrapers that collapsed.

Climatic changes: The drainage of the lake influenced the local climate, particularly in the dry season. The large water surfaces, which had previously balanced out the rise and fall of the temperatures, disappeared and the dry, salty clay was blown into superfine dust-clouds. Together with the smog produced by car exhausts and industrial emissions the clouds contributed to the unbearable air pollution prevalent during the long periods of fine weather in spring.

Under these circumstances, the basin location of Mexico City has proved a further disadvantage. Stable inversion layers get stuck between the mountain ranges and dissolve into rain only on the rare ocassions when they meet cold fronts. Then the air is clear and the volcanoes again zigzag across the horizon, just as they do on old paintings.

In general, the climate is influenced by the tradewinds prevalent in the northern areas of the tropics. The dry season lasts from November to April and the summer brings rain which occurs mainly in the late afternoon. Substantial showers tend to cause terrible floods in Mexico City, which is notoriously subject to drainage problems.

Unfortunately, the annual precipitation – at 700 millimeters (28 inches) about the same as Northern Europe – is far too little to ensure the capital's water supply. This is mainly due to the unfavorable distribution of rain between summer and winter months – there is no regular intermittent supply – but also to the increasing expansion of the city into the drained areas and rising private and industrial water consumption.

The first mechanical pumps to produce ground water were introduced towards the end of the last century. In the 1930s more distant resources were tapped, at first via a pipeline from Xochimilco, then by a connection to the springs of the Río Lerma near Toluca. Recently, plans have been drafted to get water from the rainy Sierra Madre Oriental. Apart from the difficulty of providing

In the past 100 years: Mexico City grew beyond the boundaries of the old colonial city in the 19th century. Emperor Maximilian created an avenue, modelled after the Champs Elysées, the Paseo de la Reforma, which led to his castle, the Castillo de Chapultepec. French influence on the capital's architecture, though shortlived, brought happy diversity. Villas in the French style were built along the wide Paseo de la Reforma; some of them are still there in the Zona Rosa, while others had to yield their ground to office towers and big hotels.

Since the turn of the century residential areas for the middle and upper classes have

sufficient amounts of water, there are also serious flaws in the distribution system, particularly in the growing suburban regions. Water quality, too, is not adequately monitored. Rapid urbanization, water shortage, canalization – and the far-reaching consequences of all these for the environment – are closely intertwined; the lack of water naturally affects the city's sewerage system and the health of its people.

Above, early morning in Chalco, a huge new *ciudad perdida* (lost city) in the extreme outskirts of the metropolis.

been developed in the south and west, leaving the vast Bosque de Chapultepec as a public park. Today the classy Lomas suburb, rising in the west, is an exclusive suburb with stylish country houses. At the same time the old village of Tacubaya was devoured by urbanization. The distant colonial cities of San Angel, Coyoacán and Tlalpan were discovered only later as preferred residential areas. Artists, such as Diego Rivera who belonged to the avant garde movement, relocated to these romantic towns that today are part of Mexico City.

A significant factor in the city's extension

southward along the Avenida Insurgentes in the 1950s was the generously laid out university complex, the Olympic stadium and the state-of-the-art residential development Pedregal (which means "lava") on the site of an ancient and long extinct volcano. Further colleges, government offices and American-style shopping malls (such as Perisur) were also added to the complex.

In the north, the situation is entirely different. Under Porfirio Díaz the first factories were established along with the railway line. They formed the initial stage of an industrial area which has since grown to extend well beyond the northern city limits.

trous. On the dry bed of lake Texcoco slums appeared, covered by mud in the summer and by dust in the winter. In addition to the planned suburbs, such as the monotonous Nezahualcóyotl with more than 3 million inhabitants, new spontaneous settlements with access to the public infrastructure mushroomed.

Even in the inner city there are now many slum-like neighborhoods, *ciudades perdidas* (the lost cities), which differ hardly at all from the cardboard and tin shacks that cover the hillsides of so many third world capitals. Innumerable patio-houses in the eastern part of the old town are deteriorating

The people attracted to the capital by industrial development initially lived in so-called *vecindades*, one-room apartments with cooking facilities along open hallways with one water tap for 10 to 20 families. In 1930 the city had 1 million inhabitants, but by 1950 this had increased to 3 million. This was only the beginning of a veritable population explosion. Today the metropolitan area, with its 20 million people, is the largest in the world, alongside the world capitals of New York and Tokyo.

The consequences for urban development of such a population explosion were disas-

into mass quarters in dire need of renovation.

Traffic problems: The infrastructure has not been able to keep up with the pace of change in the city, although the post-war economic boom has permitted some improvements. In the 1960s, for example, a number of urban highways were built, such as the Viaducto crossing the city along the east-west axis, or the Periferico. But they were not able to cope with ever-increasing traffic and had to be complemented by a network of four and six-lane one-way highways, the *ejes viales*, covering the entire inner city. Even these are regularly congested during rush-hour.

Use of vehicles has been restricted to certain days of the week and tough exhaust emission control laws have been passed. Under such circumstances the opening of the subway, the Metro, in 1969, was extremely important. Since then the system has been extended to eight lines totalling more than 100 km (60 miles) and ferrying five million passengers every day. The subway is the best evidence that, even in a metropolis with seemingly unsurmountable problems, it is possible to organize a reliable service for the masses. It was not even disrupted during the earthquake in 1985.

Hope for the future: However immense the

designed that not only met the needs of the population but were also aesthetically pleasing. Programs providing for the transfer of ownership to the tenants after 10 years have met with enormous success.

A master plan to stabilize traffic and to redevelop the colonial center has long been overdue. It has materialized at last and even made progress in spite of all the obstructions (the restriction on using your car on alternate days has been thwarted by those rich enough to own two cars).

There is hope, then, that this city, which seems to be growing uncontrollably, can be saved. Regular visitors express the surprise

losses caused by the catastrophic earthquake might have been, it also released enormous energies for renewal and solidarity. During the rebuilding of the poorer neighborhoods in the northern part of the inner city, local initiatives were instrumental in guaranteeing the proper completion of a public program to build 48,000 housing units. With the financial assistance of the World Bank and other organizations, small complexes were

Left, The *Casa Grande*, as described by Oscar Lewis in *The Children of Sanchez*, before and, above, after the earthquake of 1985.

each time they return that the city has not yet been completely given over to chaos. It remains to be seen whether a program transferring government offices and industries to other parts of the country will bring the expected and hoped relief on overstretched road, housing, infrastructure and population growth. But the present government is trying to set a positive example: the National Bureau of Statistics, Cartography and Computer Science has already been moved to Aguascalientes, 500 km (300 miles) west of Mexico City, and there are plans for other similar bodies to relocate.

THE GREAT EARTHQUAKE

"I stood under the doorway, as the guitar fell from the wall. Glasses shook, lamps swung ominously back and forth. Books fell from their shelves and the trembling seemed as if it would never stop. When it was finally over, I made my way to the garage. 'Good morning, that was another heavy quake, wasn't it?' I called cheerfully to a neighbor. "Yes, my most beautiful vase was broken," she yelled back quite unperturbed. So soon after the event, neither of us could yet imagine the magnitude of the structural damage the other buildings in

For days after the quake the city was without electricity and there was a shortage of drinking water. It was feared that some kind of epidemic would ensue. The telephone network suffered considerable damage, and it was weeks after the catastrophe before connections to the national and international trunk lines could be restored. For days ambulances with non-stop sirens raced through the city at all hours of the day and night and helicopters flew back and forth across the metropolis.

The reaction of everyone who had survived the disaster unharmed was spontaneous and exemplary. A new feeling of brotherhood spread among the residents of the world's largest city. Every individual was moved by

our own neighborhood had suffered.

Earthquakes are no rarity for the residents of the Mexican capital. In the early morning of September 19, 1985, everyone reacted much as usual when the first tremors hit the city. Some tried as much as possible to ignore the quake. Others stood under doorways for protection. Only a few took the precaution of stepping out into the streets. The earthquake reached the unusual level of 8.1 on the Richter scale and lasted nearly a minute. Hundreds of buildings, including schools and hospitals, collapsed, burying tens of thousands of people dead or alive beneath the debris. The number of people rendered homeless was estimated at hundreds of thousands.

the scenes of devastation and hardship to make himself useful either through donations or active cooperation. Civilians directed the traffic at street intersections where traffic signals hadn't functioned for days. Strangers organized brigades in order to provide clothing and food for the homeless or to open their own homes to those in need. Volunteers rushed to damage sites to try to dig out those buried under the ruins. Radio and television were in action round the clock providing information about the tragedy; coordinating rescue brigades; maintaining the connections to the rest of the country and the southern US and helping to locate those who were reported missing.

Although during the first days after the disaster very few people in the affected parts of the city had access to television, the news spread very rapidly among the whole population. Whoever had a working telephone put it at the disposal of strangers, took messages and passed them on to those concerned. Whoever had a transistor radio let the whole neighborhood listen in, but still it took several days before everyone could get a clear picture of the total impact. Since the Mexicans cope with their most difficult ordeals by laughing at them, the first of the often macabre earthquake jokes began to circulate through the city soon after the disaster.

Poor tradesmen soon appeared at the sites of collapsed buildings, hawking the necessary digging tools to rescue those who were trapped. Others sold refreshments (drinks, fruit, or *tacos*) to the *topos*, the moles, as the rescue workers quickly came to be called.

At the Plaça de Tres Culturos in Tlatelolco, nearly all of the buildings which had been built in recent years were partly damaged or totally destroyed. Tlatelolco lies, as does the downtown district, in the lake area which had been drained by the Spanish. In that area the destruction was especially extensive. However, it seems that the majority of the colonial homes in the city center survived on account of

their relatively low height and the materials from which they had been built (stone and brick instead of modern concrete).

On the Avenida Juárez, the 42-storey Torre Latinoamericana was one of the few buildings which suffered almost no damage. This was due not only to the outstanding quality of its construction but also its extreme height. Because of the character of the swaying, buildings with fewer than ten and more than 20 storeys were least affected.

Left, Mexicans laugh death in the face, as in these marionettes made for All Soul's Day after the earthquake of 1985. **Above**, damaged building in the Avenue Insurgentes.

For the same reasons, the Hotel Presidente Chapultepec in Polanco remained undamaged. A tourist staying on the 32nd floor testified that the building's highest part shifted from side to side, about a meter each way. After the earthquake, the Avenida Juárez was a very sad sight. Nearly all of its hotels and office buildings were either seriously damaged or reduced to piles of rubble. Tourists sat distraught in their nightshirts in Alameda Park and stared in shock at the ruins of the Hotel Regis where they had been staying only a few minutes before. There was nothing left of the Hotel del Prado except Diego Riviera's famous mural *Sunday Reverie in the Alameda Park*. Since then it has been moved to a new exhibition building next to the Alameda Park.

Only very few of the old, dilapidated houses in the inner city survived the quake. In Tepito, the Casa Blanca, which was made famous as the Casa Grande in Oscar Lewis' novel *The Children of Sanchez*, had to be cleared away along with other *vecindades*. In the Colonia Morelos stood a 101-year-old woman viewing the ruins of the house in which she had lived for over 50 years.

With the collapse of buildings throughout the city many social grievances came to light. More than 600 seamstresses were buried in the workshops of firms, some of which were illegal. Their working conditions had been miserable. The strong social movement, which grew from the protests of the survivors, resulted in the formation of a labor union.

Many parts of the city center took on a new face after the earthquake. Parks have taken the place of many hotels, office buildings and houses. The construction of public housing has been accelerated as a result of the catastrophe. However, even five years after the earthquake, many poor from the downtown district were still living in makeshift accommodation. Despite all the prophecies of disaster, the officially declared motto after the disaster, "Mexico sigue en pie" had been confirmed: Mexico City was on its feet again.

Muralismo – the art of political and public wall-painting – is a child of the Mexican revolution of 1910. Following the spontaneous uprising of the masses, a fundamental renewal of Mexican culture was to fill the ideological vacuum. Art was afforded a particular function: to communicate to the people an awareness of their own history. Artists were encouraged into the public domain, to address themselves directly to the people, in much the same way as the Italian Renaissance and colonial art had done. The Minister for Education, José Vasconcelos, took on the role of concerned patron and made available to the artists a series of centrally located buildings for their murals.

Testing ground: In 1922 the Escuela Nacional Preparatoria became the testing ground for the first phase of Muralismo. Formerly the Jesuit College of San Ildefonso, this magnificent Churrigueresque construction dates from the 18th century. The themes that would later become hallmarks of Muralismo – the clashes with the conquistadors, Mexico's social and cultural problems – are already discernible in the murals here.

Diego Rivera's *The Creation* in the main hall reveals hints of Gauguin and Renoir, but also Renaissance influences. Inspired by the philosophy of Vasconcelos, it takes the form of an allegory of a cosmic race born from a symbiosis of American peoples and cultures. If the rapt mood of the work brings to mind elements of Magic Realism, the murals in the stairwell and courtyard pertain more directly to Mexico. They arise out of a process of internal debate, whereby differing contextual and stylistic positions make themselves felt. Jean Charlot has taken as his theme a Spanish atrocity, the *Massacre of Templo Mayor*. Just as traces of Uccello are perceptible in this mural, then Fernando Leal's

Feast of the Lord of Chalma opposite it suggests the proximity of Impressionism and Realism.

Finally we come to José Clemente Orozco, who leans more towards the Expressionists. For Orozco, the Spanish conquest was essential to the birth of a new nation. Mexico grew out of the synthesis of two traditions, a condition that finds expression in a scene in which Cortéz and his Indian wife Malinche stand triumphant beside a defeated Indian.

For Orozco, Mexico's history is one of high tragedy and conflict. But he is also given to underlying symbolism: a comforting embrace from a corpulent monk for a half-starved Indian remains the ambivalent gesture of a victor. Orozco's cycle of murals in the courtyard (1923–27) depicts the several stations of proletarian life: the drudgery of work, the extravagances of the rich, the frantic activity of political agitators, fraternal feuding and the futility of struggle. Scenes like *The Trenches* and *Revolutionary Trinity* are, in his hands, unmistakeably symbols of defeat.

Placard art: Grief and protest tend to dominate Orozco's work whereas Diego Rivera, in the nearby Ministry of Education (Secretaría de Educación Pública, SEP), celebrates the people's victory. His giant cycle of murals divided over two courtyards (1923–28) is an encyclopaedic view of Mexican life. It devotes itself to conditions in pre-Revolutionary Mexico, and the fate of the farmers and miners whose freedom was won in the Revolution. As a reaction to Orozco's pessimism, it can be seen as representing the beginning of an era of happiness and justice, with the victorious revolutionary trinity of worker, farmer and soldier showing the people the way forward.

With this work Rivera is reinterpreting the Mexican Revolution from a Marxist perspective, a standpoint which simultaneously indulges a Utopian impulse and is used to correct history. His work is didactic, agitational. Fat capitalists and larger-than-

Preceding pages: Orozco's mural *Catharsis* in the Supreme Court. **Left**, The dynamic metaphorical and visual language used by Siqueiros in the Polyforum.

life heroes of the Revolution are set up as stereotypical opposites. Good and Evil are immediately apparent to the viewer. There are clear stylistic parallels with the true-to-life tendencies of the New Realists. At the same time, Rivera makes references to Courbet and Rousseau and draws on his own experiences in Paris. That becomes particularly clear in his treatment of Indian rituals and festivals, the Mexican tradition of honoring the dead, the unmistakable atmosphere of the Mexican landscape.

History in paint: Among Rivera's most well-known works is the cycle on the staircase of the National Palace (1929–35), a

deliberately wide panorama of Mexican history from its earliest beginnings to the present day. Here, too, good and evil take the shape of unambiguous social forces and symbolic figures. The Spanish conquest is portrayed as a violent offensive against a peaceful land, in which even Indians fought on the side of the conquerors (Tlaxcalteken, who hoped by allying himself with the Spanish to free himself from the Aztec yoke). The Spanish are caricatured as being motivated by greed, with the exception of those who defended the Indians, like the bishop Bartolomé de las Las Casas and Vasco de

Quiroga. Scenes from the struggle for independence, the war against the United States and the French invasion, episodes from the Revolution and contemporary life blend into one massive history lesson.

Rivera strives for an identification between the viewer and his heroes: national heroes like Morelos the priest and liberal president Benito Juárez are immediately recognizable to the Mexican public – Rivera based his figures on famous portraits. As clearly as Rivera states his sympathy for the Aztec resistance, just as unclear remains his standing towards the modern predicament of the Indians. Tribal culture may have formed the roots of national tradition, but it has to bow to industrial progress. How far Rivera's ambivalent view of history contributes towards creating its own myth is evident in a series of smaller murals in the main hall of the National Palace. The Aztec capital Tenochtitlán, a kind of pre-Columbian Atlantis, here appears as the Garden of Eden.

These works are based on what was for Rivera another important source of creativity – his archaeological studies and collaboration with anthropologists. Rivera illustrated the Mayans' holy book, *Popul Vuh*, and built up an extensive collection of pre-Columbian art, which is now to be found in a museum in Anahuacalli, which was conceived by the artist himself, in the city's Coyoacán district.

Dream in the park: Rivera's mural *Sunday Reverie in the Alameda* (1947–48), in the foyer of the Hotel del Prado on Alameda Park, marked the high point of his career. This traditional Mexican hotel was badly damaged in the earthquake, but before it was demolished the mural was rescued and given an exhibition space of its own on Avenida Juárez. It has the effect of a burning glass in uniting vital events from Mexican history, although it only starts from the colonial times. More than 40 years after its creation, it still draws regular crowds of admirers.

Starting on the left, the period of Spanish rule is represented by the burning of a heretic at the stake, and by portraits of Bishop Zumárraga and the religious poet Sor Juana Inés de la Cruz. Prominent figures from 19th-century Mexican history follow, Emperor Iturbide and Santa Anna overshadowed by Benito Juárez and his liberal comrades-in-arms. A plaque refers to the Reform Laws of 1857, which heralded a fundamental secularization of Mexican society. Rivera portrays himself as a son of the popular illustrator José Guadalupe Posada and Catrina, a *calavera* woman (Posada's famous skeleton motif). With this he allies himself with a long-established Mexican tradition, for the *calavera* reached a wide audience in pre-Revolutionary Mexico in woodcuts. Behind Rivera appear the revered Cuban poet José Martí and Frida Kahlo, Rivera's wife and a distinguished painter in

A unifying theme is provided by the representative masses in the foreground, with their balloons, sweets and fruit – symbols of a living culture in which fantasy is still part of everyday reality. The action is set within the framework of the Alameda Park on the edge of the old town, laid out in the 16th-century, and its architectural backdrop. The whole work, with its futuristic mood, combines elements of the art of social criticism, Magic Realism and popular culture, whose Indian roots are essential to an understanding of a particularly distinctive form of Mexican ambiance.

In addition, there is a glistening, dream-

her own right, whose work can be admired in the house in suburban Coyoacán where she and Rivera lived for many years. Then come scenes from the Revolution, with dictator Porfirio Díaz and the mainstays of his regime, as well as a group of armed Zapatans, and finally, on the far right, the liberal president Francisco Madero, who was a revolutionary martyr.

Left, Rivera's revolutionary trinity. **Above**, viewers experience the world according to Siqueiros from a revolving platform in the Polyforum.

like quality to the light, which casts a spell over the whole mural. This capacity for assimilating material from so many different sources is one of the fundamental characteristics of mural painting. In his best works, Rivera succeeds in blending Mexican and European heritages to create a new quality.

Walls of horror: If Orozco relied on the visual traditions of his people to spread his ideas into a national art, he also recognized early on that an abstract critique of capitalism sold well. In the face of World War II, the abuse and defilement of humanity and ubiquitous violence, he developed an aesthetic of horror, at times reminiscent of Goya. His cycle of murals in the stairwell of the Supreme Court (1941) on the south side of the national palace, are a stinging pastiche of society's hidden evils. The angel of justice sits in judgement on the henchmen of a corrupt judiciary. A new humanity rises from the cathartic flames.

Orozco developed this theme during the years 1942–44 in a series of murals in the church of the Hospital de Jesús (where Avenida República del Salvador meets Pino Suárez), founded in 1528 by Hernán Cortéz. While Orozco's vision of the apocalypse was still in the planning stage, the Church was secularized. The Christian theme became instead a permanently relevant expression of accusation and prosecution, a sign of protest against the terror and suffering brought down upon mankind. The beast and the apocalyptic wife, the demons of darkness and destruction, are symbols of imminent danger. Orozco's art is a revolution of conscience, remote from all ideological handicaps.

In contrast to this uncompromising disillusionment, a third master of the mural, David Alfaro Siqueiros strove for a political clarity. Thus he is less concerned with giving a detailed reconstruction of pre-Columbian history than celebrating individual heroes who have been seen to uphold the revolutionary cause. In his mural *Cuauhtémoc versus the Legends* (1944) in the Tecpan of Tlatelolco, a colonial building near the Plaza of Three Cultures, the Aztec hero is portrayed as the victor over the conquistador centaurs. Here too the actual course of Mexican history is reinterpreted to create a Utopian vision of the past, a technique which is in evidence in some of the artist's other works, for example the mural *Patrician and Patricide* (1945–72) in the stairwell of the Baroque Customs House located on Plaza Santo Domingo.

An avid experimentalist, Siqueiros was responsible for introducing new materials and techniques to mural painting, such as synthetic paints and the spray gun. His mural *Portrait of the Bourgeoisie* (1939) on the stairs of the Electricity Company (45, Antonio Casa) is the product of his experiences in the Spanish Civil War. Its dynamic structure is reminiscent of the formal principles of futurism. The central image is that of a torch-swinging, parrot-faced political activist. The monster, intended to symbolize fascist propaganda, is seen whipping up the brown shirts into a frenzied attack on ordinary life.

A new aesthetic: The effectiveness of murals lies not only in the breadth of their vision but also the public controversies which they trigger. Their ambivalence lies above all in the fact that they make a critical claim while at the same time being dependent on public support. Many commissions only came about by the state's need to legitimize itself. Early on, individual artists warned of the dangers of fossilizing "a waxworks of Mexican nationalism" (Octavio Paz).

There was a steady stream of exciting innovations in technique, style and subject matter. Murals appeared in government ministries, schools, churches and hospitals throughout the capital. Within 50 years, thousands of works were created of widely differing standards. Eventually, in fact, mural painting came to be threatened more by the cheap mass production of imitations and reproductions of the great masters than from any over-protectiveness exhibited by the state authorities.

As a reaction to the official version of mural art, a new aesthetic concept developed. The second generation of muralists turned with renewed vigor to local culture, but also to universal themes. The integration of mural painting into modern architecture provided further innovative impetus, and was to become even more important after the upturn in the Mexican economy. The murals and reliefs in the Centro Médico and in the new University City were the most important forerunners of this trend.

A new factor began to appear in the debate over cultural identity, one which was only too aware of its own possibilities. In his 4,000 sq. meter (43,057 sq. ft) mosaic in volcanic rock on the main university library (1949–51), for example – an attention-grabbing situation – Juan O'Gorman outlines Mexico's contribution to world culture. The four sides of the cube are decorated with allegories and symbols of pre-Columbian culture, of the colonial period and Europe, as well as of independent Mexico and the university itself. In terms of its content, the human interest eclipses the polemic of the formative phase.

The move toward modernism took a variety of paths. Siqueiros sought to preserve the revolutionary impetus in a new use of form. His *Polyforum Cultural* (1965–72) next to the Hotel de México (junction of Avenidas Insurgentes Sur and Filadelfia) is dedicated to mankind's march through history and combines architecture, relief, sculpture and wall painting. It is used as a center for

revitalized strength and renewed energy.

World example: Those who are interested in learning about the significant trends in mural painting can do so in the **Palacio de Bellas Artes**. On the top floor are murals by Rivera, Siqueiros and Orozco. Alongside are works by other masters, most notably Rufino Tamayo, who provided an early challenge to the "three greats". His mural *Birth of our Nation* (1952–53) is a powerful synthesis of pre-Columbian Indian legends and symbols and the vocabulary of modern art. Mexico's contribution to world art stems from this same technique. Another contributory facet was a geometric trend, tending toward the

multicultural performances of various kinds and always has folk art on display.

While the interior consists of a dynamic, voluminous relief frieze of the martyrdom of the masses, which the viewer confronts from a rotating platform, the exterior is made up of a series of murals bearing motifs from both Mexican and world history. Hope for overcoming conflict appears in the shape of the legend of the new man. From the center of the intricate ceiling freize, he glows full of

Above, *Sunday Reverie in the Alameda* is the title of this mural by Diego Rivera.

abstract, represented by Carlos Mérida, Mathias Goeritz and Manuel Felguérez, not to mention a movement of young political artists whose work was largely a reaction to actual events.

For all the contradictions of its "dualistic and static view of history" (according to Octavio Paz), the art of mural painting has provoked debate about the future of the nation. It has become a model of cultural identification, and for visitors it provides an invitation to search beyond the inconsistencies and look into the very heart of this fascinating country.

What Mexican isn't an artist? This is the home of the artists in corn, artists of the *taco* and the *quesadilla*, who use their hands to create the most original delicacies, and of the roadside cooks, offering an amazing variety of food in the open street. We are men of corn, part of a corn society. Our culture is a corn culture, based on corn as opposed to wheat. We build pyramids and observatories, we make gods of sound and stone, gods hidden still behind the altars of our land.

We corn types are more creative than others. But the only place we can hope to gain recognition

tion from the city's rich mythical tradition: "la Malinche", the founding of Tenochtitlán, the visions of the Virgin of Guadalupe on the hill at Tepeyac, the labyrinths of man's lonely existence... there's no artist who wouldn't come here to drink from such a deep well. In Mexico City, the artist quickly learns total, uncompromising dedication to his art.

The three great muralists – Orozco, Rivera and Siqueiros – turned the walls of the city's palaces into one endless painting, which set out to show the people their history and make them proud of

is in the capital. There's no chance of any success in the provinces. In the provinces there is nothing more than the provincial.

Jalisco is a case in point: a province that has given birth to an unusual number of Mexico's most prominent countrymen: José Clemente Orozco, Juan Rulfo, Juan José Arreola, Agustén Yanez. But Mexico City draws people like a magnet, just as Paris did for a time when it was the capital of the world. Writers like Carlos Fuentes grew up on the streets of the city, together with poets like Octavio Paz, who was born in the district of Mixcoac, comedians from the slums like Cantinflas, actresses like Dolores del Río, painters like Frida Kahlo. They all drew inspira-

their past. José Vasconcelos, Minister for Culture at the time, swamped the country with editions of the classics, in the hope that the *campesinos* would take to reading Plato and St Augustine. It is thanks to him that so many Mexicans were baptized Socrates, Parménides, Temistocles and Arquimedes.

The *estridentistas* or "Extremists," strongly influenced by the Dadaists, sought to take the mechanization of the city to its limits by giving it futuristic designs like those in Fritz Lang's seminal film *Metropolis*.

The *contemporáneos*, inspired by their muse Antonieta Rivas Mercado (who committed suicide before the main altar of Notre Dame), composed perfect sonnets, while European Modernism was introduced into Mexico by the likes of Salvador Novo, a master of language, the chemist and poet Jorge Cuesta, an extraordinary character of strong contrasts, the alchemist Gilberto Owen, Jaime Torres Bodet and Carlos Pellicer, poet and historian of the Olmec era, Enrique Gonzáles Martinez and Xavier Villaurrutia, the most talented of them all.

According to Octavia Paz, our civilization has never been so blind as it was during that period when the intellectuals used to meet in Café Paris and allow themselves to be captivated by the beautiful María Asúnsolo and her cousin Dolores del Río. Yet in World War II, the *Taler de la Gráfica Popular* (Workshop of Popular Art) filled every street corner with black and white prints opposing fascism and tyranny.

Mexico took in many refugees from war-torn Spain as well as the rest of Europe. Many great figures landed here: painters, authors, film directors like Eisenstein, writers like Anna Segher, Katherine Ann Porter, Graham Greene, D.H. Lawrence, Léon Felipe, André Breton, Léon Trotsky (who was murdered in Coyoacán), Luis Buñuel, Antonin Artaud, who used to experiment with hallucinogenic mushrooms, Jean Charlot, assistant to Diego Rivera and a muralist in his own right, historians like Ralph Roeder, author of the essential work *Juárez and his Mexico*, archaeologists and anthropologists like Rolf Stavenhagen, who – like the travelers Alexander von Humboldt and Egon Erwin Kisch before him – contributed a fund of knowledge about Mexico which has become a precious treasure. Alejandra Kollontai and the photographer Tina Modotti are other famous names to have fallen under Mexico's spell, leaving behind them a culture we now regard as our own.

There are other artists living on our streets: the *evangelistas* under the arches of the Plaza San Domingo, who tap out letters on old Remington typewriters – and make glorious grammatical mistakes. Their clients dictate the text, which the typists then embellish with flowery turns of phrase and protestations of love. The "evangelists" of San Domingo are our *literati*. Mexicans, many of whom are unable to write themselves, queue for hours outside their makeshift offices. They'll send letters to your loved one, letters to your family, even petitions to the Pope or the

president, although you'll never get a reply.

Then there are the basket makers and the flower arrangers, the folk singers and the *mariachis*. Their name comes from the French word "marriage", since they used to perform mainly at weddings. With their amorous guitars, trumpets, violins and violas, the *mariachis* have the power to transport the listener to another world. In the past they were hired by budding Romeos to serenade their darling Juliet beneath her balcony. Today there are no more Romeos, and those who want to hear *ranchero* songs or sentimental ballads have to go along to Tenampa, where the artists of the strings weave enchantment all night long with their sad chords and melancholy lamenting: "Ay, ay, ay, ay, sing, don't cry, for song,

ay, ay, ay, ay, will make your heart light."

The pickpockets in the city buses and on the Metro count as artists too, as do the bureaucrats shuffling papers in city offices, or the teachers, standing before their classes. But none is a greater artist than the *merolico* – the trader hawking his assortment of natural remedies in the market place. He's more persuasive than José Luis Cuevas or Octavio Paz when he's extolling the virtues of his corn ointment, his potions to ward off the "evil eye" or cure sudden unexplained lameness, or the medicinal herbs that claim to induce instant abortion. Small wonder, in a city with such a vast population and so many glaring social inequalities.

__Left__, the celebrated artist Rufino Tamayo looks back over 70 creative years. __Right__, José Luis Cuevas is partial to "happenings."

LOS CAPITALINOS: HIGHLIFE AND SURVIVAL

Of Mexico's 85 million inhabitants, around 20 million are *capitalinos* living in the capital, and the other 65 million would like to be. The majority of Mexicans strive to live in the capital or one of the other major cities. No one likes living in the poor countryside. By 1976, a thousand Mexicans were arriving in the capital every day. Since then, this number has quadrupled. Many returned to their own provinces after the tragic earthquake of 1985, but they came back again. Others, who only came to look for their relatives, ended up staying for good. You have to have seen it to believe it. Mexico City has the dubious honor of being the world's third biggest city.

The intellectuals: The writers Octavio Paz and Carlos Fuentes are *capitalinos*, as are actress María Felix and artists Rufino Tamayo from Oaxaca and Francisco Toledo from the Tehuantepec isthmus. No one wants to be a provincial. Intellectuals need the Librería Francesa (a French bookshop) on Paseo de la Reforma. Just as in the 1950s and 60s they needed the bookstores that sold French editions of Henry Miller, whose works still had to be smuggled into the US, where they were still banned. Similarly, artists need the Palacio de Bellas Artes, a cake-like construction in white marble with various creamy layers, endowed by the dictator Porfirio Díaz and slowly being devoured by the earth. For – as everyone recognizes, and visitors above all – the city of Tenochtitlán-Mexico was built on a lake and the earth is pulling its buildings downwards, sucking them under, letting them slowly sink.

Rich writers and painters (almost all of them are rich) have their villas in Cuernavaca or Tepoztlán, which they drive out to at the weekends, but all of them continue to live in the incredibly ugly city, in

spite of the traffic, the jams, the water cuts and a future which looms mournfully over it. The *capitalinos* can't live without their great city; they need the culture, the art galleries, the festivals and gatherings, the gossip and the problems to make them feel they're alive.

In the last 50 years, villages which once lay outside the city – Tacubaya, Tacuba, Azcapotzalco, Mixcoac, San Angel, Coyoacán, Tlalpan – have been integrated into it, along with several other villages

belonging to the adjoining federal state of Mexico like Naucalpan, Tlalnepantla and Ecatepec. Once upon a time, those who lived in the center, around the Zócalo, used to say they were going for a walk in the market gardens of Coyoacán, Tlalpan and San Jerónimo. These days the popular Sunday afternoon resorts are part of the city. It's sad but true that even places which are still weekend retreats, like Cuernavaca, Tepoztlán or Cuautla, will soon become *barrios* (districts) of one of the most heavily populated cities of all time, a city the like of which has never been seen on this earth.

Preceding pages: bright Sunday bargains from an urban street trader. **Left**, San Angel's young Saturday chic. **Above**, "Carnation for your buttonhole, Señor?"

Marías of the streets: The *capitalinos* are very sharp; they know all the tricks a person needs to eke out a life in this city. They get around by Metro, Pesero, Combi, Minibus and Ruta 100, a magic bus that gradually extends or can blow itself up rapidly like a balloon, according to the number of passengers on the route.

Drivers never seem to mind that passengers are hanging out of the windows and doors, and Mexicans – whether they're working or not – travel like this from one end of the city to the other. In the mornings they leave their homes, regardless of whether they have jobs to go to. If they're not work-

and lottery tickets, which the sellers wave enticingly in front of your windscreen. "*Andele* (come on!) Señor, buy a ticket, *ándele* (okay, don't then), look at this cute little number, *ándele*, you could travel, you could fly to Europe, you don't even have to take me with you." Sometimes it seems there is hardly an inch of space anywhere that some enterprising vendor hasn't set up his little stall. The entrances to the subway stations are often so full of salesmen that the police have to crack down to make room for travelers to get in. But within hours the vendors are back again on their patches.

The streets of Mexico City are unusually

ing, they wander the streets and squares, buying whatever's for sale: the latest craze in toys, like models of Garfield the Cat or Topo Grigio, a talking mouse, or Mickey Mouse and girlfriend Minnie, and all sorts of chewing gum (incidentally, the gum tree was "discovered" in Yucatán and chewing gum is, like chocolate, one of Mexico's cultural gifts to the world. The chicle workers used to chew little balls of gum while they drew off the white sap from the trees, a thankless task in the enervating subtropical heat).

There are plenty more bargains on offer in the streets – Kleenex tissues, for example,

rich in images. You'll see the *golondrinos* (street musicians) and the *marías* – the Otomí and Mazahua Indian women with their embroidered blouses and plaits braided with brightly colored ribbons. Their tradition as traders is inextricably bound with their history as the oldest race in the land. In the past they used to sell fruit; now they approach the slow-moving traffic with trays of plastic toys. In short broken sentences (for they barely speak Spanish) they offer their meager wares to the captive audience of immobilized drivers. And all the while they tend their children, embroidering them little caps and vests in bright colors to ward off the spirits and protect them from the evil eye of the elders.

Although the Mazahua and Otomí women are outstanding needlewomen, they have no desire to work in factories, preferring the streets. They find it more sociable outdoors, more exciting and infinitely more varied than sitting indoors, sewing on a chair by the window. For a house wouldn't be the same as the big city with all its cars and attendant dangers, nor would they earn the 50, 100, 200, 500 pesos that they can make during an eight-hour day out on the streets.

Behind high walls: Their men arrive at the

All, or almost all, are unemployed or without full-time work, according to the economists. Many of them are farmers, who work on the land for one or two months of the year and have nothing to do the rest of the time.

They come to the city because they think they will have a better standard of living here than in the country. Here they can see electric light, walk on tarmacked pavements, sit in the shade under the trees in the city's parks and, when they look up, there are skyscrapers to marvel at. There's no shortage of distractions to take their minds off their hunger. Even if these refugees from the country have to live in miserable hovels,

DF (Distrito Federal), husbands and others who aren't their husbands, the fathers of their sons and the friends of their childhood, seducers of the moment and silver-tongued promisers of the future. They come from the country, their *sarapes* (woollen capes) slung over their shoulders, their faces shiny and clean-shaven. They jump down from the bus and stumble into the best job they can find, usually hawking cheap goods in the streets.

Left, children form the majority of the city's population. **Above**, "Who says we don't know how to wash our own trousers?"

they still don't give up hope of one day winning the lottery or attracting the favor of some magical benefactor who will somehow help them to make their fortune in the city. As a rule, though, they remain the poorest of the *capitalinos*.

The richest have their own residential districts, entertainment and travel – mostly to Las Vegas. The upper classes live in Tecamachalco and Lomas de Chapultepec (which used to be known as Chapultepec Heights, Bosques, Herradura and Valle Escondido). They dress in US fashions and build themselves modern houses, which they surround with high walls to deter casual onlookers – for no one should be allowed to criticize what lies beyond.

When these people aren't flying to Las Vegas, they jet off to Houston "for some shopping" or for a medical check-up. The Mexicans are renowned for squandering their money. They maintain houses they have built on the international border – "Taco Towers", as they've become known – and keep their fortunes in North American banks because they're worried about the inevitable devaluation of the peso. Their children attend universities in San Diego or San Antonio. Many of the major chain stores

would go out of business if the Mexican shoppers stayed at home.

Divided world: The Mexicans who count themselves among the upper echelons live in the south of the city, in Coyoacán, San Angel, Chimalistac, San Angel Inn, Tlacopac, El Pedregal and San Jéronimo. They prefer traditional Hispanic-Mexican architecture, and their taste tends towards the colonial style, visible in their choice of furnishings and pictures, although they also like Tamayo, Soriano and other modern artists.

They organize festivals in the historic city center (the *Centro Histórico*), charity ba-

zaars full of tasteful knicknacks and "ladies' garlands", posies of flowers bound together in classical style. They distance themselves from the rest of the population and from the overcrowded, noisy streets full of traders, clowns, beggars, car washers, balloon sellers and gum sellers, fire eaters – all those we collectively call *mil usos* ("of a thousand uses") because between them they practise all the professions in the world. Except of course banking – that's the province of the upper classes.

The affluent members of society meet in the San Angel Inn, go to art exhibitions, frequent art galleries, visit each other's homes, lunch and dine together, go away for weekends to their houses in the country.

The miserable plight in which the vast majority of the remaining *capitalinos* find themselves has led to an increase in violence, in the number of muggings and the number of people in prison. The rich will readily give advice to visitors: ay, ay, ay, only keep the bare minimum of money on you if you're walking around the streets, ay, ay, ay, and leave your passport and any valuables at hotel reception. Ay, ay, ay, it's better to go out in groups, rather than on your own, ay, ay, ay

For the spirit of solidarity that was so much in evidence and appeared so strong in times of crisis like the 1985 earthquake has petered out again in everyday life. In the city only a very few have time to care about anyone other than themselves. Sadly Mexico has too many politicians and too few true public servants.

The dizzy pace of city life slows down on Sundays. Public life takes a rest. The smoke from the factory chimneys stops; television – the so-called "idiot box" – starts up, and in the sports stadia the atmosphere is high. No one is left standing on street corners waiting for something to happen, for this is a day for getting together, for the family, for walking. This is the day to visit your mother-in-law – for after all, what we are talking about here is a matriarchy.

Left, as an industrial worker, he is one of the better off. **Right**, "My range of goods is my best advertisement."

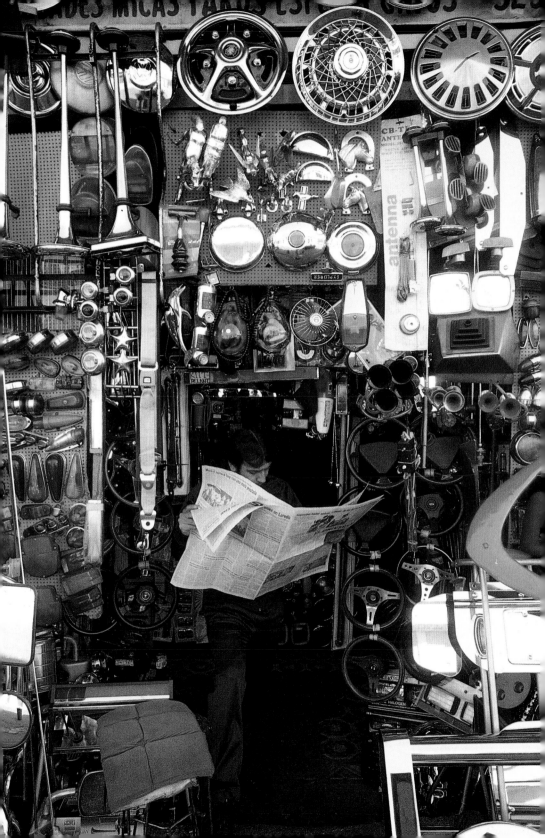

Post-Revolutionary Mexico became the classic land of asylum for Latin America, which accepted revolutionaries of every color and creed. Indeed, others who were persecuted have reason to be grateful to the Mexicans.

Spanish Republicans forced into exile by Franco as well as Jews and anti-fascists expelled from Hitler's Germany found refuge in Mexico. After Pinochet's overthrow of Salvador Allende, Chileans sought safety here and during the torture-junta in Buenos Aires, Argentinians fled to Mexico. Mexico has since accepted many political and economic refu-

Mercader, acting on the orders of the Soviet secret service, succeeded in assassinating Trotsky after having insinuated himself as a friend of the house. The exiled Soviet leader's ashes are preserved in an urn in the garden of his house in Coyoacán, now a museum.

In 1939, after Mexico and the Soviet Union were the only countries to recognize the Republic during the Spanish civil war, President Cárdenas announced that Mexico was ready to accept Republicans fleeing from Franco. Among these were a high percentage of artists, scientists, and intellectuals who have enriched

gees from El Salvador and Guatemala.

One of the first to take advantage of the generosity of the Mexican government under Lázaro Cárdenas was Leon Trotsky. The founder of the Red Army and his wife Natalia Sedova found refuge from Stalin's persecution in Mexico City – at first with the painters Diego Rivera and Frida Kahlo who were husband and wife. Later Trotsky moved into a house in the suburb of Coyoacán which he had had fortified. But in spite of all his security measures, he was nearly killed in an attack by an armed commando of Communists under the direction of muralist David Alfaro Siqueiros. Three months later, the Catalan Communist Ramón

the country's cultural life. Fritz Pohle, in his book *The Mexican Exile*, notes that not only humanitarian reasons lay behind Mexico's immigration policies. One of the demographic objectives of the Mexican state has been the increase of the number of *mestizos* among the population through the assimilation of foreigners, an objective the Spanish seemed most likely to guarantee. Indeed, they became integrated relatively quickly. Even before the Spanish Civil War, refugees with skills and qualifications had been privileged for economic reasons, since they were needed to further the country's development.

In view of the desperate refugee situation

created by the outbreak of World War II in Europe many European émigrés arrived in Mexico after hazardous journeys of many kinds. Among them were several prominent German writers and journalists who, with the administration's consent, made Mexico the center of anti-Nazi resistance in Latin America. The journal *Freies Deutschland*, which began in November 1941, published the texts of authors living in Mexico: Anna Seghers, Ludwig Renn, Paul Westheim, Egon Erwin Kisch, and others.

Most of the refugees lived in Mexico City, since the climate of the high-lying metropolis was pleasant for the Europeans. As the country's political and cultural center, the city was also the communications link to the outside

possibilities open to him than an illiterate native moving from the countryside to the city. Bruno Frei recalled in his autobiography (*Der Papiersäbel*): "From our windows in newly built apartments on the city's edge, we could see the viscera of the city. The real Mexico consisted of barrack settlements where the Indio woman wrapped her new-born children in rags, held it up to the Mexican sun to ensure survival. Hardly a single day went by that a man with saddened eyes didn't leave the barracks with a roughly constructed child's coffin. Although our stone house was a slum, it seemed like a palace to the Indio children."

Other authors have also written about their exile in Mexico. Egon Erwin Kisch's *Entdeckungen in Mexiko* (Discoveries in Mexico)

world. Finally, the exiled found better living and working conditions here than they could have found in the Mexican provinces.

Most of them lived in what, by their standards were modest conditions, but, compared to the poverty around them, conditions which were quite privileged. Many European emigrants found cheap lodgings in former maid's rooms under the roofs of the city, but none of them had to work as servants. The penniless European refugee in exile in Mexico had more

Left, President Cárdenas with Spanish refugees. **Above**, Leon Trotsky and Natalia Sedova in their refuge in Coyoacán.

appeared in 1945 from El Libro Libre (The Free Book) Publishers, and remains very instructive even today. Twenty years after his return, he published two poetic stories about Mexico: *Chrisanta* and *Das Wirkliche Blau* ("The Genuine Blue"). Of those exiled who stayed in Mexico, some have devoted their efforts to the service of the country. The art historian Paul Westheim produced an inimitable description of ancient Mexican art in his *The Sculpture of Ancient Mexico* (Doubleday 1963). Gertrude de Duby, originally from Switzerland and now in Chiapas, has dedicated her energies to the Lacandon Indians and the protection of the tropical rainforest.

OFF-DUTY IN MEXICO CITY

On Saturdays a sigh of relief runs the length and breadth of the city. Rich and poor alike yearn for the great outdoors. Those who can afford it jet off for two days to the coast, to Acapulco or Cancun, but even the hour's drive to Cuernavaca brings a change of climate. The city slickers indulge themselves here amidst the lush, subtropical vegetation. Since some of the smog has now dispersed over the provinces, the air in the city is more bearable too, and pedestrians are winning back the center.

Relaxing in the parks: Those who don't have at least a clapped-out old banger or *carcacha* to their name to drive the family out to the countryside, go walking or camping in the Alameda. Or husband, wife, children, uncles, aunts and grandparents will get together for a picnic in Chapultepec Park. Even before lunch, areas are already marked out with strings of balloons to show there's a children's birthday party taking place later that afternoon.

Children are kings and queens of the park on Sundays. Their little heads dive blissfully into huge mountains of pink candy floss. Spellbound, they watch the traders' brightly-colored windmills spinning. Their laughter rings out from a circle gathered around a clown, drawn there by the merry sound of his penny whistle. They can ride through the zoo on the miniature train, be rowed around the park on the artificial lake, or have their photos taken on a wooden horse, dressed as mini-revolutionaries.

On the *montana rusa,* the massive roller-coaster in the Pleasure Park (Parque de Diversiones) in the southern part of Chapultepec, parents' screams compete with those of their offspring. It's a colorful change for people who spend their everyday life between gray city walls. Everyone needs some fun – adults too.

Another place to spend holidays and get

Preceding pages: taking a break on a park bench. Left, homage to King Football against the majestic backdrop of Popocatépetl.

closer to nature is Xochimilco. On Sundays the packed gondolas (*trajineras*) are propelled nose to tail along the canals. People pack hampers of food and crates of drink, or buy tacos and drinks from the *canoas* paddling up and down. Flower sellers, ice-cream sellers and steaming food stalls are all part of the service. Other boats sway along, filled with photographers and *mariachi* bands with their violins and trumpets, who'll tag along behind your boat for a few songs. Sometimes you'll meet another boat carrying a *marimba*, a large Caribbean xylophone, to make a Mexican pot-pourri. "Ay, ay, ay, ay – sing, don't cry."

women's sides – regularly fight it out on the dusty pitches alongside the highway.

This land was previously the bed of a lake. The suburb has developed from a giant slum into an established satellite town, and is now the home of a huge stadium, where the top clubs in the national league play their matches. Visitors who want to see a top-class Mexican football match should find out who is playing on Saturday and Sunday afternoons in the "Azteca", "Universitario" and "Neza" stadiums.

Football *à la mexicana* is whatever the players and spectators choose to make of it. The *ola*, the crowd "wave" around the sta-

King football: Many *chilangos* (city dwellers) are so exhausted by the time the weekend arrives that they want no more than to swing gently in a hammock between two trees in Chapultepec Park. Others turn to sport to let off steam – either as active participants or committed spectators. Join the convoy down Avenida Zaragoza heading towards the Puebla highway, and at Nezahualcoyotl you can sample what has become Mexico's favorite game: football, the imported game which has become the opium of the masses. At "Neza" alone, well over 100 amateur teams – including several

dium was invented by the fans of player Hugo Sánchez.

The old Mexicans were early masters of the art of staying on the ball, even before the Europeans invaded. Their sport of *tlachtli* was in no way "just a game" but a fundamentally serious matter. The ball symbolized the sun and the team which let the sun go down – i.e. dropped the ball on the ground – was sacrificed to the gods. The rubber ball, considerably smaller in size than today's football, was not allowed to be touched with feet or hands, only with the elbows, knees, hips and bottom, but these parts of the body were protected with leather or cloth padding. The major attraction of the game, however – for only the nobility were allowed to play – seems to have been in the betting that accompanied it. Huge sums changed hands, sometimes in the form of gold, feathers, clothes – even slaves – and many unfortunate gamblers found themselves ruined for life.

Bull-fighting in the world's biggest arena: The Mexicans came up against the ritualistic nature of the *tlachtli* in some of the games introduced by the Spanish, for example bull-fighting, also a matter of life and death. All debate for and against is futile, for the *aficionados* – those avid followers of bull-

insight into the soul of the Mexican people.

The Plaza México seats 50,000 spectators, which makes it the largest bull-fighting arena in the world. From December through to May, the best matadors display their courage and grace in this ring. During the summer months, the *novilleros* use it to practise their routines. It is far from easy to get a seat in the shade because, like the grand opera, seats here are booked on a season-ticket basis. You may well end up sitting next to some delicate bourgeois housewife, who when asked whether she comes to these things often, says proudly: "I've been coming since I was a girl." For you'll find women

fighting – are deaf to criticism. Those who go to a bullfight just once, drawn by curiosity and a desire for spectacle, are unlikely to understand much of what goes on and will wonder why the deep, reverential, admiring "Olé" rises at precisely the same moment from a thousand throats.

But for the open-minded spectator, the atmosphere in the imposing Plaza México and all the trappings of the event should prove fascinating, giving as they do a brief

Left, "Helados!" is a welcome cry. **Above**, the line-up for the *charreada*, the Mexican rodeo.

and children in the audience here, too.

Dress tends towards two different styles: classical Spanish with flat-brimmed black hat or Basque cap, and the Mexican ranchero look, with boots and cowboy hats. As bottles are forbidden in the arena on safety grounds, people make do with Spanish leather flasks, which they hold at arm's length in traditional style, aiming a stream of red wine into their open mouths.

Punctually at four in the afternoon a trumpet fanfare sounds and the *corrida de toros* begins with the ceremonial entry (*paseo*) of the *toreros* dressed in their tight-fitting, gold-embroidered suits. They are followed by their helpers on horseback, the *picadores*, then the *banderilleros* and others whose task it is to drag the dead bull from the ring by three white horses. As the bull storms into the ring, it is teased by the *capeadores*, who wave their *capas* (short bull-fighters' capes). This skirmishing is followed by the *suerte de varas*, in which the *picadores* on horseback attack the bull with lances, thrusting them into his back. From this point onwards, anyone who can't stand the sight of blood should concentrate instead on the crowd's reaction.

In the next part of the fight, the

"cross" – the vulnerable spot between his shoulder blades is laid bare. If the torero strikes this exact spot, the bull is fatally wounded. His death throes may last a little longer, but they don't appear to hold much interest for the crowd.

The fight is over with that fatal thrust: the spectators stand, the men light themselves fat cigars and the women nibble on pistachios or eat ice cream. This is perhaps the most gruesome part of the whole bullfight.

The ritual is repeated six times in one *corrida*, each of the three *toreros* competing against two bulls. The matador is not always the victor. Sometimes the 1,100 lb (500 kg)

banderilleros shower the bull's neck with three pairs of *banderillas* (long, barbed sticks decorated with bright ribbons). Sometimes the *torero* will join in at this point, before demonstrating the full extent of his skills in the *hora de la verdad* – the hour of truth. With his cape (*capote*) he leads the bull around in tight circles, rewarded by suitable applause from the crowd for particularly daredevil manoeuvres bringing the bull close to the body.

It is crucial that he picks the right moment for the fatal thrust. The bull's head has to be lowered, his feet close together, so that the

bull catches him on his horns and the victory falls to him.

The noble sport of *Charreadas*: The *charros* also put their manly prowess on public display at the Mexican rodeo or *charreada*. At the risk of insulting them, you could compare these gentlemen to north American cowboys. They share a common background as professional cattleherds, whose skill in handling horses and the lasso makes a stunning display north or south of the border.

The Spanish introduced horses and cattle to Mexico, and the traditional *charro* suit, with decorative silver buttons on the trousers and a short jacket, brings to mind the festival costume of the men of Salamanca on mainland Spain, while the sombrero resembles the wide-brimmed Andalusian hat. To the rest of the world, the proud *charro* is the popular image of a Mexican.

Charreadas are a fashionable sport in Mexico City nowadays, based around specialist clubs. For the participants, they are an expensive form of entertainment, because the horses have to be stabled and the *charro* costume, along with the elaborately decorated saddle and bridle, are unbelievably expensive. For spectators in the *lienzos charros*, the *charreada* arena on the outskirts of the city, entry is usually free.

The *jaripeo* tournament begins with the *cola de caballo*: riders enter the ring at a gallop, then bring the horse to an abrupt standstill, before turning it in a circle. Then, in a manoeuvre known as *coleadero*, they seize the cattle by the tail and try to throw it off balance by whirling it round. They demonstrate their skill with a lasso by rounding up wild horses, and the climax of the show comes with the daring leap from the back of a galloping horse onto an untamed wild horse. Women riders also take part in *charreadas*, although they have their own competitions and elegant side-saddles – no doubt so that they don't risk stealing the men's limelight.

Place your bets: Punters desperate for a gamble would do best heading for the race course, the Hipódromo de las Américas (Tuesday and Thursday through Sunday). There is also betting at the Basque Jai Alai in Frontón México (Plaza de la República), open every evening except Monday and Friday. This is probably the world's fastest ball game, involving either eight individual players or eight pairs. The ball is hurled and caught using banana-shaped baskets (*cestas*) and is only allowed to touch the ground or the wall once. Betting plays a large part in the activities and the gamblers, too, use a ball – a tennis ball with a slit in it to hold their stake which they throw to the bookie.

Other sporting events that the Mexicans get excited about are boxing (Saturday evenings) and *lucha libre*, all-in wrestling. Those who want to put in a spot of training themselves can take a morning jog through Chapultepec Park, or swim, play tennis or golf at one of the expensive private clubs. Some are open to visitors (take your passport and tourist card with you).

The *chilangos* are expert in enjoying themselves without feeling guilty – even in times of economic crisis. They eat out with family or friends in restaurants, where they like to pay musicians to play for them while they sing along to well-known folk songs.

Extravagant hosts, they like holding parties, or enjoying themselves at the various sporting events in ring or arena.

Cultural and educational pastimes are available at very little cost, because they are subsidized by the state. Entry to most museums is free on Sundays and theater and concert tickets don't cost the earth. Many make the most of these bargains. Those who have the chance to relax in their hammocks or let off steam in sport and games have refueled their energy by Monday and can hurl themselves back into the hectic everyday of Mexico City with renewed vigor.

Left, glass bottles are banned at bull-fights, but there are ways round the problem. **Right**, *toreros* should show daring and grace.

No visitor should miss the pleasure of Mexican cuisine or fail to sample Mexican delicacies. The wide variety of dishes stems from an intermixing of different eating habits and has some surprises even to those who think they know it.

The country's real culinary art has little in common with what is known abroad as Mexican cuisine. Outside the country's borders one rarely finds such familiar menu specialities as *caldo tlalpeño* (a tasty chicken

"Montezuma's revenge", don't subject your stomach to excessive strain.

The many different types of *chile* peppers are an ubiquitous part of Mexican cuisine. They are used as spicy garnishes and very sharp condiments in cold sauces (*salsa verde, roja* or *Mexicana*) or stuffed with meat or cheese (*chile relleno de carne* or *de queso*). If you should find them too spicy, the best antidote is a *tortilla* (maize pancake) which is a surer way than an icy glass of

soup with Mexican vegetables), *tamales* (maize semolina croquettes), or *chiles en nogada* (peppers in nut sauce with pomegranate seeds).

Mexico City offers a broad culinary spectrum as well as a price range. It ranges from the simple *taco* (a rolled maize pancake, usually filled with meat), to the *comida corrida* (a three-course *menu de jour*), to the exquisite *mole poblano* (chicken in a dark sauce which is prepared with more than 17 ingredients – among them chocolate). One should, however, be careful when first trying Mexican cooking: if you want to avoid

water to neutralize a burning tongue.

Tortilla is the staple food of the population, part of practically every meal, not only as a side dish but as a main course: as rolled *tacos* with all sorts of fillings such as meat, vegetables, spices, cheese, etc; as *enchiladas* with tomato-chili sauce, or roasted as *tostadas*. Rice (*arroz*) and brown beans (*frijoles*) are the most common side dishes. *Puntas de filete* (filet ends), *carne asada à la tampiqueña* (a juicy strip of broiled beef) *huachinango à la Veracruzana* (red bass prepared according to the Veracruz recipe) are only a few select main dishes. The curious should also try a cactus leaf salad (*ensalada de nopales*) or the crisp fried agave worms (*gusanos de maguey*) with *guacamole* (avocado paste with chopped onions and tomatoes, fresh coriander and lemon juice), a Mexican delicacy.

A *tequila con sangrita* (agave spirit and a glass of spicy tomato juice) is an aperitif to be recommended. Local wine or superb Mexican beer goes with any meal. Fruit and scented waters (*aguas naturales*) made from tamarind, melons, limes, guavas, hibiscus (*jamaica*), etc., are also particularly good thirst quenchers.

Before going to a restaurant remember *haciendas* are among the "best addresses" in the city and are a favorite with the city's business community. The Fonda del Recuerdo and the Restaurant Focolare are among those with live Mexican music and typical cuisine. Both offer Veracruzan specialties and folklore expressive of the Mexican's festive character. The Kino Mexikatessen, in the Palanco quarter, specializes in the "exotic" dishes of the pre-Spanish period.

Princes, princesses and other prominent guests such as Robert Kennedy or Brigitte Bardot have dined in the romantic San Angel Inn with its luxurious dining room (beware:

that, in Mexico, one eats relatively late. Lunch is served between 1 and 3 p.m. and dinner between 8 and 10.30 p.m.

The list of Mexican restaurants in the capital is inexhaustible and it is difficult to make any selection. Many prefer the rich atmosphere offered in the former mansions of old *haciendas*, such as the Antiqua Hacienda de Tlalpan, with its wonderful garden, or the Hacienda de los Morales. The former

Left, the roofed patio of the Tile House is the flagship of the Sanborn chain. **Above**, in high spirits at the Fonda del Recuerdo.

diners will not be admitted in the evening without appropriate attire, e.g. dinner jacket and tie for men). One should definitely try the *taquerías* which can be found on any street corner. These Mexican "snack bars" offer good, reasonably priced tortilla-based food with real Mexican ambiance.

Visitors to Mexico who cannot even stand the smell of maize or are reluctant to eat anything unknown or exotic can relax; there's something for them too. This world metropolis, like any other, has a large choice of international cuisine available alongside the native food.

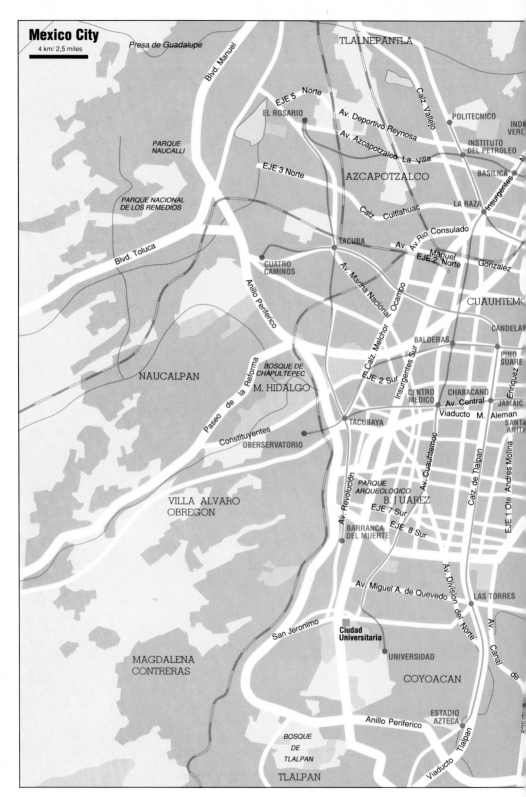

Mexico City

4 km/ 2,5 miles

Presa de Guadalupe

TLALNEPANTLA

Blvd. Manuel

EJE 5 Norte

EL ROSARIO

Calz. Vallejo

POLITECNICO

IND
VERD

Av. Deportivo Reynosa

INSTITUTO
DEL PETROLEO

PARQUE
NAUCALLI

Av. Azcapotzalco La Villa

EJE 3 Norte

AZCAPOTZALCO

BASILICA

PARQUE NACIONAL
DE LOS REMEDIOS

Calz. Cuitlahuac

LA RAZA

Insurgentes

Blvd. Toluca

Av. Rio Consulado

TACUBA

Av. Rio Consulado

Manuel

CUATRO
CAMINOS

Av. Matha Nacional Ocampo

EJE 2 Norte

Gonzalez

Anillo Periferico

CUAUHTEMO

NAUCALPAN

BALDERAS

CANDELA

PINO
SUARE

BOSQUE DE
CHAPULTEPEC

EJE 2 Sur

M. HIDALGO

Insurgentes Sur

CHABACANO

JAMAIC

Calz. Melchor

Paseo de la Reforma

CENTRO
MEDICO

Av. Central

Viaducto M. Aleman

SANTA
ANITA

Constituyentes

TACUBAYA

OBERSERVATORIO

PARQUE
ARQUEOLOGICO

Av. Revolución

B. JUAREZ

Av. Cuauhtemoc

Calz. de Tlalpan

Andres Molina

EJE 1 Ote

VILLA ALVARO
OBREGON

EJE 7 Sur

EJE 8 Sur

BARRANCA
DEL MUERTE

Av. Miguel A. de Quevedo

Av. Division del Norte

LAS TORRES

Av. Canal de

MAGDALENA
CONTRERAS

San Jeronimo

Ciudad
Universitaria

UNIVERSIDAD

COYOACAN

ESTADIO
AZTECA

Anillo Periferico

BOSQUE
DE
TLALPAN

Tlalpan

Viaducto

TLALPAN

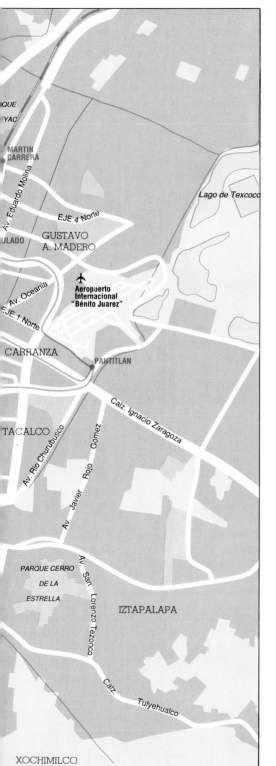

PLACES

Flying over the seemingly endless sea of houses into today's Mexico City the visitor might wonder how it is possible to find one's way around. The reality is of course that he is likely to stay in a relatively small portion of the metropolis: the area bounded by Chapultepec Park to the west and the Zócalo – that vast plaza which forms the heart of downtown – in the east. Although these east-west extremes are too far apart for a casual stroll the area is comprised of cozy-sized smaller units, most of them adjacent or close to the main street. This is the broad and beautiful Paseo de la Reforma which runs from the edge of the park, past the touristy Zona Rosa, bisecting Avenida Juárez beside the downtown Alameda Park.

Chapultepec Park contains half a dozen of the capital's finest museums including the National Museum of Anthropology which is probably unequalled in the world. During the weekends this park is the place to glimpse the private lives of Mexicans.

In contrast, there is the modern architecture in and around the university campus. To the north of the city center is Tlatelolco with its "Plaza of Three Cultures" bearing witness to different civilizations which have thrived in the city's history. Even farther north is the shrine of the Virgin of Guadalupe, the Mexican national patron saint. The Mexican bares his pious soul in front of the Virgin but it is in the markets, where all sorts of mysterious means to influence one's fortunes are offered, that one encounters his superstitions.

No visitor should miss exploring at least one of the city's markets: the vast Lagunilla or Merced markets selling virtually anything, or such smaller *mercados* as the folkcraft-filled Centre Artesenal or the Saturday-only *Bazar Sabado* in suburban San Angel (whose "neighbor" Coyoacán is notable for its museums devoted to Leon Trotsky and painter Frida Kahlo).

Preceding pages: a Mexican soup chef; the Saturday market at San Angel; "Voladores" in action near the Museo de Antropología.

TIPS FOR SHORT TRIPS

Some travelers in Mexico have only time for a short stay in the capital – especially business people. This chapter aims to help those travelers to get the best use out of that time.

First in the Old Town: One should definitely get to know the historic city center. To get in the right mood, a good start is a substantial breakfast at Sanborn's on the Calle Madero (in the famous Tile House) or in the Café Tacuba. From there it is only a few steps to the **Zócalo** and the **Cathedral**, the **Palacio Nacional** and the excavations of the **Templo Mayor**. The roof terrace of the Hotel Majestic (which also has a good Sunday buffet) has a commanding view of the city's main plaza.

It is also worth making an excursion to the nearby **Plaza Santo Domingo** with its old hand-set printing presses and itinerant secretaries. The Restaurant Prendes on Calle 16 de Septiembre has been the meeting place of Mexican politicians and business people for decades, and the turn-of-the-century Cantina La Opera is also rich in tradition. This restaurant has a genuine Mexican ambience and is seldom visited by tourists.

It is well worth attending an orchestral concert or performance by Mexico's brilliant Ballet Folklorico at the **Palacio de Bellas Artes**, thereby not only enjoying this magnificent art deco building as a museum but also seeing it as a lively cultural center.

An excellent museum in the city center is the **Museo Franz Mayer**, a private collection of art treasures from the colonial epoch which belonged to a German who emigrated from Mannheim in the 1920s. From there it is easy to take a taxi to the **Zona Rosa**, a district of restaurants, cabarets, galleries, jewelers, handicraft shops, and boutiques devoted to fashion and other things to interest tourists. In the pedestrian zones, it is pleasant to relax at street cafés and watch the life in the big city go by.

There is something for everyone, for every age and for every time of day in and around **Chapultepec Park** to the west of the city. Anyone in the least interested in the ancient Indian cultures should definitely visit the **Anthropological Museum** here. Mexican history since the Spanish conquest is unfurled in the **Historical Museum** in the **Palace**. In three other excellent museums, there are exhibitions of modern art: **Museo de Arte Moderno** in the park, **Museo Rufino Tamayo**, and the well-appointed **Centro Cultural de Arte Contemporáneo**.

Between these attractions there are walks in the park, with lakes, the zoo and children's playgrounds. The elegant hotels on the park's perimeter have live music or international discos in the evenings (the hotels Camino Real, Nikko, and Stouffer Presidente). This is the place for a romantic evening

Bargaining in the Bazar del Sábado

for two with dancing at the Restaurante Del Lago on one of the ponds in Chapultepec Park.

Weekend specials: If you have a weekend available for Mexico City, it is worth going to the **Bazar del Sábado** (Saturday bazaar) in San Angel if just to see the concentration of arts and crafts from all over Mexico. Or alternatively you could take a boat trip along the canals of **Xochimilco** and afterwards have lunch in one of the old *hacienda* restaurants in the south of the city. The cultural center (**Centro Cultural Universitario**) of the national university (UNAM) also lies in this part of the city with its cinemas, theatres, and one of the world's best concert halls called **Sala Nezahualcóyotl**. The journal *Tiempo Libre*, which is available from any newsagent, provides a weekly listing of the cultural events in the city.

The biggest shopping center in Mexico City, the **Perisur**, is also near the university. There you can find anything from a toothbrush to a tuxedo or a new car (Perisur is closed on Mondays).

If you want to spend the evening "á la Mexicana" you should drive to the Plaza Garibaldi where the *mariachi* bands play; they also perform in some of the nearby restaurants. *Mexico City Daily Bulletin*, a free daily newssheet found in most hotels, also has information about night clubs, bars with shows and cabarets, and your hotel's bell captain should also be able to tell you what's going on.

Mexicans are also fond of the places where Caribbean music is performed (*música tropical*), e.g. the Salón Margo, the Antillanos, the Bar León or the Peñas, and night spots with Latin American folk music such as the Mesón de la Guitarra, and El Condor Pasa.

If you'd like to see Mexico City from above, the view from the **Torre Latinoamericana** almost opposite the Bellas Artes Palace downtown is very impressive at night. From there the endless sea of lights in the city spreads out before you as the city changes shift.

A drink in view of the flag ceremony.

Mexico City Center

400 m/ 0,25 miles

E. Ancona

Dr. Gonzáles Martínez

Av. Insurgentes Norte

Saturno

EJE 1 Poniente

(Guerrero)

Cda. Estrella

Diaz Miron

EJE 1 Norte (Jose Antonio Alzate)

Main Railway Station

(Mosqueta)

Cda. Camelia

CUAUHTEMOC

Amado Nervo

Plaza Buena Vista

Pedro Moreno

Paseo de

Central Lazaro Cardenas

Plaza Gar

Ribera de San Cosme

(Guerrero)

Edison

Puente de Alvarado

Templo de San Hipolito

Santo Tomas de Villanueva (Hotel Cortés)

Templo de San Juan de Dios + Museum Franz Mayer

Museo de San Carlos (Palacio de Buenavista)

(Rosales)

HIDALGO

Plaza Sta. Veracruz

Templo de La Santa Veracruz

El Cal

Plaza de la Republica

Monumento a la Revolución

Pinacoteca Virreinal

ALAMEDA-PARK

Diego Rivera Museum

Post

Pala

Antonio Caso

Insurgentes Centro

Palacio de Bellas Artes

Av. Juarez

Ca (H

Torre Latinoamericana

Templo de San Francisco

P de Itu

JARDIN DEL ARTE

Paseo de la Reforma

EJE 1 Poniente

Mineria

Columbus Monument

(Bucareli)

Plaza Ciudadela

Plaza de San Juan

Roma

Handcraft Market

Plaza Vizcainas

EJE Central Lazaro Cardenas

Circular de Morelia

Arcos de Belen

BALDERAS

Plaza Morelia

Dr. Rio de la Loza

Pla el

Puebla

Dr. Lavista

Puebla

Plaza Romita

Dr. Lucio

Dr. Pascua

Plaza Rio de Janeiro

Frontera

JARDIN TABASCO

Dr. Claudio Bernard

Diag. 20

EJE 2 Norte

Plaza de las
Tres Culturas

Av. Peralvillo

(Av. del Trabajo Boleo)

Plaza
de la
Concepcion

EJE 1 Ote

(Canal Norte)

F.C. Cintura

Circunvalacion

Sastreria

...forma

Plaza Sta. Ana

Glez. Bocanegra

Panaderos

Imprenta

EJE 3 Ote

Rayon)

(Heroes de Granadita)   EJE 1 Norte

Ebanisteria

Jardineros

Av. Ing. Eduardo Molina

Plaza de
Sta. Catarina

Carmen Castellanos

Plaza Torres
Quintero

(Vidal Alcocer)

F.C. de Cintura

Tapiceria

Albaniles

Chile

Templo de
Santo Domingo

Templo
de Loreto

Rep. de

Plaza
Loreto

CENTRO

Monte de Piedad

Templo Mayor

Cda. Tomatlan

Cathedral

Sagrario

a Catolica

Zócalo

Palacio Nacional

Templo de
La Santisima

E. Zapata

City Hall

20 de Noviembre

J. Ortiz de Dominguez

Templo de
San Augustin

Plaza
G. Bravo

(Anillo de Circunvalacion)

CANDELARIA

Av. Congreso de la Union

Museo de la
Ciudad de Mexico

Plaza
General
Anaya

Gral. Anaya

Hospital de Jesus

Misionero

Plaza
Carrizal

Maria Izazaga

San Pablo

C. Robelo

PINO
SUAREZ

La Merced
(Market)

PARQUE
BALBUENA

Fray Servando Teresa de Mier

EJE 1 Ote

AROUND THE ZOCALO

The heart of the largest city in the world is appropriately grand: the Zócalo, the main square, has always been the center of the city and of the entire country. Every edifice on the square bears witness to the metropolis' eventful history. The holy temples of the Aztec Tenochtitlán, whose ruins have by now been unearthed by archaeologists, lie right next to the square. The Spanish built their own cathedral and government offices on the Plaza Mayor in what was the capital of New Spain.

Before the middle of the 15th century Tenochtitlán was already a magnificent, crowded city of as many as 400,000 people and the great temple was the symbolic as well as the physical center of the Aztec empire. Since the city's founding two centuries before it had been enlarged and rebuilt on numerous occasions.

The modern name came about because, in 1843, the dictator Santa Anna ordered the erection of a monument to independence in the square, but the monument was never finished. After the empty pedestal (in Spanish *zócalo*) had been there for years, the people started to call the square "**Zócalo**" – a name which now designates the main square in any Mexican city.

During the reign of the Habsburg Emperor Maximilian the square was transformed, trees were planted, a pavilion was built for concerts, a kiosk, candelabras, statues, benches and fountains were imported from Paris to give it maximum French atmosphere. Today the Zócalo is empty again, except for a flagpole with the Mexican flag. Compared to the overcrowding which one normally associates with the downtown area it is almost unimaginably spacious and is the ideal site for festivals, parades and demonstrations. Everyday life for the people unfolds on the streets around the Zócalo like a series of picture postcards – an experience that certainly should not be missed by any visitor.

The Aztec temple: On February 24, 1978, construction workers discovered a cut stone weighing 8 tonnes, with delicate, well-preserved reliefs, behind the cathedral. According to archaeologists the decapitated figure on the stone is the powerful Aztec moon goddess Coyolxauhqui. They also discovered that the oval monolith, which is 3.25 meters (10 ft) in diameter, marks the spot where the sacrificial victims, falling from the Great Temple, would hit the ground.

They deduced that the Templo Mayor, otherwise the **Great Temple of Tenochtitlán**, therefore had to be somewhere close by. In the years that followed, houses and historic buildings from colonial times covering an area four times the size of a soccer field were torn down to enable further excavation work, which was completed in 1982.

The archaeologists unearthed several

Preceding pages: view from the "Torre". Below, the Palacio Nacional.

buildings and more than 6,000 artifacts – testimony not only to the Aztecs' cruel religious rites but also to the size of their empire: sculptures from Oaxaca, clay vases from the Guerrero region, burial urns from the Gulf of Mexico, anthropomorphic figurines and fish and shell ornaments were part of the tribute that the subjugated tribes had to pay to the Aztecs, who themselves lived primarily from fishing.

The temple sites are best explored following the path which leads to the **Tzompantli**, an altar made of 240 stone skulls. It strongly resembles the real Tzompantlis, that is the walls on which the skulls of the beheaded sacrificial victims were displayed. The colorful reliefs that decorate the houses of the "Caballeros Aguila", the Eagle Men, a military caste in the Aztec society, are also remarkable. The original of the monolith of the moon goddess Coyolxauhqui, whose head first came to light in 1825 in the foundations of a house being built on Santa Teresa Street, east of the Zócalo, is now in the museum of the Templo Mayor; the sculpture exhibited here is a copy.

Museum for the beheaded: After the foundations of the Templo Mayor had been so spectacularly uncovered, scientists and politicians demanded a museum right next to the archaeological site. Mexico's famous architect Pedro Ramirez Vazquez, who had already designed the **Museum of Anthropology and History** in the lovely Chapultepec Park, drafted the plans for the new exhibition halls, whose interiors were modified according to the progress of the excavations. On October 12, 1987, the anniversary of the discovery of America, the museum was inaugurated.

The stone tablet of the moon goddess Coyolxauhqui is on display in the central part of the museum behind the building's only window. The relief shows a naked female torso without head, arms or legs.

Coyolxauhqui was an important goddess in Aztec mythology. The legend

The Zócalo, a stage for many events.

goes that she was dismembered by her brother Huitzilopochtli, God of War, because she wanted to kill her mother Coatlicue, the earth, and did not approve of human sacrifices.

In the museum, the monolith can be viewed from two perspectives: on the first floor, flat in front of the visitor, or from the second floor through an opening in the ceiling. The artist who created this relief succeeded in showing life and death side by side so that at close range, the goddess seems to be both alive and dead at the same time. This seeming contradiction is intended to express the antagonisms within the world of the Aztec gods.

At the time when the renowned German traveler Baron von Humboldt visited Mexico in 1803 the statue of Coatlicue was languishing under a foot of earth at the University of Mexico to which it had been consigned on the orders of the Spanish viceroy, who feared this "devilish idol" could provoke anarchistic ideas. With the aid of

his friend the Bishop of Monterrey, von Humboldt succeeded in having the statue dug up and it is on exhibit in the museum today.

The design and organization of the new museum was planned to transcend traditional concepts. The museum therefore avoids display cases so that no glass barrier stands between exhibit and visitor. A receptacle representing Tlaloc, the rain god, is suspended above a small fountain, clarifying the object's symbolic meaning. Passages from the different Codices explain the customs and traditions of pre-Hispanic peoples. Unfortunately, there is no English translation for foreign visitors.

Eight exhibition halls with artifacts from the history of the Aztecs are arranged on four levels around a central patio. The four halls in the southern wing are devoted to the legend of Huitzilopochtli, god of war, and to war, sacrifice, tribute and trade.

Hall 1 shows the migration of the Aztecs to their permanent place of set-

The stone of of the Coyolxauhqui.

tlement in Tenochtitlán. In Hall 2, war and the sacrifices necessary to reconcile the gods and the sun are dealt with. Tribute and trade as the Aztecs' bases of existence are explained in Hall 3, while in Hall 4 the most important monoliths are on display: the eagle warrior, the god of fire and the eight standard bearers, which had already been found in 1978 near the stairs to the altar of Huitzilopochtli. Some of them showed traces of paint and shell-incrustations on their bodies and obsidian in their eyes. Up to the present day the archaeologists have failed to agree on significance of this. Some of the recently discovered objects had already been covered by earth and thus forgotten by the time the Spanish arrived.

The four halls of the northern wing are the realm of Tlaloc, god of fertility and water. Pieces found in the area of the Mixtek tribe which was as far as 560 km (348 miles) away, illustrate the god's manifold presence. In the room marked "Fauna", skeletons of sacrificial animals are shown: crocodiles, turtles, eagles, pumas, poisonous snakes, snails and sharks. The seventh gallery deals with everyday life and religion: childbirth, education, the concept of the Aztec universe and the significance of the Great Temple in the cosmology of the Aztecs. The "Conquista" hall shows the arrival of the conqueror Cortéz and his followers.

The contemporary historian Bernal Díaz wrote that the conquistadors "saw things unseen, nor ever dreamed" and he records that four days after his entrance into Mexico, Cortéz and his chief captains were taken by Montezuma "to look at the great city and all the other towns nearby on the lake and the villages built on dry land... This great accursed temple was so high that from the top of it everything could be seen perfectly... So having gazed at all this and reflected upon it we turned our eyes to the great marketplace and the host of people down there who were buying and selling: the hum and murmur of the voices could have been heard for more than a league. And among us were soldiers who had been in many parts of the world... and they said they had never seen a market so well ordered, so large and so crowded with people."

Spanish ceramics and columns built on Aztec structures illustrate the decline and fall of Aztec society. A gold bullion bar reminds us of the fact that the conqueror melted gold and precious jewelry to send to the *madre patria*, the motherland, as proof of his excellence.

Latin cross: The **cathedral** of Mexico City is probably the biggest and most important Christian building on the South American continent. It combines the three major architectural styles of the 16th to the 19th century – which are the three centuries of its construction: from Gothic through Renaissance and baroque to the neoclassical era. The baroque facade is framed by two neoclassical bell towers and the clock tower designed by the architect Manuel Tolsa. The layout of the cathedral is in the

Gilded pomp in the cathedral.

shape of a Latin cross, built on a square 109 by 54 meters (358 by 177 ft).

Hernán Cortéz had the first Christian church on the Plaza Mayor built with materials taken from the Templo Mayor. Up to 1552 the church was Franciscan, but in 1544, archbishop Montúfar began the preliminary work for a new cathedral, modeled on the cathedral of Seville. Although the foundation stone was laid in 1573, only 50 years after the Spanish conquest, it wasn't until 100 years later that the cathedral could be dedicated and the basalt and limestone facade was finished only in 1689. Another 100 years went by until architect Damian Ortiz de Castro inaugurated the bell towers. Manuel Tolsa finally finished it off, adding a dome and balustrades.

The interior of the cathedral consists of one main and two minor naves as well as 14 altars along the sides. The most significant work of art in the choir is the **Altar de Pardon** (altar of forgiveness) in the 18th-century Churrigueresco style. Some years ago, the altar, together with the cedar-wood choir stalls, were all but destroyed in a fire but have since been renovated. The choir-lattice – a mixture of gold, silver, and bronze – comes from China. The vestry features Gothic vaults and two major frescoes by Villalpando and Correa.

The prize exhibit is the Altar de los Reyes in the apse, behind the onyx main altar, carved over a period of 10 years by Jeronimo de Balbas. Note the *estípites*, pillars which taper off at the base, which recur in many buildings of the colonial period. Here the paintings by Juan Rodriguez Juárez depict the *Adoration of the Magi* and the *Assumption*. The cathedral itself is dedicated to the Virgin Mary. Seven chapels are arranged along the aisles, and a statue of Senor del Cacao to whom the Indians gave cacao – to them it was a currency – as a sacrificial gift for the construction of the church, can be seen in the third chapel to the left of the entrance.

The Sagrario: To the right of the cathe-

Left, in the Chapel of Fear in the cathedral. Right, the Sagrario Metropolitano.

dral, in 1749, the Spaniard Lorenzo Rodriguez began to build the Sagrario Metropolitano, the sacristy, in which books with the names of all believers were kept. Although it was Balbas, with his Altar de los Reyes, who introduced the Churrigueresco style, Rodrigues took up its most important element, the *estípites*, and turned them into the most dominant feature of the Sagrario's facade. Ever since, this and other Churrigueresco elements have been imitated on hundreds of churches throughout the country.

With the use of the *estípites* on the Sagrario the architect created a harmonic, well-proportioned churchfront which is made to seem less stark by the use of volcanic red *tezontle* stone among the gray basalt blocks.

eft, in the rcades. ight, ivera's ural in the alacio acional.

The interior of the Sagrario is impressive, with its Greek cross layout above which rises an octagonal dome. As with other buildings in the city, the foundations of the building have sunk into the soft ground of the dried-out lake Texcoco on which the city is built.

Political center: Ever since the foundation of the Aztec empire, the **Palacio Nacional** has been the place where the political fate of the nation has been decided. The Spanish viceroys resided in the palace and since the proclamation of the Republic, it has been the official residence of the Mexican president. The building, filled with art treasures, depicts a nation in search of its identity for hundreds of years. It was destroyed – but immediately rebuilt – during an insurgency in the 17th century. In the 18th century the Conde de Revillagigedo had the public market removed from the interior court and cleaned up the dark, foul-smelling places. The last viceroys revelled in their love of French architecture and design and gave the palace its European character. During the War of Independence the building had to serve as the military headquarters on many occasions.

Since independence the Palacio has housed the federal government, the leg-

islature and the Supreme Court. The precious furniture and works of art date from the days of the Habsburg Emperor Maximilian when the palace served as residence for visiting dignitaries. General Porfirio Díaz had the building modernized, installing telephones, lights and elevators. During the Revolution, the palace once again was used for military purposes, and between 1924 and 1928 President Elias Calles added a new facade and a third storey.

In the course of 20 years the great muralist Diego Rivera decorated the staircase and the first floor galleries with scenes from Mexican history and his particular vision of humanity and class struggle.

Above the main entrance there is the liberty bell with which, on September 16, 1810, Padre Miguel Hidalgo rang in the country's independence in the little village of Dolores. Every year, on the eve of September 16, the national holiday, the president repeats the *grito de la independencia* before cheering crowds.

The Avenida Pino Suarez leads to the **Museo de la Ciudad de Mexico**, the city museum. As pre-Spanish history is documented much better these days in the Templo Mayor, this museum has lost some of its significance. Nevertheless the colonial building, a former ducal palace, is well worth a visit. Across the street is the **Hospital de Jesus Nazareno**, built, according to legend, on the very spot where Hernán Cortéz first met Montezuma. It was the first hospital in the Americas and still treats patients – mainly from poor classes. The mortal remains of Hernán Cortéz rest in the hospital's chapel which was built in the 17th century and painted in the 1940s by muralist José Clemente Orozco. Cortéz, who actually died in Seville but whose body was carried back to Mexico, is remembered by a simple plaque bearing the inscription "Cortéz – 1485–1547" to the left of the apse.

School premises: On the Calle Ildefonso there is the sombre Jesuit school **Colegio de San Ildefonso** (1740). In its past this has served as a dormitory for the students, as a place for religious exercises and it also housed a big library. Until 1975 it was Mexico's most famous public school, the **Escuela Nacional Preparatoria**. The baroque front is made of *tezontle* stone. Inside, a stone marks the place where the building is sinking into the ground. Worth seeing are the murals in the staircases, the patios and the Simón Bolívar amphitheater: the first examples of Mexican *muralismo*, already here showing its typical popular and social content as well as its characteristic monumental nationalism.

One of the most famous paintings is *La Creacion* (The Creation) by Diego Rivera (1922) in the Simón Bolívar amphitheater. It combines elements from the Italian renaissance, symbolism and Art Deco as well as Christian scenes and allegories from the sciences. The young muralist Alfar Siqueiros has also worked on the walls of the college: in the painting *Los Elementos* (The El-

Scribes and printers in the Plaza Santo Domingo.

ements), lyrical scenes are found side by side with odes to the solidarity of the working class. Over a period of three years, Clemente Orozco has painted his visions of corruption, demagogery, lack of moral integrity, fear, pain, and the tragedy of life itself.

The modern **Ministry of Education** (Secretaria de Educacion Publica) lies in the Calle Argentina. Beautiful *murales* by Juan O'Gorman, Carlos Merida and Diego Rivera decorate the walls of this colonial building, which was founded in the 18th century as a nuns' cloister, Nuestra Senora de la Encarnacion. Since the creation of the Ministry of Education, the building has been remodelled several times to accommodate the needs of the institution.

Iglesia de la Santísima Trinidad is one of the most beautiful examples of Churrigueresco. The church, built in the 18th century, lies on the corner of the Calle La Santísima and Calle Emiliano Zapata. The facade with its delicate stone carving work is particularly re-markable: busts, semi-reliefs, papal crown and keys, the twelve apostles and the Trinity.

While in the area, a little detour to the **Plaza Santo Domingo** is recommended. This picturesque square, with its Dominican cloister church, nestles between the Calles Brasil, Venezuela and Cuba. It is bordered by the former Customs House, the tribunal of the Inquisition and other buildings from which the Catholic authorities surveyed all Mexican publications and punished those who transgressed Catholic moral beliefs.

A statue of the heroine of the Revolution, Josefa Ortíz de Domínguez, called "La Corregidora," overlooks the square. Under the arcades here is where you will find the public secretaries and printers seated at battered typewriters on which they compose all kinds of letters for their often illiterate clientele, ranging from love letters to official correspondence with the daunting machinery of government.

Art Nouveau in the Gran Hotel.

There is nothing you might wish to buy in Mexico City for which you might conceivably have to enter any of the city's modern supermarkets and department stores. Everything necessary for daily life is offered for sale in one or another of the traditional markets.

To bargain on the street, to make your purchase from an itinerant vendor or a trusted *marchanta* is no furtive delight – it is an open passion of the Mexicans. Shopping is part of the daily activity of the Mexican housewife or her maid. Who knows whether the Indian or Spanish heritage is the more

by street vendors. The city fathers have repeatedly tried to keep the streets and squares free from commercial activities. They have built many indoor markets in those areas where the vendors' stands accumulated. The indoor markets were also introduced in an attempt to control the hygienic conditions under which foodstuffs were sold, but the majority of vendors who cannot afford to rent a place inside continue to spread over the streets and sidewalks.

Some markets in the city are especially interesting for travelers. Among these are La Merced,

significant in this? In any case, we know from contemporary reports that the Spanish conquerors were amazed at the size of the great Aztec market of Tlatelolco when they were first led through it.

The word *tianguis*, still used as a synonym for market, comes from the Indian *náhuatl* language. *Tianquistli* means "every five days", the cycle of the pre-Spanish weekly market. Today it indicates a particular day of the week when a street within a neighborhood is closed off by market stands with their colorful sun shades or the *mercado sobre ruedas*, the market on wheels.

There is supposed to be a law which prohibits the obstruction of vehicle and pedestrian traffic

the former great market which, with its 7,000 stands, covered 110 streets and five squares in the old city center. Now it is mostly collected under one roof, reached by Metro line No. 9 at station "Merced". Visitors emerging from the underground into the center of the market are greeted by the overpowering odor of onions.

La Merced is a colorful, turbulent world of its own. All the country's fruits and vegetables are represented – sometimes artfully piled into pyramids by the vendors. Here you can become acquainted with *chirimoyas* (sugar pears), *jicamas* (a bulbous fruit), *tunas* (cactus figs) and the spicy *cilantro* (coriander herb), as well as many varieties of chiles. This corner of La Merced is only one of six sections. In addition, clothing, sweets and flowers are sold here. Then there are the *comedores*, the small market restaurants.

The Mercado de Sonora with its *herbolaría* (herb market) is surely one of the most mysterious parts of La Merced. Here the vendors sell homeopathic medicines against every sort of illness in hundreds of large and small sacks, and here superstition also flourishes. The merchant-sorcerers are ready to offer aid for nearly every imaginable problem – difficulties at work or in the marriage bed; protection from the evil eye or a variety of other curses. Magical curing properties are attributed to black candles, snakes' skins, shark's jaws or deer's eyes.

Sensitive souls would do better to avoid the adjacent animal market. They would be sorely tempted to free a small kitten from its cage next to fat pigeons or perhaps to adopt a puppy to release it from its wooden crate. Or perhaps one would wonder who and to what end would buy a poisonous tarantula or snake.

Most visitors end up going to the flea market La Lagunilla (only Sundays; on the right hand side when driving down the Paseo de la Reforma in the direction of Tlatelolco). Here not only junk is displayed. You can also find valuable antiques. Next to bombastic Victorian-style beds hang art nouveau figures next to martial swords and old pistols or a treasure chest full of old coins. The green camouflage suits on sale could probably be used by the dealers themselves when the police make their raids in search of *fayuca* (smuggled contraband), which they often do.

Folk art and handicrafts from all regions of the country are also on sale. The Ciudadela Market, with its small businesses and stands, is centrally located near the old citadel (Avenida Balderas). The Bazar Sábado, in San Angel (Plaza San Jacinto) is open as its name suggests only on Saturdays. While shoppers browse through the various stands filled with expensive handicrafts non-shoppers can enjoy a Mexican-style meal on the patio of an old mansion. Outside in the square artists exhibit their paintings or sculptures and in the adjoining plaza are the regular stands of the modest provincial traders.

For how long has the fat *marchanta* from Xalitla been coming here with her colorfully painted *papel amate* (bark paper) hanging in a

row? The Indian masks and embroidered blouses and dresses are also gaily colored, making a feast for the eyes and a danger for the purse – not only because of the temptation to collect souvenirs but because one can easily lose one's wallet in the seething crowd.

The Mexican markets, with their wealth, color, delicate scents and strong smells, may be an extravaganza for the foreigner. For the people who move about behind the sales counters they are a matter of economic survival. Just the location of the stall is the end result of a complicated game. It is not enough to pay the required stall fees to the local administration; powerful merchant *caciques* allow only those who pay protection money to sell their wares (*cacique* was originally

the Indian word for a chief or local tyrant). The city has virtually no control over these market czars who often have thousands of dependent vendors on their books.

The Indian women who have just recently left their village for the city appear to be quite defenceless in these markets, ignorant of the hierarchical structure. They sit on the sidewalk with small piles of limes or peanuts in front of them, a child in their arms. The city dwellers call them *marías*, a condescending term for Indian women. These women wait patiently, not only for a few pesos, but to somehow understand what it is that is behind the incessant movement in this monstrous city.

Above, greengrocers at their stall. **Right**, miraculous remedies for all ailments from the Mercado de Sonora.

AROUND ALAMEDA PARK

The elevator stops at the 42nd floor. From *mirador*, the observation deck of the **Torre Latinoamericana** (The Latin American Tower), the second tallest skyscraper in Mexico City, one can't exactly see all of Latin America but, at least the greater part of this infinite cityscape is visible from here. The view, however, is dulled most of the time by the gray veil of smog, which seems to contend with the Torre for the distinction of being the city's modern landmark. The panorama from the top of the tower is particularly enchanting at dusk when a glorious sunset coats everything with a pink hue and night falls with its thousands of lights. It's a spectacle best savored over an aperitif or dinner at the restaurant Muranto, up on the 41st floor.

Torre with a view: To the east of the tall, 181-meter (594-ft) high building lies the Zócalo, split by the elegant Calle Madero, whose flat roofs support their own untidy worlds. On the west side, right at the foot of the Torre, the dome of the **Palacio de Bellas Artes** rises. The **Alameda Park**, behind the Palacio, formerly the green lung of the city center, now suffers from acute consumption. Today the name of this city park, which is old and rich in tradition, is but a faint memory of the poplar (*alamos*) grove that viceroy Velasco had planted in 1592 "for the decoration of the city and the edification of its citizens." Now it is the ash trees that, viewed from above, sprinkle the stone desert with dark green dots. Down in the park, however, the stroller will notice that many a tree has lost its battle against the smog and died on its feet.

Dream and nightmare: Neverthless the Alameda Park, with fountains and monuments, is still a peaceful oasis in the din of the city. Innumerable statues all over the city bear witness to the incessant adoration of the nation's heroes. The main monument on the south side, with its semi-circle of white columns, is dedicated to former President Benito Juárez.

A famous foreigner was generously granted a corner close to the Palacio de Bellas Artes: Beethoven. In 1921, the German community donated the monument including the composer's black death mask. Five centuries ago the Alameda Park was an Aztec market its different areas designated for specific things such as foodstuffs, gold, silver and precious stones, clothing and even slaves. Later the area became an execution ground for the Spanish Inquisition's victims.

During the week not only tourists who are tired of sightseeing, but also the ordinary working people relax on the Alameda's lawns and benches. On Sundays, the place of rest turns into a big circus, immortalized in Diego Rivera's famous mural *Sunday Reverie in the Alameda* with historic figures from different eras (pictured on *page 85*). Up to 1985, this monumental fresco by Rivera, covering 72 sq. meters (775 sq. ft), was the pride of the Hotel del Prado until the latter was hit by the earthquake. The mural was saved in a spectacular rescue mission and given its very own exhibition site next to the Alameda Park on the Avenida Juárez.

The face and life of the city was changed dramatically by the earthquake. A string of famous hotels once dominated the center. In addition to the Hotel del Prado, there were the Hotel Alameda and the Hotel Regis, both of which no longer exist. A part of the nightlife has died with the hotels. Like a phoenix, the Torre Latinoamericana rose from the debris and during the earthquake its special construction allowed it to sway flexibly, saving it from serious harm.

Marble muse: Also indestructible was the art nouveau splendor of the **Palacio de Bellas Artes**. The Palacio, commissioned by Porfirio Díaz during his final term of office, was intended to replace the old national theater that had been torn down in 1901. The Italian architect Adamo Boari designed Don Porfirio's *pièce de résistance* in white Carrara marble. However, because of several hiccups in its construction it was not inaugurated before 1934. The building, with its heavy steel skeleton, was an adventurous undertaking right from the start considering the soft former lake-bed upon which it was built. In 1907, during the first phase of construction, the complex had already begun to sink into the ground. Concrete and calcium injections have helped to prevent further sagging but a slight slant is visible nevertheless.

The war of the Revolution brought construction work on the Palacio to a halt. In 1916, architect Adamo Boari fled Mexico leaving behind him a completed outer shell. In 1930 the Mexican Federico E. Mariscal was asked to finish it off. The result is that the interior of the Palacio is all post-Revolutionary art deco with its geometrical functional-ism, and the decorator obviously revelled in colorful Mexican rather than Italian marble, creating a special, unique elegance.

The **stage curtain** of the large theater, which seats 2,000 in stalls and boxes, is remarkable. The curtain alone weighs 22 tons, and on it glitter one million opalescent glass pieces, punctiliously assembled during a time period of 18 months by Tiffany jewelers. Based on a design by the Mexican painter Dr Atl (Gerardo Murillo), it shows the mountain valleys of Mexico with the two volcanoes Popocatepetl and Ixtaccihuatl.

The spectacular theater is home to the Ballet Folklorico, which is eminently worth seeing. Here also famous actors delight the audience, ballet dancers perform their *pas de deux* and opera divas sing immortal arias (Mexico does not have an opera ensemble of its own). Famous artists from all over the world acknowledge the applause in front of the glittering curtains.

Preceding pages: Bellas Artes in the window. Below, folk art in the Fonart shop.

The **Museo de Artes Plásticas**, also in the Palacio, presents changing exhibitions in its seven halls. The upper level, right below the dome, houses the **Museo Nacional de Arquitectura**.

The most famous painters of Mexico have decorated the hallways and lobbies of this museum. Two huge paintings by Rufino Tamayo adorn the corridors on the second floor: they are titled *Birth of our Nationality* and *Mexico Today*. On the third floor, the muralists José Clemente Orozco, Diego Rivera and David Alfaro Siqueiros have left their heavily metaphorical works for posterity. Rivera's notorious mural is the second version of a piece commissioned by and for the Rockefeller Center in New York; because of its condemnation of capitalism, the original of *Man at the Crossroads* was rejected and destroyed.

Fantastic realm of folk art: Not only do the fine arts reside at the Avenida Juárez but folk art is to be found here too. The **Museo Nacional de Artes e Industrias Populars**, in the former Corpus Christi Church of 1724 (44 Avenida Juárez), is the place to fall in love with Mexican folk art, whose vivacious colors and patterns have been a constant source of inspiration for modern Mexican painters and sculptors.

In addition to the museum on the first floor, a sales exhibition on the ground floor assembles specialties from all over the country: grotesque dance masks, painted ceramics which branch out into "life trees", colorful lacquer work, silver jewelry, earthen figurines ranging from the comical to the obscene (called *Ocumichus*), chess boards and sculptures from onyx, Indian woven textiles and embroideries, fantastic woollen pictures made by the Huichol Indians. The list could continue ad infinitum. The museum store is run by the Mexican Indian Institute (Instituto Nacional Indígenista).

Remember the Revolution: More indigenous art can be found in the public FONART store, down the Avenida Juárez in the direction of the Paseo de la Reforma. In the distance, the open-domed edifice of the **Monumento a la Revolución** rises from the Plaza de la Republica. The 67-meter (220-ft) high monument to the revolution was constructed from the ruins of the unfinished parliament. It exemplifies the functionalist architecture of the post-Revolutionary period, and its bulky voluminous pomposity clashes with the light wit of the colonial Churrigueresco and the art deco.

These huge blocks of stone, arranged in a strictly geometrical pattern, are interrupted by four openings, with the light streaming and the wind howling through them. Four presidents, Madero, Carranza, Calles and Cardenas have found their final resting place in the four corner pillars which are crowned by massive sculptures.

The interesting **Museo de la Revolución** is underground, right beneath the monument. It helps to have at least a slight knowledge of Spanish to **Siesta in the park.**

best appreciate the enormous collection of newspaper stories and documents exhibited but there are also drawings, photographs, weapons, uniforms and furnishings.

Colonial picture galleries: A tour around the Alameda also reveals colonial treasures. On the west side of the park the **Pinacoteca Virreinal**, one of the most important collections from the era of the viceroys, is now in the former monastery church of San Diego, which dates from the early 17th century. The nave, renovated in the classical style, is an appropriate environment for the works of art of three centuries, mainly interpreting religious themes. Andres de Concha (16th century), Cristobal de Villalpando (17th century), and Miguel Cabrera and Jose de Ibarra (18th century) are the most famous artists represented here. The lighting and captions in the gallery, however, leave much to be desired.

On the Avenida Hidalgo (No. 85), the southern border of the Alameda, a most pleasant surprise awaits the unsuspecting visitor behind an unassuming colonial facade of reddish volcanic stone (*tezontle*). The cross above the entrance, enhanced by baroque sculptures, bears witness to the original purpose of the building: it was the hostel Santo Toma de Villanueva of the barefooted order of the Augustinians. Today it accommodates tourists as the **Hotel Cortés**. Those who are not fortunate enough to stay here (the hotel has only a few rooms) should stop to sip a coffee under the big sun umbrellas in the quaint patio or should at least cast a glance at the secluded little world within it.

Crossing the Paseo de la Reforma to pass the **Iglesia San Hipólito** (17th century) and continuing down the Calle Puente de Alvarado, one reaches the **Palacio de Buenavista**, a classical town mansion of the Spanish architect and sculptor Manuel Tolsá. It is now the home of the **Museo de San Carlos**, an exquisite collection of Mexican and European paintings – from Gothic to Impressionist. Rembrandt, Tintoretto and Rubens are among the illustrious artists represented here.

German collection: Those more interested in the "applied arts", arts and crafts of the colonial period, are advised to continue their Alameda tour through the Avenida Hidalgo. A diminutive square, now several feet below street level, connects two 18th-century churches, **Santa Veracruz** and **San Juan de Díos**, the latter easily recognizable with its shell-shaped front. Next to this church is the **Museo Franz Mayer** in the former San Juan de Díos hospital, in which the monks of the Order of St John of Jerusalem achieved virtually superhuman feats helping the victims during the bubonic plague epidemics in the 18th century.

Franz Mayer, the founder of the museum, was born in Mannheim, Germany and spent 70 years of his life in Mexico. He donated his whole art collection to the Mexican people. Impressively and

The Monument to the Revolution.

carefully arranged, the exhibits fill the lovingly restored building: precious colonial furniture, silverware, religious sculpture and crucifixes, and Mexican fayence (*Talavera de Puebla*). In addition to the arts and crafts collection, there are paintings by European and Mexican artists. With its classical music and the soft murmur of the fountains, the patio is the ideal place to sit, relax and meditate. Book lovers will want to look at the old library. The **Museo Nacional de la Estampa**, the museum of Mexican prints, is also located on the Plaza Santa Veracruz.

City of palaces: Passing the back of the Palacio de Bellas Artes and crossing the main artery of the city center, Eje Central Lázaro Cárdenas, one reaches the main post office, a true **Palacio de Corréos**. Its eclectic style combines Moorish, Gothic and Renaissance elements, artistically arranged by beaux-arts architect Adamo Boari.

The **Palacio de Minería**, at the corner of the Calle Tacuba is in pure neoclassical style. The former School of Mining was built between 1797 and 1813 according to plans by the architect Manuel Tolsa. Inexpensive Sunday evening classical concerts sometimes take place upstairs.

Across the street, in front of the Palacio de Comunicaciones, dating from the Porfirian era, Manuel Tolsa's famous monument to King Carlos IV of Spain, nicknamed **"Caballito",** found an appropriate final resting place after having been sited in several other locations through the city. Weighing 26 tons it is among the world's biggest bronze cast statues.

Today, the Palacio de Comunicaciones serves as the **Museo Nacional de Arte**, its galleries providing an excellent overview of all the various artistic movements in Mexico from pre-Hispanic times to the present day.

The Avenidas Tacuba, 5 de Mayo and Madero connect Alameda Park with Zócalo. Pedestrian malls with tiny, old-fashioned restaurants and shoe and

Some architectural jewels glitter along the Avenida Madero: the **Iglesia La Profesa** (1720) and the **Palacio de Iturbide** (17 Madero), one of the city's most beautiful baroque palaces, now belongs to the National Bank. The rich decor of its facade casts tiny shadows like filigree. The **Casa de los Azulejos**, so called because of its tiled facade, is the former town mansion of the Duke of Valle de Orizaba. Today, the villa is part of the Sanborn's department store chain. A popular restaurant is located in the skylit patio and Mexican arts and crafts are sold in the gallery.

Straight across from the department store, the **Iglesia San Francisco** with its artistic Churriguerresco facade continues sinking into the ground while the "Torre" next to it reaches for the sky. The 16th-century church, founded by the earliest Franciscan friars to reach the country, was the preferred place of worship of all the early viceroys and at one time sheltered the body of the conquistador Hernán Cortéz.

Below, tiles in the Casa de los Azulejos. **Right**, in the Museo Franz Mayer.

PASEO DE LA REFORMA AND ZONA ROSA

When high, high, high society degenerated to mere café society in the 1950s, and the aristocracy became the jet set (managing by a bit of work and the magic power of money to live in Mexico exactly as they did in Paris, Madrid or New York), Mexico City's "Zona Rosa" came into being – a district of elegant restaurants, smart boutiques and glitzy galleries.

Pâtisseries and designer shops sprang up in the French-style houses, built with attics and pitched roofs against the snow (this in a land which has no winter). Bespoke tailors appeared, like Campdesuñer, to make suits for politicians, not to mention the plastic surgeons, snipping away at the bodies of politicians' wives.

Mexico's Champs-Elysées: Zona Rosa is the area beween Paseo de la Reforma and Avenida Chapultepec. It is like a little Europe, with streets named after European cities: Florence, Stockholm, Dresden, Strasbourg, Rome, London, Lucerne, Hamburg.

The construction of the Paseo de la Reforma was begun by Maximilian, who envisaged it as a Mexican Champs-Elysées: a broad majestic avenue stretching from Zócalo to Castillo de Chapultepec, the castle to be broadly based on Maximilian's own Castle Miramare in Trieste, Italy.

The emperor did not live to see the magnificent thoroughfare completed. He ended up in front of a firing squad in 1867. Ten years later, by an irony of fate, the avenue was to be named after a presidential triumph of Benito Juárez, the man who ordered his execution. Juárez was himself responsible for the reform laws of 1861, which called for the division of property between church and state.

Even before it was finished, Paseo de la Reforma witnessed an age of splendor: huge French-style residences

Previous pages: the angel stands night watch.

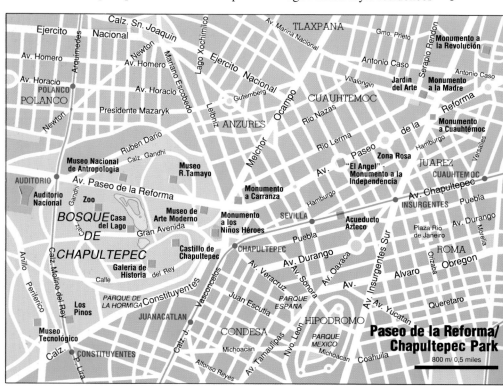

Paseo de la Reforma/ Chapultepec Park
800 m/ 0,5 miles

with horse-drawn carriages, Parisian fashions, Italian millinery, and distinguished gentlemen riding down on their fiery steeds from the castle mount to Zócalo, right up to the front of the cathedral and the Palacio Nacional. Chapultepec Park was a favored spot, thanks to its *sabinos* (Montezuma cypresses). Today their branches are bare. Pollution has killed off all the leaves, and Paseo de la Reforma resembles nothing so much as Eugene Ionesco's *Bald Singer*. The trees are bare, the lawns too, the flowers have gone, and there are now no signs of the children who once used to chase balloons and balls along the pavements.

Today the still-majestic Paseo de la Reforma is a street for Mexicans who barely lift their eyes from the ground as they walk, and for countless vehicles which thunder along it on their rubbered tyres. At almost every intersection, as in other parts of town, the itinerant lottery ticket salesmen can be seen with their sheaves of tickets on long sticks. The headquarters of the National Lottery itself – an art deco building of some style – can be found where Juárez intersects Reforma and is worth admiring. Admission is free.

Guardian angel: Curiously enough, we Mexicans are sufficiently *macho* that we still call the **independence statue** "El Angel", addressing it in the masculine. The monument is a tall Corinthian column, at the top of which is posed an angel, balancing on the chubby toes of its right foot, its wings outstretched ready for take-off. In its right hand it holds a laurel wreath. Despite the rounded breasts like two golden oranges, and the obviously feminine features, we still call the figure "El Angel". He is our guardian angel – he watches over the city, which is in dire need of angels, archangels and the rest of the heavenly host for that matter.

The angel rises out of a *glorieta*, a circular garden ringed by famous hotels. *Glorietas* or traffic circles take an infuriatingly long time for a pedestrian

to walk around but are even more infuriating to motorists who are unfamiliar with local driving etiquette and have been known to circle several times before being able to achieve their preferred exit.

Other *glorietas* on the Paseo de la Reforma encircle other monuments, like *Christopher Columbus*, a work of the French sculptor Charles Cordier, or that to the great Mexican hero **Cuitláhuac** where the Paseo de la Reforma crosses the Avenida de los Insurgentes. At almost 28 km (17 miles) long, the Insurgentes is the longest avenue in Mexico and possibly the world. The **Cuauhtémoc monument** has its own fountains, where the children love to splash until the police come and haul them out.

Two sculptures have disappeared from the Paseo de la Reforma: one of Karl IV known as the *Caballito* (little horse), which newspaper sellers and medicine men used to climb to watch the military parades and protest demon-

strations, and the *Diana Cazadora* (Diana, goddess of the hunt), which was censored by the city's moralistic contingent. The voluptuous nude, known to all as Diana, excited the bus and taxi drivers to such a dangerous extent that eventually the statue had to be hidden in a little copse, well away from the casual public gaze.

The **Monumento a los Niños Héroes** (Monument to Our Young Heroes) commemorates those famous figures from our past, the heroic cadets from the military academy who defended Chapultepec castle against North American invaders in 1847. But it's nowhere near as popular as the angel or the huge flag which flutters in the centre of the Zócalo, opposite the cathedral and the Palacio Nacional.

The black rose: Among the ash trees and the *sabinos* of the Paseo de la Reforma, a black rose suddenly sprouted. Its petals opened seductively, exuding a strange perfume. The streets Niza, Genova, Hamburgo, Londres and Amberes (Antwerp) were now alive by night as well as by day.

Black are the high walls of the cabarets, black the jackets of the waiters, black the pianos playing light music in the bars, black the shadows, black the trousers of the existentialist girls, black the heavy doors of the Benjamin Franklin library, black the soutanes of the Roman Catholic priests, black the designer carpeting in the galleries, black the drummers in the jazz bands, black the coffee in the round cups, black the roses between the teeth of the young girls searching for themselves, black the slates of the Mexican-American Cultural Institute on Calle Hamburgo where the private secretaries come to learn English and longtime residents somewhat shamefacedly try to acquire a smattering of Spanish.

And black too is the smoke of the candles in the Italian restaurants La Góndola and Alfredo, Delmónicos and Honfleur (where the menu includes spinach, Gruyère and Gran Marnier

Left, the feminine angel. **Right**, a tree becomes another monument on the Paseo.

soufflés), Passy, La Calesa, Raffaello, Rivoli, La Pérgola and the Chalet Suizo, the "Swiss Chalet" with its cozy fondues for two. The *konditori* (café) tables meander across the pavements, and waiters run to and fro with open sandwiches of German black bread and liver pâté, salmon or herring, real German sauerkraut and large tankards of beer. The Focolare and other top restaurants are like precious caskets lined with velvet, like the petals of the fabulous rose with its piercing scent.

The classical *sanborns* – tearooms and Viennese-style coffee houses like **La Marquesa** and the wonderful **Snob** – round off the culinary attractions of Zona Rosa.

The black rose may have bloomed at night, but it struck its roots long ago – during the time of Don Porfirio, in fact. Colonia Juárez, Colonia Cuauhtémoc and the streets Niza, Genova, Londres, Amberes and Hamburgo were home to the best families and their blooming daughters. Among the gray houses of a second Paris, with their pitched roofs, cellars, winter gardens and attics, the dictatorship of Porfirio Díaz faded and withered. The Revolution broke into the houses, tore the petals from the roses, trampled on every established custom and belief, and in the cellars the ghosts wailed and lamented.

But beneath the ground the giant black rose lay in wait, lurking, ever lurking, a panther of velvety petals and thorns, waiting for the moment, one fine day, when it would break through the hard asphalt of the streets.

Chic and costly: Zona Rosa is the most chic, most exclusive district of Mexico City, and the most expensive. On its European streets you'll find European boutiques, branches of the famous French couturiers and parfumiers, as well as Italian shoemakers, Swiss pâtissiers, Viennese chocolate shops and German delicatessens.

First to appear was the Hotel Genève (now the Calinda), to which tourists flocked by the thousand. Silver jewelers

ating al esco in ona Rosa.

(*tane*) and craft shops appeared at its side and clung there through the passing years. The Porfirian houses craned their necks shyly to see what was going on. And the melancholy old women who were the survivors of that period sat themselves down to wait it out, until one of them – the smartest of all – finally dared to knock in her ground-floor windows and put in a plate-glass shop front instead. The French basements were transformed into elegant, exclusive shops.

In one such basement, in the Amor family home in Abraham González street, the **Galería de Arte Mexicano** was founded. Exhibitions were staged there by Rufino Tamayo, Diego Rivera, Clemente Orozco, Juan Soriano, Leonora Carrington and Carlos Mérida – all great Mexican artists.

The shops behind these elegant facades were from the start rather snooty. Porfirian ladies descended the creaking wooden stairs from their second floors and opened bookshops, picture-framing studios, galleries selling religious art, furs or leather goods. Then pizzerias began springing up, complete with checked tablecloths and glasses of beer, or gondolas and Chianti. The **Fonda del Refugio** opened its doors.

Scandalizing the locals: It was over this bar that Carlos Fuentes lived and here that he wrote his novella *The Death of Artemis Cruz*. At one time Fuentes was a familiar face in the Zona Rosa, along with Antonia Souza, the manager of the gallery which exhibited all the young painters who were later to become so famous: José Luis Cuevas, Franciso Toledo, Manuel Felguérez, Pedro and Rafael Coronel. José Luis Cuevas painted his first short-lived mural in a building in the Zona Rosa, and later he staged many artistic "happenings", which scandalized the district's devout churchgoers.

The art of the Zona Rosa today, packaged and confined as in so many other places of its kind is actually less interesting to view than that of Sullivan Park (sometimes known as Jardin del Arte) a few blocks away. Here, between Calles Sullivan and Villalongin a Sunday afternoon art show is always packed with visitors inspecting the casual display of sculptures, paintings and engravings, more than a few of them actually attended by the artists themselves.

The cuisine of the Zona Rosa was international: mixed salad and cocktails christened "Silk Stockings". Everything that happened on Niza Street happened – and happens still – in English. Many Mexicans followed the tourist herds to Zona Rosa, among them a group of intellectuals known as Los Divinos ("the divine ones"), who somehow managed to mouth the word *revolución* while in the same breath ordering giant crabs in garlic sauce in the Ballinhaus.

José Luis' **El Parador** on Niza Street is still a traditional bar, where you can sample first-class cuisine, prepared by the same Pueblan angels or nuns who invented the black *mole*, which the **The French touch.**

French call *poulet au chocolat* (chocolate chicken).

In the name of the rose: A newspaper column once christened the Zona Rosa "the zone of art and good taste", and today commercial enterprises wave this under our noses unashamedly. The boutiques offer cigarette-holders, key rings, wallets, room scenters, picture frames and Japanese flower arrangements. Floral stylists thread little wires through crysanthemum blooms to make the petals stand out like arrows. Florists display tortured-looking Bonsai trees, and the shop windows are full of Chinese figures, ashtrays and glassware artistically arranged on twisted trunks and dwarf-like branches.

Nature is anathema, it seems, to the residents of the "zone of art and good taste". They can't cope with it in its raw state. To appreciate it aesthetically they have to stylize it, scale it down and make it "artistic". Even the women on Niza, Liverpool, Hamburgo, Florenzia, Paris and Berlin street are driven by this compulsion. They all seem to be wired up. A thin pin, a stiletto heel, keeps them upright, and on their heads perches a triumph of artistry, a sensational, puffed-up thicket of a hairstyle, so enormously wide that you'd think a lot of them would lose their lovers in their hairdo. But ultimately there is a proverb in their defence: "You may see the face, but you can't see into the heart."

The black rose continues to grow in its solitary plot. A hothouse bloom, it is sheltered by a protective glass dome. Vain about its beauty, obsessed with its personal appearance, it demands a lot of care and attention. It fluffs itself up in the hands of the experts.

But despite the eulogies, the rose no longer looks as fresh as it once did. There are nights when it even seems to be growing old before its time. Dark bags are beginning to show beneath its eyes. One day, people will finally discover it is artificial. For like it or not, on this our planet there is no such thing as a black rose.

old jewelry on display.

The traffic light turns green but the police officer at the intersection holds up the traffic with his hand. Multi-toned honking of horns breaks out and continues until the first police motorcycle patrols have driven past, clearing the way for a limousine: a politician who wants to get to his appointment on time.

In an instant, the horns sound together – three short blasts and two long ones – *"chinga tu madre"* ("fuck your mother"). For a Mexican this is the maximum insult, an expletive that is more easily sounded from the horn of an auto than spoken. People who, moments before, had been

others from driving further. Thousands of trucks, oil tankers and trailers that provide services for the city form an additional, enormous burden.

Mexico has made great efforts to keep up with the growing demands on the city's transport network. However, by the time most of the projects have been completed, the situation has already moved three steps ahead of the planners. The development of Mexico City's infrastructure is hopelessly behind the real expansion rate: the city is growing by 3,000 people per day, almost a million new inhabitants every year.

When the Anillo Periférico was finished at the

cursing each other as if they were personal enemies and using the horn signals and hand movements which constitute the Mexican car-driver's language, are instantly united against a collective opponent – the tangible sinner who caused the traffic jam.

There are many reasons why traffic jams have become part of the everyday life in the Mexican capital and not just because politicians over-ride the traffic lights. Defective vehicles sometimes block traffic for hours. During the rainy season, whole lanes turn into lakes. With the heavy rainfall, the overloaded drainage system shoots water back into the streets instead of carrying it away. Many vehicles get stuck in the water and prevent

end of the 1960s – it was designed to connect the suburbs of Satélite in the northwest and those of Villa Coapa in the southeast with the downtown Paseo de la Reforma – some people criticized the extravagance of such a luxuriously wide street. Today these outer regions have long since melted into the metropolis, and the new edge of the city extends as far as the federal highway. The Periférico, which has up to five lanes, has long been too small for today's traffic demands. The 28-km (17-mile) long Avenida de los Insurgentes crosses the city from north to south.

The Paseo de la Reforma, the imperial parade built by Maximilian, links the city center with Mexico City's most exclusive residential neighborhood, Chapultepec, as far as the federal highway to Toluca. All of these streets have been widened over the years but they still remain too narrow to allow anything resembling an even traffic flow.

In the middle of the 1970s, the *ejes viales* (principal routes) were built to provide the city with north-south and east-west connections. Numerous houses and green areas were sacrificed. Despite early protests, today one cannot imagine the Mexican capital without the *ejes viales*.

The road construction measures of the last couple of decades have helped, but they are just as ineffective at reducing the transport chaos in what is probably the world's largest city as the helicopters which fly daily across the city at rush hour to provide radio reports of the traffic situation for

drivers, and deliver police support to the critical points throughout the city.

According to conservative estimates, over three million motor vehicles, often with defective exhaust systems, circulate daily through the Mexican capital. They are responsible for a substantial part of the 11,000 tonnes of air pollutants which are emitted daily, contributing to the destruction of the atmosphere in a city once praised for its excellent air quality. The blankets of smog cause serious health problems especially when, in the cooler winter months, the thermal inversions

Left, a dangerous post. Above, entrepreneurs sell goods and services at red traffic lights.

in the Valle de México prevent the necessary air movement to carry the smog away.

Even the increase in available public transport over the last few years has done little to help the traffic problem. Although the Metro will eventually be expanded from three to nine lines it has not grown fast enough to meet demands. And most of the day buses and *colectivos* (minibuses) are always overcrowded.

Musicians, singers, and vendors push their way through the crowds on the buses and subway trains, do their business between stations and collect their money. One can also buy all sorts of different things at street intersections while waiting for the light to turn green: chocolate, chewing gum, lottery tickets, rear view mirrors for cars or a Popeye doll for the baby.

At the junction itself, children play and juggle, dressed as clowns. Sometimes they concentrate so hard on their performances that they do not notice the lights changing to green and must run for their lives without receiving a single peso for their performances. Cyclists and moped drivers are even rarer in the heavy traffic than pedestrians, since they are in even greater danger. The main reason is the continuous changing of traffic lanes. The worse the jam, the more frequently the drivers move pointlessly from one side of the street to the other, and the more frustrated everybody becomes.

Mexican automobile drivers more often follow their own senses than the traffic rules – which many do not even know – yet the system functions amazingly well, and although accidents are part of everyday life in a huge city, they are also relatively rare. The Mexican driver is prepared for aggressive driving and knows how to handle it. He is only irritated when he cannot drive any further. "*Ni modo*" (So what!) said one man about the hopeless traffic situation and proceeded bravely into the evening's traffic turmoil.

"I've long ago given up going to the theater. Either one gets there too late on account of the traffic or one can't find a parking place," notes another with resignation. With the help of an emergency plan, the government has also tried to bring the traffic problem under control in order to reduce the stress, noise and smog level by a restriction on automobile use. One day in the week drivers, including those from out of town, are prohibited from using their cars. Which day is determined by the last number of the registration plate. Although it was initially given a trial period of four months, the program has been extended indefinitely because of its obvious success. But the city is growing further, and the public transport system is bearing up badly under the strain.

CHAPULTEPEC PARK

The great Paseo de la Reforma leads from the city center right up to Chapultepec Hill and the castle. As you emerge from Chapultepec metro station, the first thing you see are the tall white marble pillars of the **Monumento a los Niños Héroes**, crowned with bronze eagles, which forms the entrance to the city's treasured park.

Divided into three areas, covering 260 sq. miles (670 hectares) in all, Chapultepec Park is the city's largest open space. But it's not only a place to unwind – to bring a picnic at the weekends, or go for a walk or a jog. People also come to take advantage of the wide-ranging cultural and sporting facilities on offer. Dotted around the landscape, which no amount of careful tending can save from the ravages of air pollution and overuse, there are a range of attractions: man-made lakes, the zoo, a good children's center (*Centro de Conviviencia Infantil*), a botanical garden, sports pitches and a funfair, not to mention some first-class museums. At the same time, the park also bears witness to significant events in the city's history which have helped to shape it.

"Grasshopper Hill": Numerous stories and legends have grown up around Chapultepec, the "grasshopper hill". In 1266 the Aztecs held their first "new fire" ceremony here. The extinguishing and relighting of all fires heralded a new calendar every 52 years. In 1325 they appointed Chapultepec a "holy place" and erected a temple on Chapulín Hill.

Montezuma Ilhuicamina ordered the building of the first aqueduct in 1465 to carry water from the Chapultepec springs to Tenochtitlán. Montezuma Xocoyotzin (Montezuma II) was concerned only with his personal well-being, and had an opulent palace built, surrounded by swimming pools and fishponds. Here he would come to relax after hunting in the Chapultepec woods.

Previous pages: entrance to the Museo de Arte Moderno. Below, the monument to the "Young Heroes" at the foot of the castle.

On May 26, 1521, these woods were the scene of a bloody battle between the Spanish and the Aztecs. The conquistador Hernán Cortéz took the Chapulín with the intention of laying siege to Tenochtitlán, and by destroying the aqueducts he cut the enemy's water supply. Then he fortified the hill to defend himself against Mexican attack.

After the country had been overrun, the viceroys followed the example of the Aztec rulers and used Chapultepec as a kind of spa resort. On the site of the Aztec palace they erected a summer residence, as well as a pilgrimage church dedicated to San Francisco Xavier and a remembrance chapel. In 1537 Emperor Karl V decreed, at the request of Viceroy Antonio de Mendoza, that the hill and woods of Chapultepec belonged to the capital of New Spain and should be used for the edification of its inhabitants. Cortéz's stronghold was turned into a gunpowder factory, which blew up in 1784. At the behest of Viceroy Bernardo de

Empress Charlotte's bedchamber.

Gálvez construction then began on a castle on the Chapulín. It was completed three years later.

Shortage of funds meant that the castle and its woods came under the hammer for 130,000 pesos in 1788. Count Revillagigedo intervened to try and prevent the sale. In a desperate attempt to raise the necessary funds to finish the castle, both festivals and bullfights were organized.

After the declaration of independence in 1810, both the castle and the woods were declared public property and in 1826 Mexico's first president, Guadalupe Victoria, announced the creation of a botanical garden. Meanwhile the castle remained empty, until in 1841 it was turned into a military academy. During the French and North American invasions of the 19th century, the capture of Chapultepec was an important strategic goal.

The castle was almost destroyed in the US invasion of 1847. Nine hundred Mexican soldiers and 47 cadets of the military college attempted to defend the castle and the Monumento a los Niños Heroes commemorates the six young cadets of the academy whose staunch defence cost them their lives.

In 1864 Maximilian von Habsburg made the castle his imperial residence and had both interior and exterior substantially rebuilt and improved, as befitted his status. He also initiated the construction of a street connecting the park with the city, but it was only completed as the Paseo de la Reforma after the end of his fateful three-year sojourn as emperor.

With the re-establishment of the republic, the castle was appointed the seat of the president, but General Porfirio Díaz was the first to take up official residence in 1876.

Castle museum: Lázaro Cárdenas, the popular president of the Revolution, whose puritanical streak was displayed when he closed the city's brothels and gambling houses, did not wish to surround himself with such luxury, and during his period of office (1934–40) he moved into the modern Residencia Presidencial de los Piños on the western edge of the park. This remains the official address of the Mexican president to this day.

Cárdenas designated the castle as the **Museo Nacional de Historia**, but as rebuilding took until 1944, it fell to General Manuel Avila Camacho to perform the opening ceremony.

Unfortunately the lift in the hillside is no longer in use, but it is worth the 15-minute climb to the **Castillo**, not so much for the castle's rather plain architecture but for its historical collections, the rooms used by Maximilian and his wife Carlotta, the old coaches and – on a clear day – the magnificent view over the city from the terrace. In the main western wing of the Castillo, 20 rooms take you on a tour of Mexico's history, from the conquistadors to the Revolution. The Mexican history paintings merit a special mention, as do works by European artists who traveled through Mexico in the 19th century and left behind a permanent record of their impressions. Among them are the Germans Rugendas and Nebel.

In several rooms famous Mexican muralists have interpreted significant excerpts from Mexican history in wall-paintings. These include Juan O'Gorman's vision of independence (see the chapter on *Muralismo* starting on page 81), and José Clemente Orozco's violent interpretation on the theme *Juarez, the Church and the Imperialists*. Vivid frescoes executed in the 1930s by muralist Siqueiros can also be admired.

In the east wing (Alcazar) you can visit the rooms used by the Mexican dictators when the castle was the presidential seat. A favorite with the children who make the pilgrimage up here is the stunning display of historic coaches, which includes Maximilian's state carriage from Milan and the plain, black coach in which Juarez entered the city after the defeat of Maximilian. The chambers where the Habsburg emperor dwelt with Carlotta are furnished in the style of the times with pieces purchased at a later date. There are also two full-length portraits of the unfortunate Maximilian and Carlotta who were respectively 32 and 24 when they arrived in Mexico.

Descending again to the park, you might like to follow in the footsteps of the empress – discribed by one historian as "brooding, haughty and highstrung" – on the **Escalina de Carlota**, the Carlotta Steps. Beneath the castle you'll find the **Galería de Historia**, the work of the architect Pedro Ramírez Vázquez, also known as Museo del Caracol because it is shaped like a mussel. A highly accessible presentation of the Mexicans' historical battle for freedom, from the first days of independence to the Revolution, is once more paraded before visitors' eyes.

Artistic pilgrimage: At the foot of the castle you are not far from a second big museum – the steel and glass edifice of the **Museo de Arte Moderno**, also designed by Ramírez Vázquez. The building is the perfect setting to display all the contemporary trends in Mexican art. Among the museum's most important collections are works by José Maria Velasco, an important forerunner of modern Mexican painting, and paintings by Dr Atl, Orozco, Rivera, Siqueiros, Kahlo, Tamayo and Goitia. The second half of this century is represented by artists including Cuevas, Coronel, Felguérez and Toledo. The museum grounds are used to display sculptures and feature commemorative works by Zúniga, Goeritz, Guirría and Silva among others.

The **Museo Rufino Tamayo** on the other side of the Paseo de la Reforma is another celebration of modernism. This monumental construction features a breathtaking interior with rooms of varied dimension and varying perspectives, and was designed by the architect team of Abraham Zabludovsky and Teodoro González de León. Inaugurated in 1981, the museum houses Rufino Tamayo's outstanding international collection, as well as the Mexican artist's own work. With this museum which bears his name, the "Grand Old Man" has ensured himself a lasting place in the Mexican avant garde. It was here that the artist, now in his nineties, celebrated over 70 working years with a major retrospective.

The main body of the museum is built around two vast exhibition spaces, housing paintings, drawings and wall-hangings by some 150 contemporary artists from around the world, among them works by Picasso, Dalí, Francis Bacon and Mexican artists. Between lies a covered patio, reserved for sculptural work. The rooms on the second floor are devoted to changing exhibitions. The museum also boasts an auditorium in which to stage various cultural events and a cafeteria.

The Museo Rufino Tamayo is another impressive example of the standards of excellence of Mexican museum architecture and presentation. The worldwide reputation it now enjoys is largely in response to the neighboring **Museo Nacional de Antropología** designed by Pedro Ramirez Vasquez which opened in 1964 and which is dealt with in the following chapter.

To whet the public's appetite for the Indian artefacts displayed within, there are regular performances in the museum courtyard of a spectacular ritual dating from the pre-Spanish era. In the past such rituals were celebrated in many areas of Mexico to honor the god of spring and fertility, Xipe Totec.

Today the tradition of the *voladores* or "flying men" is preserved mainly by the Totonaken on the Gulf coast and in the Sierra de Puebla. The *voladores* climb a tall pole, wound around with ropes which are fastened on to a rotating wooden frame (see picture on *page 112*). The *capitán* takes his place at the top of the pole, playing a flute and beating on a drum. When he gives the word, the four fliers, who have each tied

Chapultepec's large lake.

themselves to the end of a rope, somersault backwards from the wooden frame. The ropes unravel from the pole and after 13 revolutions of the frame the men land safely on the ground. Multiply 13 by the number of fliers and you get 52, the old Indian "century".

Behind the anthropological museum (and its massive car park) is the **Centro de Arte Contemporáneo**, belonging to the TV company Televisa. Televisa has an extensive collection of modern art and holds international exhibitions in these premises.

Los Lagos: If you cross the Paseo de la Reforma near the anthropological museum, you arrive at the largest of the park's man-made lakes. At the weekends it teems with rowing boats. If the pace gets too frantic for the resident ducks and swans, they can always retire to their islands. The **Casa del Lago** on the lakeside belongs to the National University and is the venue for cultural events like poetry readings, plays, concerts and exhibitions. On Sundays in particular this more traditional part of Chapultepec, between the castle and the lake, is the province of casual strollers, traders selling pink candyfloss and brightly colored windmills, and photographers with model horses and pony traps for the children. The nearby zoo is home to more than 2,500 animals of over 300 species. A major attraction is a family of pandas, whose young were born here.

On the left, before the Paseo de la Reforma crosses the city highway, the Periférico, is the **Auditorio Nacional**, the city's largest assembly and concert hall. The whole complex is known as the **Unidad Artística y Cultural del Bosque** and houses several theaters, administrative offices, etc.

On the far side of the Periférico, the second part of Chapultepec Park, opened in 1972, continues. From the highway you can see the massive rollercoaster (*montaña rusa*) in the adult's pleasure park. Next door is the electricity company's **Museo Tecnológico**, which is devoted to developments in technology. To the south east, beside another small lake, the **Museo de Historia Natural** provides a guided tour through the history of evolution. A miniature railway (*Ferrocarril Escénico*) chugs around the artificial lake, passing through a tunnel of terror and a tunnel of love. On the banks of the other lake in the part of the park you'll find the select restaurant Del Lago.

Resting place of the famous: Between the second and third sections of Chapultepec stretches a huge cemetery, the Panteón de Dolores. Eighty nine eminent Mexicans are buried here in the **Rotonda de los Hombres Ilustres** (on Avenida Constituyentes), founded in 1876 by Porfirio Díaz. Among them are the best of the muralists: Orozco, Rivera and Siqueiros, as well as the composers Jaime Nuñó and Agustín Lara.

The third part of the city's great park contains additional leisure attractions. In the sea-water aquarium **Atlantis**, sealions and dolphins perform their tricks. And in **Aguas Salvajes** you can yourself safely simulate riding the rapids. The only real danger is accidentally getting too close to the archers who have a practice ground nearby. Barbecues are banned in this more remote part of the park.

Bread and games: The presidents of modern-day Mexico who live on the edge of Chapultepec Park in **Los Pinos** (between Periférico and Avenida Constituyentes) are only too aware of the advantages of this old and proven method for keeping the people happy. But the park's excellent museums and countless monuments to historical figures, like Gandhi and José Martí, ensure that it is not only used for relaxation but that it plays a part in the wider education of its visitors. Attractive and relaxing as the park is in the daylight hours, it is not recommended for visits at night any more than the urban parks of most visitors' hometowns would be safe havens. By night, its population is quite different than by day.

A genuine Mexican.

THE MUSEUM OF ANTHROPOLOGY

Water signifies life in the ancient cultures of the highlands. Through water, the rain god Tlaloc guaranteed bounty to his believers. A massive monolith of Tlaloc at the entrance to the Anthropology Museum reminds beholders of this belief, and as a further testimony the interior courtyard of this impressive building is occupied by an enormous fountain. Even in Aztec times the problem about water was always that there was too little or too much.

The Anthropology Museum has proved to be an inspiration for a whole generation of modern Mexican museums. That flat-roofed building was designed by a team of architects under Pedro Ramírca Vasques, and opened in 1968. Before this time the art treasures of pre-Columbian Mexico had been collecting dust in warehouses, and the sculptures of the Aztecs were walled into or buried in public buildings. But now, clearly displayed on the ground floor of the museum, a selection of first class art from ancient Mexico leads visitors through the millennia of Indian high culture. The tour through the individual artistic landscapes is laid out anticlockwise, and on the second storey there is displayed a collection of contemporary Indian art.

To the right of the entrance is a hall devoted to an **Introduction to Archaeology**, which has a useful map of the Mexican regional cultures and artistic landscape. The next gallery, the **Sala de Orígen** deals with man's occupation of the New World. During the last two periods of the Ice Age until about 18,000 BC, big-game hunters migrated across the Bering Strait which was then a land bridge between Siberia and North America. They came in pursuit of mammoth and bison. It took these hunting groups at least 10,000 years to cross the north and south sections of the American double continent. We know from

The inspiring Museum of Anthropology.

excavations that they finally reached the southern tip of Tierra del Fuego about 8000 BC. The Ixtapan mammoth find, not far from present-day Mexico City, produced evidence about the way of life and hunting practices of these big-game hunters.

Initially the animals were chased into swamps or off cliffs, effectively killing themselves. After gutting the animals, a clan of hunters could live for a long time from the catch. However, around 8000 BC the climate changed. Precipitation became more and more infrequent and savannahs became steppes and then deserts. Herbivores like the mammoth or the giant sloth lost their subsistence base. Along with the improvement in hunting techniques, this climatic catastrophe led to the extinction of those giant beasts whose bones we admire today. Under these new ecological conditions the desert cultures came into being, and the hunters started to concentrate on small animals or gathering seeds and fruits.

The cultivation of maize: The first cultivated plants appeared in Mexico around the fourth millennium BC. Avocados, pumpkins and tomatoes were grown and maize was developed from the cross-fertilization of different grass types. It is hard to believe that the surplus production of these insignificant, small cobs (which were not even 3 cm/ 1½ inches in length) was essential to the development of the high cultures of the New World, but it was the classic triad of maize, beans and pumpkin that formed the basis for the rise of pre-classical Mesoamerican cultures in the second millennium before Christ.

The variety of clay maternal figures representing fertility took on especial significance at that time. In the next gallery the first animal sculptures and anthropomorphic pottery, such as the now famous acrobat with wildly contorted limbs, tell the story of the increasing importance of the arts to the new society. In this period the social preconditions for an artisan class first

eft, the crobat of latilco. ight, in the useum atio.

emerged, with the artists specializing in working clay, stone, obsidian, bone, wood or shells.

The pre-Columbian metropolis: The urban architecture and handicrafts displayed in the **Hall of Teotihuacán** were dictated by the requirements of the powerful priestly class which had by then emerged in the new society. Binding conventions determined the exact depiction of human likenesses in the stone masks, the small clay figures and above all the image of the rain god Tlaloc. He appears on urns and clay vases and on brightly colored frescoes in the large pre-Columbian city of Teotihuacán which, along with the reconstructed facade of the Quetzalcoatl pyramid, provide an impression of what the original ceremonial center must have once been like (the pottery was all made without potter's wheels, which were only introduced with the invasion of the Spanish).

Also in the hall is a depiction of happily dancing skeletons which was saved from a palace on the periphery of the city. The rain god crouches over the dancing dead, spewing forth colorful streams of life-giving water which came from his paradise to the dry world of the high valleys of Teotihuacán. In the middle of this hall is a 4-meter (13-ft) high statue of Tlaloc's wife Chalchiuhtlicue which has a somewhat magical and overall threatening effect on the visitor.

After the fall of Teotihuacán (AD 600), the power monopoly of the priests was destroyed and a warrior civilization prepared the way for the rise of the Aztecs. In the **Hall of the Toltecs**, jaguars and coyotes, which at one time guarded the entrance to the temple platforms, appear to spring at the visitor. The Atlantes who carried the roof of the temple of the Morning Star god are carved as likenesses of these warriors: fully armed with the *atlatl* (a kind of discus), shield and spear.

The Toltecs preserved the skills of the Teotihuacán craftsmen. Priceless inlay

Huge head from the Olmec era.

work, such as the warrior head which shows through a coyote's jaws, alabaster vases, and large stone face masks were found among the ruins of the capital, Tula.

Tyrannical Aztecs: The great sculptures of the Aztecs are impressively displayed on the front side of the **Hall of the Mexicas** across from the main entrance to the museum. A reproduction of the Codex Boturini describes the migration of the tribe from their mythic ancestral home, Aztlan, to the lake of Texcoco. Along the way, the tribes found the carved wooden idol of their god, Huitzilopochtli, who would later become the focus of the blood sacrifices in the Templo Mayor, the most important Aztec temple. Other pages of the picture book tell of the defeat of their neighbors and one-time masters of Colhuacan and Tenayuca. The replica of a feather headdress gives an impression of the splendor of the Aztec kings and nobility.

Codices, primitive fold-out "books"

filled with hierogliphics written on bark paper or sometimes deerskin are understandably rare; filled with records of such matters as religion and astronomy, they are still largely obscure today.

Blood and heart sacrifices took on great significance among the Aztecs. As the warriors pushed farther and farther into new territories, so the gods became ever more greedy. Even though the sacrificial knives and bowls were very artistic, they only served a very cruel purpose. Here there are also reproductions of the painted lists which recorded the tribute of the subjugated peoples, who sent their prisoners for sacrifice to their gods as well as all manner of luxury items. Such sacrifices also served to tyrannize those whom the Aztecs conquered.

The colossal statue of Coatlicue, the Aztec mother goddess, is among the most impressive in the hall. The two snake heads which replace the human one signify the gender duality of the deity. A complex symbolism is con-

In the hall of the Mexica or Aztecs.

tained within the goddess's form: a snake skirt, wild cat's paws with eyes, two human hearts and two pairs of human hands on the breast, a deaths-head, feathers, a double mouth and multiple sets of eyes.

The "sun stone," also mistakenly called the "calendar stone," is filled with similarly diverse symbolism. The "sun stone" dominates the other exhibits from the middle of the hall. It depicts a tribute, turned to stone, to the sun god, Tonatiuh, whose face can be seen in the middle of the slab. The bloodthirsty god was once colorfully painted like the whole stone. On both sides of the face are claws that clutched human hearts. The claws with eyes inserted between them also form faces, and they themselves are part of the central face with its two rectangular wings extending from top to bottom.

This sign of *olin*, further qualified by four discs indicating the date "4 olin" shows the day on which the world of the Aztecs, the fifth world according to

their beliefs, should come to an end. The four previous worlds are signified by the wings of the symbol.

Three other dates and the four directions of the heavens are represented by a symbol cluster within the figure. Beginning anticlockwise from the apex, an outer ring shows the symbols for the 20 days. Snakes and deific images on the edge of the sun stone depict the various attributes of Tonatiuh, the sun god.

Superb animal sculptures such as coiled rattlesnakes, oversized grasshoppers, jaguars, coyotes, and lizards, are another facet of Aztec art. Using only a very few strokes, these artists were able to capture the essence of these symbolic animals in highly polished stone sculptures.

Before visiting the other side of the museum with its exhibitions of the cultures of southern and western Mexico, try the museum's very good restaurant with its respectable Mexican menu. Or alternatively have a rest by the fountain in the courtyard. The bulrushes in the water are meant to resemble the environment of Tenochtitlán as it was once, on the swampy islands of the Lake of Texcoco.

Olmec influences: The visitor to the **Hall of Oaxacan Cultures** is greeted by a reproduction of fabulous, almost abstract, wall patterns from the Mixtecan palaces in Mitla. A map here provides an overview of the mountain landscape of Oaxaca where the Zapotecs and the Mixtecs lived. In the wide, fertile valleys of Oaxaca, since the first millennium BC, these cultures expanded around the most important of their ceremonial centers, Monte Alban.

The *Danzantes*, fragments of large stone reliefs depicting dancing figures, were sculpted around 600 BC. The significant influence of the early Olmecan culture of the Gulf coast on the Oaxaca can be seen. One can imagine the role of shamanistic practices and the ritual use of drugs depicted in these reliefs from the grotesquely distorted limbs and the hands pressed against the abdomen.

Xochipilli, the Aztec flour prince.

The Zapotecs of Oaxaca took great care in the construction of the tombs of their priests. Clay urns in the form of the gods stood on cornices above the tombs' entrances. A replica of one of the famous tombs from Monte Alban is also shown here.

In the **Hall of the Gulf Coast** the exhibits date back to the beginnings of the Olmec cultures. The ingenious Olmecan stonemasons created the enormous heads, perhaps portraits of some of their chiefs, using stone age techniques. Deified jaguar-human beings or "baby-face" figures resembling mongoloid children were principal themes among the puzzling peoples of this pre-Christian civilization. The highly valued jades and emeralds were made into polished ceremonial hatchets. In a famous archaeological find, near the important site of La Venta, a group of small jade figures was found among a setting of stone megaliths. It is believed that these figures had some sort of ritual significance.

A model of the Totonac temple of El Tajín is also on show here. Of a very high artistic quality are the *hacha*, *palma* and *yugo* stone sculptures exemplifying elements of the ritualistic ball game around which so much upper-class leisure was centered.

The complex **World of the Mayas** forms the central theme of the next gallery. The pinnacle of classical Mayan culture from the 3rd through to the 10th century can be seen in the diverse artefacts and replicas: finely worked sandstone stelae from Yaxchilán with depictions of priest-kings and complex symbol texts; colorfully painted, life-like clay figures from Jaina island near Campeche; jade and shell jewelry from the lowlands; and fantastic pyramid and palace architecture. Later the center shifted to the Yucatán peninsula.

With a new wave of immigration, pilgrimage centers like those adjoining the sacred Cenote, the well of Chichén Itzá, experienced new importance. A copy of the Toltec city of Tula was built, where the Mayan rain god Chac stood alongside the Toltecan Quetzalcoatl.

In stark contrast are the cultures of **Northern and Western Mexico**: in the last two galleries of the ground floor, the ceramics displayed read like a library in clay of the daily life of the Indians. Depicted here are animals, acrobats, ball players and complete scenes of indoor and outdoor life. The essence of this art as found in their graves shows that for these people nature and daily life had actually replaced the gods as their main concern.

If you still has enough energy after standing and examining so many display cases, the upper storey of the museum offers an excursion through the contemporary life of Mexico's Indians. The exhibits include traditional costumes, festivals, handicrafts and traditions which form the components of life for the surviving Indian cultures. And after all that, you still ought to leave time for the outstanding museum shop.

◀An eternal smile from the Totonacs.

The most colorful photos of Mexico City are mostly taken in Xochimilco. At weekends, the traffic is as busy as anywhere, but here the gondolas are painted with cheerful designs, their canopies wreathed in flowers, and the Mexicans certainly don't sit still in well-behaved rows listening to the driver's commentary. Instead they hold rowdy parties on board the rocking gondolas, liberally supplied with tacos, beer and tequila, to the strains of a hired *mariachi* band performing raucous renditions of *Las Mananitas* the Mexican birthday serenade.

To experience this side of Xochimilco, choose a Sunday to visit. But be prepared to join a steady steam of cars heading out of the city for the countryside – the journey may take you an hour. By Metro, you simply zip along to Taxqueña station and change there onto the quaint tram (*tren ligeno*) to Xochimilco.

Once there, you're faced with the dilemma of choosing between the 2000-odd *trajineras* (that's what they call gondolas here) working the waterways. Of the five quays or *embarcaderos*, Nativitas is the biggest and best known. It's here that most of the market stalls and food stands congregate at the weekends.

Maybe the name of the boat, hiding among the flowers, will help with your choice. Look a little closer and you'll realize that nowadays the floral decorations are made of paper, but the names they frame are all the more flowery as though to compensate: Graciela, Lupita, Angelita, Isabel, Esperanza, Carmelita...

"*Xóchitl*" is the Aztec (*nahuatl*) word for flowers, and "Xochimilco" means "in the flower fields". Flowers and vegetables are still grown here, but no longer in the legendary *chinampas*, the "floating gardens" of the Aztecs. Only one motorboat is now allowed to chug around what remains of the "Venice of the New World" – that belonging to the Mayor of Xochimilco. On this you can travel through the canals, the air heady with the scent of camomile and carnations which wafts from the banks, out into the open lagoon.

In 1890 the travel writer Ernst von Hesse-Wartegg found some of these same "curious islands" drifting against his boat: "A tangle of long dark roots, quite independent of the seabed, forms the base of the floating bodies. The fertile clouds of dust that blow from the stubble fields during the dry season, together with the accumulation of decaying plant and animal matter, in time laid down a layer of soil, the wind brought plant seeds, and thus the green islands were created ... They move around the lake in the wind, ... run aground on the banks in heavy storms, one on top of the other, soon growing into each other, and when they tire of their vagrant life, they form part of the proper mainland."

The fertile black soil of the *chinampas* always gave a high yield, irrespective of the rainy season. There were harvests up to four times a year. The people who lived on the banks used to anchor the little islands with posts so that they could work them. Sometimes they also built their huts on the islands and let themselves float off around the lake. Not only did they carry their homes with them like snails, but also the land on which and from which they lived. It was this independence that von Hesse-Wartegg so envied in the great *chinampa* farmers.

In the past they used *canoas* (dug-out canoes) to carry the harvest to market in the center of the city. During colonial times, the largest of these barges would have been anything up to 15 meters (50 ft) long, capable of transporting several tonnes of maize.

Today, 190 km (120 miles) of Xochimilco's canals are still navigable. The German Rowing Club "Antares," with a long tradition in Mexico, trains here. A section of the canal was widened to create the course for the 1968 Olympics. Many of the canals are barely passable, so completely are they covered with water hyacinths, which the farmers happily scattered on their fields as fertilizer. But agriculture is slowly returning to Xochimilco, homes are appearing on the *chinampas*, and now machines are working at clearing the canals from their carpet of plants.

Meanwhile other dangers are threatening Xochimilco. The problems of the city's growing population are spilling over into the surrounding countryside. A quarter of the city's water supply is drawn from the groundwater to the south east of the city, above all from Xochimilco. It's not hard to envisage a time when these reserves will be exhausted; some canals have already dried up.

At the same time, large areas of Xochimilco are subject to flooding during the rainy season. In 1987 UNESCO declared Xochimilco part of the "cultural heritage of mankind" and the Salinas government initiated an "ecological protection program" for the canal system. On the one hand this called upon the population of Xochimilco to take action to help themselves – by keeping the

canals clean and planting more trees, for example. At the same time, the government plans recommended the installation of a sewerage system and the construction of overspill lakes to counter the danger of flooding to the city. Finally, private investment in the scheme was to finance a massive leisure park.

The people of Xochimilco remain skeptical, however, suspicious of the fact that under the aid program they will be forced to surrender over 1,000 hectares (2,500 acres) of land if all the planned projects are to go ahead. They are preparing to fight. Since the Revolution of 1910, the authorities here are no longer afforded the blind respect they once were where land is concerned – the land on which one lives and works.

From the back of beyond, where you'd be lucky to catch a hazy glimpse over the distant snow-covered peaks of Popocatépetl and Iztaccíhuatl (at their most imposing on a winter afternoon), the one motorboat slowly makes its way back towards the center of Xochimilco. Narrow *canoas* rock past it, laden with red and white geraniums. Unlike the gondolas, they have no names, but the aphorisms painted along their sides bear witness to the people's almost fatalistic attachment to their watery environment: *Soy feliz entre las flores* ("I'm happy among the flowers"); or *Navegar es mi destino* ("I was destined to be a sailor"). The Xochimilco flower market does great credit to the ancient name of the city.

Left, during the week Xochimilco is a peaceful place. **Right**, waiting for customers amidst the enticing rainbow of painted gondolas.

COYOACAN AND SAN ANGEL

In order to escape the hectic life of the Mexican metropolis, one doesn't necessarily have to leave the city. Within the capital area, there are various possibilities for getting away from it all. In different parts of this enormous city there are tranquil sections which have preserved a certain cultural integrity of their own, where everyday life seems slower and more easy-going than in the outside world.

Coyoacán and San Angel are among the most beautiful of these hamlets within the city. Coyoacán is much older than San Angel and its residents have a stronger sense of tradition. But in both these suburban communities you can detect the intertwining of three different cultural epochs: the pre-Spanish, colonial, and modern styles.

Urban idyll: The Mexicans love their **Coyoacán** with its small, sleepy streets that take the visitor into another era. Behind the green of the trees, palms, and ivy and the bright blossoms of the bushes and shrubs, are some of the most beautiful colonial houses in the city with facades that are decorated with huge portals made from carved wood, often interrupted by narrow, wrought-iron balconies. Poor cottages can also not infrequently be seen alongside the villas, since rich and poor often live side by side in this district.

The name Coyoacán goes back to the pre-Spanish epoch. It is derived from the *nahuatl* word *Coyohuacan*, place of coyotes. Nearly 100 years before the Spanish conquest, the Aztecs conquered this area and subjugated the former metropolis of Tenochtitlán. Hernán Cortéz found the inhabitants of Coyoacán willing allies and set up his headquarters among them.

After the Spanish conquest, the colonial masters erected their summer residences in Coyoacán, and even today, the center of the district retains the

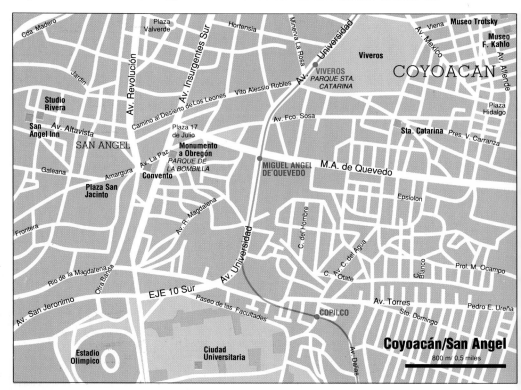

Coyoacán/San Angel
800 m/ 0,5 miles

character created by the typical colonial architectural style.

Home to intellectuals and artists: Many famous artists, politicians, and intellectuals lived and died in Coyoacán: the highly original painter Frida Kahlo whose anguished life at the side of the great Diego Rivera moved the whole world; or the Russian revolutionary, Trotsky, who in his flight from Stalin's henchmen barricaded himself in his own house here, where he was eventually murdered at the hands of a treacherous interloper who supposedly came to woo his daughter.

Both these houses are now preserved as museums, the Kahlo house (in which she was born in 1910 and in which she lived with Rivera from 1929 until her death in 1954) being filled with Kahlo's works and also much of the pre-Columbian art that she collected.

Even today, Coyoacán is the artists' and intellectuals' quarter. They come here to the **Parnaso** in search of like-minded people. In this bistro-like café

with an adjoining bookshop, they sit over a cappuccino conscientiously studying the daily papers. Only a few streets further away, soldiers guard the residences of several former Mexican state presidents.

For many Mexicans, Coyoacán is also the part of the city where you can buy the best ice cream. Next to elegant restaurants there are small, modest taverns. As unpretentious as these places may seem, everyone knows that only here can you get the best *pancita* (pig's stomach) or the best *pozole* (a type of casserole) which is prepared in a huge pot in the open entrance of the restaurant. Even elegantly attired businessmen come a long way through the morning traffic to begin their workday with a hearty breakfast in Coyoacán.

There are many ways of getting to Coyoacán. Buses, taxis and the Metro bring the visitor as far as the **Plaza de Hidalgo** which is in the heart of the district. The Metro also stops at the **Viveros**, a large parkland. A walk from

there to the centre of Coyoacán can be an experience in itself.

Green lungs: Viveros translates literally as nursery but for the locals it means first of all the essential "green lungs" of the southern part of the capital. A rich Mexican named Miguel Angel de Quevedo (an important street is named after him) willed this enormous green area to the city. His heirs carefully ensure that the space is used only as a nursery or for recreational purposes. Quevedo's will specifies that should the grounds be used for any other purpose then they would revert to the private possession of the family.

In view of the high real estate prices in Coyoacán, the Quevedo legacy and its rules is the best guarantor that Viveros remains protected against intruders. In the past 20 years, several state research institutes settled on the edge of Viveros. However, after lengthy court battles, they were forced to move and their premises were demolished.

In the middle of Viveros is a garden-like market in which the most varied kinds of flowers and green plants are sold. On the way out of the market is a small, cobblestone lane which leads to the dreamy **Jardín Santa Catarina**. This shady garden is scattered with restaurants and handicraft workshops in colonial style. A church from the colonial epoch is the architectural highpoint of the garden.

Colonial mansions: The **Calle Francisco Sosa** runs directly past the garden and is one of Coyoacán's most beautiful streets. Numerous art dealers, galleries, and antique dealers are housed in the street's lordly colonial villas. Francisco Sosa opens into the great park, **Jardín del Centenario** which adjoins the **Plaza Hidalgo** with its **Iglesia San Juan Bautista**. It was originally built in the 16th century as a Franciscan cloister but through the centuries has been remodelled several times.

The Plaza Hidalgo and the Jardín, laid out in the former atrium of the cloister, form the heart and the social center of **Idyllic resting places.**

Coyoacán. Shoeshines, peddlars, organ grinders, and ice vendors with their little bell-ringing carts belong as much to the Plaza and the Park as the different visitors and residents of Coyoacán. In numerous cafés you can watch the colorful activity in the park over a coffee or freshly pressed fruit juice.

Unfortunately the large area of Viveros and the many smaller gardens are not enough to keep the air of Coyoacán clean. As the trees of the Jardín del Centenario began to die, artists have used the opportunity to make original sculptures out of their remaining trunks and branches.

At the weekend, the park belongs to the children. Every Saturday and Sunday, the Jardín changes into an enormous open-air theater when Miko arrives with his big suitcase from which he magically takes rabbits' tails, wolves' furs or a little red hood. "I need two more piggies – no, you are not fat enough, I'll need you later on. And now, everyone sing along!" Every weekend hundreds of children join Miko, wait breathlessly for their turn, laughing, shouting, clapping and singing.

Original museums: To the left from the church of San Juan Bautista into the **Calle Hidalgo**, is No. 289, the **Museo de las Culturas Populares** (Museum of Popular Culture), where there are temporary exhibitions. The **Museo Frida Kahlo** is also a few minutes away from the Plaza Hidalgo. During the ethno-historical tour through this blue-painted house, the visitors are likely to forget that they are in a museum. The ambiance is such that you feel more that you are being a charmed guest in the Kahlo-Rivera household.

The rooms have retained their original style and the walls are decorated with numerous paintings from both artists. On boxes, cabinets, and shelves is a harmonious collection of household appliances and folk art of Indian origin, which symbolizes the attraction which both artists felt towards traditional Mexican culture and certainly demon-

In the Bazár del Sábado.

strates their zeal as collectors. Most remarkable are the many papier mâché figures in the shape of skeletons or devils with red or black horns. The figures accompany the visitor from the entrance to the patio.

The patio, like the house, has a romantic, dream-like atmosphere into which the many pre-Spanish sculptures from the couple's private collection fit seamlessly. Here the death's heads are also prominent. Frida's presence dominates the house, but in neighbouring San Angel is the Studio-Museum devoted to Diego Rivera in an immense building designed by the celebrated muralist to preserve his pre-Hispanic collection.

"I return to the people the artistic heritage I was able to redeem from their ancestors" is the dedication that Rivera had inscribed in the entranceway and which gratifies the visitor of today. Among the exhibits is a scale model of the ancient sacred ball game around which so much of the upper-class Aztec social life revolved.

Not far from the Museo Frida Kahlo is the "fortress" on Calle Viena where Leon Trotsky lived the last years of his life as his own prisoner after his ideological – and subsequently fatal – clash with Stalin. Despite heavy steel doors and round-the-clock armed guards Trotsky was unable to prevent infiltration of the household by a supposed "friend" who struck the communist exile in the head with an ice-pick on August 20, 1940, creating severe wounds from which Trotsky later died. In the home's rear garden is Trotsky's tomb designed by Juan O'Gorman and the house itself is a **museum** which can be visited.

The **Museo de las Intervenciones**, which documents the history of foreign intervention in Mexico, is in the former **Churubusco Cloister**. It can be reached by taking one of the large taxis with the sign "Metro General Anaya" from the Kahlo Museum.

Returning to the Avenida Insurgentes

Sur, the visitor passes the **Monumento Alvaro Obregón**, a monument which stands on the actual spot where the Revolutionary president was murdered in 1928.

San Angel: Colonial architecture also dominates the town of **San Angel** which extends westward from the Avenida Insurgentes Sur. The borders between the two communities have long since disappeared. In contrast to Coyoacán, which is very mixed, the population of San Angel is far more homogeneous and the residents belong primarily to the upper middle class, particularly the wealthy. Many Germans settled there in the first half of this century and as a result there are many places where German cuisine and delicacies can be be purchased.

A beautiful route to San Angel is the Callejón del Monasterio, a narrow, tranquil lane with high walls. A parallel street also leads from the Avenida Insurgentes Sur past the **Peña El Condor Pasa**, an artists' pub with Latin-

Romantic wedding in San Angel.

American music and poetry readings.

Both streets open into the Avenida Revolución (Mexico's best bookshop, the **American Bookstore**, is at number 1570). To the right stretches a long flower market. To the left is the former 17th-century cloister, the **Convento del Carmen**. Today it houses the ethnological and socio-anthropological departments of the Mexican Institute for Anthropology and History. The rest of the cloister with its fine courtyard serves as a museum, housing colonial art and an intriguing collection of mummies of priests, nuns and nobles.

Diagonally opposite the cloister is the **Plaza San Jacinto**, where artists exhibit their paintings and sculptures on weekends. On Saturdays, the Plaza and the nearby streets are filled with the **Bazar del Sábado**, an enormous handicraft market that extends from a beautiful old patio-house through the neighboring streets and lanes, and has drawn hundreds of delighted visitors for at least three decades.

On the patio itself you can eat and drink to the soft sound of *marimba* music or simply gaze at the things offered for sale around this courtyard: pictures, clay, onyx or wood figures and pottery, clothing, jewelry. Even if you want to resist the many distractions and buy nothing, a Saturday excursion to the Bazar del Sábado can be a rewarding and stimulating experience.

In one of the houses on the Plaza is the private art collection **Alvaro y Carmin T. Carrillo Gil**. The **Casa del Risco** (meaning "the house of broken porcelain" – a reference to the tiled fountain in the couryard) epitomizes the 18th-century colonial style in its interior appointments as well as its exterior construction. There is a small admission fee. The extremely elegant restaurant, the San Angel Inn, is located in an old town-house which dates from more or less the same period.

Just like Coyoacán, San Angel has many **art and antique shops** with an abundance of objects for sale. In the many galleries artists from all over the world as well as Mexicans with pre-Spanish roots exhibit their works.

In one gallery, in an elegant colonial house, the artist, a Huichol Indian, receives visitors. He wears the traditional attire of his people: a shirt and three-quarter-length cotton trousers which are loosely cut and richly embroidered. His hair is long and he wears handmade leather sandals on his naked feet. Next to him stands his wife, a delicate, blond Polish woman. The couple explain that they live in a traditional Huichol village and have only come to the capital on account of the exhibition.

In his pictures made of wool threads in bright natural colours, the artist integrates those symbols created and used by his ancestors long before the Spanish conquered Mexico. But the exhibition represents much more than the traditions of his people. It is also an example of the combination and juxtaposition of pre-Spanish and modern Mexico which is embedded in the colonial background of San Angel.

rom the
nountains
nto the city:
Huichol
ndians.

THE MODERN
UNIVERSITY CITY

The **Universidad Nacional Autónoma de México** (UNAM) can be reached along Avenida Insurgentes Sur or by Metro to the "Universidad" stop. The main part of the university was built in 1950–55 under the supervision of Carlos Lazo to plans by Enrique del Moral and Mario Pani. Flamboyant may not be a word usually associated with universities but it's not too out of place here. The campus, and particularly such buildings as the 10-storey library, covered with murals by Juan O'Gorman, has become a tourist site in its own right and, of course, is of special interest to those with an architectural bent. There are always visitors wandering around taking photographs and both they (and you) are welcome to patronize the inexpensive university cafeterias.

On the lava field: As early as 1553, South America's first university was opened in Mexico by Viceroy Luis de Velasco. After several changes of site, it ended up in the Zócalo, but had to move again when the new Supreme Court was built in 1935. Plans for the revolutionary new complex were helped by several factors. Under the presidency of Miguel Alemáns (1946–52), Mexico had opened itself up to industrialization. A national architecture based on simple lines and constructed according to the latest techniques was consistent with the modern drive for profit. The country was also endeavoring to espouse modernism. The neocolonial style that was still in favour in the Zócalo for the centers of power was considered obsolete elsewhere.

The ground plan of the campus is based on a wide square, around which cluster the groups of faculty buildings. The strict geometry of the modern blocks is broken up by an asymmetrical layout. Thus the white towers which house the natural science and psychology departments face one another across the edge of the main walkway.

The **Chancellery** is a particularly lavish building, designed by Mario Pani, Enrique del Moral and Salvador Ortega. The 15-storey tower block comprises a vertical and a horizontal section, embellished with Siqueiro's bas-relief *The People for the University, the University for the People* (1952–56), an amalgam of painting, sculpture and glass mosaic. The right-hand corner of the Chancellery adjoins the **Library**, designed by Gustavo Saavedra and Juan Martínez de Velasco and renowned worldwide for Juan O'Gorman's monumental mosaic, which expresses a vision of Mexico's past and future. The library has space to house over two million books. Beneath it are administrative offices and reading rooms, while a pond and a terrace hewn from the volcanic rock and decorated with pre-Columbian motifs create a pleasant setting.

The library embodies two very different trends, which are united to experimental effect in UNAM – in the international style, seen as synonymous with progress, and the urge to find acceptable solutions for today's problems from Mexico's own, age-old culture.

Colorful building materials, the covered walkways essential during the rains, the grassy inner courtyards based on the patio house, the involvement of educational artists – all are part and parcel of Mexican tradition. Particularly Mexican is the co-ordination of several styles, the ability to integrate and assimilate different trends. A concrete example of stylistic extremes co-existing in one building is the pavilion of the Institute of Cosmic Ray Research, designed by Félix Candela and J G Reyna (1953), or the sports facilities to the south of the campus, especially Alberto T Arais' *Frontones*, which draws on pre-Hispanic traditions.

The integration of art into the campus became a hallmark of UNAM. It's not a question of individual components but the clever juxtaposition of similar elements, seen for example in the medical faculty building. Designed by Roberto Alvarez Espinosa, this features Franciso Eppens' glass mosaic *Life, Death and the Four Elements* (1952). Steps are used to accentuate the different levels of the lava field. The visitor is offered a continually changing perspective, enriched by vegetation and sculptures. The apparently loose layout rests upon a strict design.

A city within a city: UNAM is a complete city in itself, with over 100 buildings, numerous squares and its own infrastructure of museums, shops, chapel, botanic gardens, post office, bus station and campus service industries. For this reason it is also known as *Ciudad Universitaria* ("University City"). The university reflects the explosive growth of the megapolis. Originally planned for 26,000 students, 300,000 are now studying there. Over the years new buildings have sprung up, notably for the natural sciences, most of them conventional constructions without any architectural pretensions. UNAM has left its mark on a wide area, with a network of housing blocks, bars and supermarkets. It has turned into the most ambitious project of post-Revolutionary Mexico and has long been a place of pilgrimage for art and architecture historians. Its international influence is undisputed.

The **Olympic Stadium** on the west side of Avenida Insurgentes also counts as part of UNAM. This is the work of architects A Pérez Palacios, R Salinas and J Bravo (1953). Structurally it resembles a cone-shaped volcano, with a giant oval bowl sunk into the crater as an arena. The exterior is decorated with a mosaic relief by Diego Rivera, using motifs from the history of sport.

Arts center: To the south of UNAM on a slight incline is the arts center, bordered by Avenida Insurgentes and the Periférico Metropolitano, and scenically framed by the nearby volcano Xitle, Mount Ajusco, the UNAM buildings and the whole panorama of

Mosaic riddle on the library.

the Mexico valley – and on rare clear days the twin volcanoes Popocatépetl and Iztaccíhuatl, too. In contrast to the building of UNAM, where the whole terrain was planned, the natural topography here was largely left untouched and instead integrated into the design. Any geometric similarities to pre-Hispanic places of worship, and especially to Teotihuacán, are far from coincidental. The ground plan lies around a similar longitudinal axis. These bearings confirm the complex as part of UNAM.

The north side is defined by the Unidad Bibliográfica (the National Library, Hemerothek), the south by the concert hall buildings, the theater, cinema and dance center. A transverse crosses this between the concert hall and the northern edge of the dance center in the right-hand corner, and runs across the square where Rufino Tamayo's totem-like sculpture stands, leading into the Centro Universitario de Teatro, which lies a little to one side.

The sloping entrance of the theater

building, as well as the northwest side of the Centro Universitario de Teatro, run parallel to the axis which appears to divide the concert hall in two. The point of intersection of this axis and the transverse points to the significance of the square as the center of this site. Framed by terraces, walkways, entrance halls and vegetation, the square provides a scenic space for open-air events.

The plans for the arts center were drawn up by a team of architects from UNAM, under the leadership of Orso Núñez Ruiz-Velasco, Auturo Treviño Arizmendi and Arcadio Artis Espriú. The concert hall, Sala Nezahualcóyotl (1976), named after an Aztec poet prince, admits daylight only through windows and doorway in the entrance hall, which leads to a flight of steps. It was designed for optimum acoustics and, next to the Amsterdam Concertgebouw, is one of the most successful concert halls in the world. Almost every day of the week there are performances by the UNAM Philharmonic or a visiting

international ensemble on the stage in the center of the wood-panelled auditorium.

The theater complex houses the Teatro Juan Ruiz de Alarcón and the smaller Foro Experimental Sor Juana Inés de la Cruz (1979), named after two writers from the colonial period. The theaters seat 430 and 250 people respectively. The high-rise section houses the fly tower. Two entrances lead up a flight of steps and into a foyer. The ground plan is elegantly mirrored by the interior, which in turn reflects the functional purpose. Thus an exciting alternation of right-angles and 45 degree angles in both ground plan and elevations creates a constant of form, crucial to the overall impact. This formal principle is common to all constructions which are built around a variety of focal points.

The building opposite also links two functional areas by a common foyer: the Miguel Covarrubia ballroom and the Miguel Chávez recital room, used for chamber music. In addition the complex houses two cinemas, a bookshop and the center's admininstrative offices. A diagonal towards the square passes through a high foyer into a series of passageways which form the heart of both complexes, their layout determined by the fall of light and shadow.

Clever orchestration: The Unidad Bibliográfica is physically set apart from the complex but closely related in terms of texture, color and style. It houses a large part of the million-volume national library founded by Benito Juárez in 1867, as well as treasures from the ancient university and secularized monasteries and valuable early literature. An old books' department is located in the old town in what was once the monastery of San Agustín, the previous home of the National Library.

Massive cuboids adorn the facade of the library. A flight of steps leads up to a small courtyard. Across this runs a glass entryway into the foyer. The fortress-like quality is moderated by the

Villa in the Pedregal lava field.

three-dimensional outer skin, which isn't much in keeping with the internal structure. The lofty inner courtyard of the five-storey building is particularly unusual, and is adorned with sculptures by Frederico Silva and Hersúa.

The interaction of the parts that make up UNAM's whole becomes clear by passing through them. Walk through the campus and it opens out around you, but drive around it and it blossoms to particularly aesthetic effect. According to your position, individual buildings come into view, only to "disappear" again into the lava field.

It is necessary to head down Avenida Insurgentes for another mile or so to reach the sculpture park, **Espacio Escultórico** which, though separated, is regarded as part of the university complex. Once discovered, however, the visitor quickly realizes that the park successfully bridges architecture and topography. Established in 1978–80 it is the result of a collaboration between the Mexican artists Helen Escobedo, Manuel Felguérez, Frederico Silva, Hersúa, Sebastián and Mathias Goeritz, a German. It includes a lava field framed by colored blocks of concrete, a kind of Mexican Stonehenge of almost earth-force energy.

This collectively planned space for quiet reflection is also an answer to the nearby **Round Pyramid of Cuiculco**, a meeting place firmly rooted in Mexican culture which was covered in lava for thousands of years until its excavation in 1922. Goeritz achieved a worldwide reputation for his **Towers of the Satellite City** (1957–58), which you pass on the way out towards Querétaro. He also instigated the **"Street of Friendship"**, an imposing avenue of sculptures created by artists of all continents which runs alongside the Periférico right up to the Aztec stadium.

The modern dilemma: Besides the arts center, which is one of the city's main attractions, a series of ambitious construction projects is concentrated in the south. From the artistic tension between tradition and the avant garde, Mexico's architects are developing a distinctive style of their own. An example is the **Colegio de México** on the road to Ajusco, an elite university founded in 1975 to plans by the architects González de Léon and Zabludowsky.

Mexico has invested its volatile fortune in petrol dollars in modern administration blocks, clinics, schools and highways, as well as hotels, banks and shopping centers like **Perisur**. The current economic crisis is necessitating more modest projects.

In individual districts like Pedregal, with its luxury villas, less imposing purpose-built estates for the middle classes and sprawling slums on the outskirts for the poor, the social injustices are drawing increasing attention. The scope for city planning has been exhausted by the pressures of the megapolis. The splendor and highflown rhetoric of modernism only serve to conceal the threatened collapse of the overpopulated valley of Mexico.

Perisur
Shopping
Paradise.

THE TRAGEDY OF TLATELOLCO

Three cultures, separated by several meters of earth and centuries of time, come together just north of the city in the quarter of Tlatelolco: the Aztec era with its pyramids, the colonial era with its 17th-century church of St James of Tlatelolco right in the middle of the grand esplanade, and the modern era with the tall, airy buildings of the Foreign Ministry.

Tlatelolco is the surest proof that Mexico City is a city built in layers. Here one sees the walls, altars, steps, the *tzompantli* (the stone skull scaffolds) next to the colonial church of St James which seems as if it would conceal everything

an object of fascination for archaeologists, anthropologists and historians. At the time the verdict on Aztec sculptures and gods was, if you believe British writer D. H. Lawrence, a colorful heap of detestable and disgusting stuff, and the ceramic and silversmith works hideous and uninteresting – so much so that one look at them made one depressed.

According to the description of the Franciscan teacher and chronicler, Bernardino de Sagahún, the children of the Aztec nobility were taught in the imperial school of the Santa Cruz cloister, right next to the church of St James, by his fellow

around it. In fact, it was the will of the Spanish conquistadors that any pre-Hispanic art be buried. In the name of the Father, the Son, and the Holy Ghost, get thee behind me, Satan. They believed that the gods of fire, water, and fertility were in union with the devil, and that these evil spirits must be driven away from the Indians. Conversion to Christianity meant destroying all that existed previous to the conquest, obliterating it, putting everything to the torch.

It is common knowledge that the Spanish not only annihilated the indigenous peoples but with them destroyed a whole way of life and a highly developed and differentiated culture. They thereby destroyed art which was much more than

Franciscans. Today, the cloister serves as the Foreign Ministry's historical archive where many valuable documents are preserved.

Tlatelolco not only remembers the Aztec empire but is also witness to its decline and the new race which thereby came into being, the *mestizos*, the people of today's Mexico. According to the historian, chronicler, and scholar Siguenza y Góngora, in 1692, the starving people (*mestizos*, poor Creoles, and Indians) rose up against the white colonial masters who were eating all of their sacred staple food, maize. The Spaniards' answer was a massacre here on this plaza. Tlatelolco was to be the scene of a bloodbath which overshadowed the end of the 17th century.

The square is not only of great historical significance for Mexico but it is also the home of more than 80,000 people living in a public housing complex originally encompassing 102 buildings. The complex was built in the 1950s according to the latest scientific and engineering concepts. The residents cross the Plaza de las Tres Culturas daily without paying much attention to what they are walking through. Children walk to school; students to the university, passing pedlars with their lottery tickets promising great fortunes: "Look, isn't this a beautiful number!" they say. In the Jardín, the small park of Santiago Tlatelolco with its stone benches and balustrades, you can buy balloons, ice cream and miracle cures.

The square was also the grave of the 1968 students' movement that preceded the Olympic

Games. On the "Night of Tlatelolco," the government's security forces shot at demonstrators during a protest meeting. Tlatelolco became a death trap for those students who had assembled there since no one knew where to run once the shooting began. The pre-Hispanic ruins were covered with the shoes and blood of fleeing protestors. Those who ran for cover in the colonial church found themselves shut out by the Franciscans who refused to open the doors. The windows of the Foreign Ministry buildings were smashed by a hail of bullets.

Above and right, the Plaza de las Tres Culturas was the setting for several catastrophes.

Just as the *mestizos* revolted against the viceroyalty, injustice, and poverty in 1692, the student's rising of 1968 was against the government. With the help of the one ruling party, the Partido Revolucionario Institucional (PRI), the Revolution had been usurped and in its place a financial oligarchy was established which worked hand-in-hand with the US. Those who had once worn sombreros and wielded rifles for the Revolution had become politicians, bureaucrats and civil servants, members of the new business, social and intellectual elite. It was in their interest to thrust Mexico into prominence on the world stage; make her presentable and dress her in the finest available clothing.

When the Olympic Games came to Mexico in 1968, the government spent millions on modern accommodation for the athletes as well as for the Olympic stadium and other sports facilities. At the same time, the students carried banners to their demonstrations that condemned the poverty and oppression of the normal people and demanded justice and freedom, and as the demonstrators began to cry "People unite!", so the government stood up and took notice. The students tried not only to sabotage the games (rumors circulated that bombs had been laid in the stadium) but they wanted also to expose the government before world opinion. On October 2, 16 days before the official opening of the XIX Olympics, there was a bloodbath on the Plaza de las Tres Culturas in which children, pregnant women, students and the elderly were killed. (According to one English newspaper, *The Guardian*, there were a total of 325 dead.)

But this was by no means the last tragic event for this part of Mexico City. In 1985, Tlatelolco was threatened with the heaviest earthquake in our history, but the underground movement didn't break up the plaza itself; instead, the residential blocks of the surrounding area were seriously damaged. Above all the "Nuevo Leon," a building which had starred in the 1968 uprising when the leader of the students had addressed the masses on the plaza from the third floor window, came crashing down.

For Mexican author Octavio Paz, Tlatelolco is a sacred and mysterious place, which seems to be destined to witness the human sacrifices that the greedy and choleric gods demand time and again. Here are celebrated sacrificial rites, rites of vengeance, sacrifices to the sun by the people of the sun, a people who love rituals. Religious celebrations, ceremonies of life and death, games, dances and fireworks spring from this place, rise to the sky from below, from the plaza, the market, the Zócalo, the Plaza de las Tres Culturas.

THE VIRGIN OF GUADALUPE

To North Americans and northern Europeans, even if they are themselves Catholics, Latin-American piety is something exotic. A visit to Mexico City's Virgin of Guadalupe can prove to be an experience which highlights that special Mexican mixture of religiosity and patriotism.

The vast site of the shrine 6 km (4 miles) north of Zócalo consists of an enclosed atrium of 46,000 sq. meters (55,000 sq. yds) facing six churches and chapels at the foot of the park-like **Tepeyac**. The summit of the hill is crowned by another church. The best means of getting there is on the Metro to the station "Basilica" or by bus in the direction of "La Villa".

Two one-way streets, continuations of the Paseo de la Reforma, lead to the gates to the shrine: the Calzada de Guadalupe and the Calzada de los Misterios with its prayer stations presenting the 15 "mysteries of the Rosary." The pilgrim, who naturally makes his way from here on foot, can pray 10 *Ave Marias* and one *Pater Noster* in between each of them.

The Madonna, known as *Tonantzin*, "our little mother," was visited by thousands of Indians who came to make sacrifices and to pray to her but also to benefit from the healing powers of the sulphuric springs which are at the bottom of the hill.

After the conquest of the Aztec capital these heathen practises came to a swift end. The temple of Tonantzin was destroyed, just like all the others. But places of pilgrimage tend to retain a life of their own, no matter what they are called or what they symbolize. They attract gods, saints and believers, and this is exactly what happened with the Tepeyac. In New Spain, the re-titled Mexico City under the Spanish, new shrines had to be erected for the Virgin Mary, who was so passionately adored

Preceding pages: the climax of the Guadalupe cult is the midnight mass on 12 December. Below, dancers in front of the basilica.

by the Spanish conquerors. Tepeyac was ready to appear in a new shape for its new mistress.

Juan Diego and the manifestation: The legend of the icon differs from other such legends in so far as the Virgin did not appear to a young boy or girl, but to an adult man. Cuauhtlatohuac, "Talking Eagle" was one of the first converts of the 12 Franciscans who had come to Mexico in 1524. The 57-year-old landowner had taken the name Juan Diego at his baptism.

On the morning of December 9, 1531, on his way to church, Juan passed the Tepeyac and saw his vision: a dark-haired, brown-skinned woman who demanded that a church be built on the hill and to reinforce her message caused roses to bloom on the barren hillside. After that the Virgin Mary appeared five times altogether, finally convincing the obdurately skeptical Bishop Zumarraga of her authenticity by causing her image to appear on the inside of Juan Diego's coat.

Today the picture of a young woman with light brown complexion but not very pronounced Indian features is ubiquitous in Latin America. She has entirely replaced the first Virgin of Guadalupe, the miraculous dark statue of the Madonna with Child from Extremadura. However there are no original testimonies from the first 100 years of the Virgin of Tepeyac. There are only references to a cult which caused the missionaries considerable alarm, especially when the newly baptized Indians called the Virgin Mary "Tonantzin," just like their old pre-Christian goddess.

All doubts and suspicions have long been overcome. Tradition says that the icon immediately caused miracles: first, the healing of Juan's uncle; then the healing of a young Indian, injured during a procession to place the image in the new shrine. Since then there have been countless healings and rescues from spiritual and material need as well as other help for which the Virgin has

been responsible. Votive images, now on display in the museum near the old basilica, testify to the infinite misery as well as the infinite hope of man.

First protectress of the city: Soon the Virgin of Guadalupe proved helpful not only for individual believers, growing into her role as patroness of the City of Mexico, the whole country and finally of all Latin America. The first opportunity to demonstrate her power arose in September, 1629, when torrential rains as well as the rising lake threatened to flood the city. The icon was carried in a holy procession from the Tepeyac to town and the danger was diverted. Ever since then Guadalupe has been the official "First Protectress" of the city against floods.

In the end there was little else to do but call upon divine assistance to fend off the epidemics (smallpox, plague, cholera, measles, etc.) which the Spanish brought to the city and which had decimated the Indian population. By 1520 when the Aztec capital was rebuilt

after a disastrous flood, its population of more than 350,000 made it one of the three largest cities in the world. Today it is the largest.

The need for divine protection for this growing mass was universally agreed upon by all – the town administration, the religious authorities and viceregal officials. In time, Guadalupe had become the symbol of the newly developing Mexican identity. When appealing to the brown-skinned Mary, the Spanish, *Mestizo* and the Indians in their misery, all forgot their feelings of hostility. The Criollos or Creoles, particularly the Spanish born in Mexico, were devoted to the Virgin whose image rose from Mexican soil.

From the middle of the 17th century, the cult of the Virgin of Guadalupe became a commitment to Mexican identity, as well as to political and spiritual independence from Spain. In 1810, waving the banner of Guadalupe, Father Hidalgo waged the Mexican struggle for liberation. Since the independence in 1821, both Mexican politicians and revolutionaries have called upon her for protection for their side. Even today no trade unionist would neglect to celebrate her feast day, December 12.

Days before that special celebration, pictures of the Patroness are decorated with flowers and candles throughout the country. Masses of people flock to her shrine. Outside the enclosure, there is plenty to eat and drink. Indian groups dance in front of the churches. Most of them wear costumes which date from before the Spanish invasion but some also dress in baroque velvet and silk or as Christians and Moors in fierce battle. As always, Tonantzin-Guadalupe especially protects "her children", the Indians. And the Church itself is resigned to the fact that, after hundreds of years of controversy, it still has little say in the matter.

Controversy: Only through willing self-sacrifice on the part of the local population has it been possible to build

Endless streams of pilgrims.

the many churches and chapels which stand, adjoin and sometimes seem to tumble over one another.

In 1976, the **new basilica** and **baptismal chapel** were consecrated. With all due respect to the architect Pedro Ramírez Vásquez, who also built the impressive Archaeological Museum in Mexico City, the new basilica resembles something like a sports stadium on the outside and the interior of a discreetly luxurious hotel lobby on the inside. It has neither the quality of a gold-glistening magic chamber, as do the churches of the colonial period, nor that of a god's throne as did the old pyramids. The modest icon itself appears even smaller in its new hall, which is intended to hold between 10 and 20,000 worshipping pilgrims.

To make up for the distance they are away from the image, enthusiastic celebrants are allowed to get close to the icon by way of a passage behind the altar. For a few seconds you can glance at the picture before following one of the carpeted paths to the stalls which sell devotional items.

The **old basilica**, built between 1695 and 1709, was not only too small but suffered the fate of so many other buildings that were built on a site that had formerly been a lake: it sank into the ground and began to lean. It has been constantly under repair ever since. Adjoining it is the church of the Capuchin nuns who founded a cloister here.

A few steps further on you can find the place where the first prayer station for the Virgin was erected. Today's structure, the third, dating from 1695, is modest and dignified. Next to it is a fountain for the refreshment of pilgrims. The fountain chapel "**Pocito**" is a playful round structure with three domes covered with blue and white tiles. It dates from 1791.

The visitor who is already too exhausted to climb one of the two 50-meter (165-ft) high stairways to the hill's summit, will miss not only an impressive view of the whole area but

tiny Aztec.

also the original sacred place where the Temple of Tonantzin once stood.

In 1660 a pious couple first ensured that the original pile of stones with a cross on top of it was replaced with a chapel. The church which now stands in its place was built decades later. Adjoining it is a cemetery with fascinating gravestones. Once the ramps and gardens were laid out in the 18th century, the hill became a favorite place for Sunday excursions.

Anyone who wants to see how the site most probably looked in the pre-Spanish epoch can set out by a car and inspect two well-restored Aztec temples. The pyramid of **Tenayuca**, 6 km (4 miles) northwest of downtown, is guarded by 138 especially threatening snakes, a living echo of the row of serpents' heads along the pyramid's base.

Not far away is the small village pyramid of **Santa Cecilia** where you can see the temple construction and the sacrificial stone. Today it is a very quiet place for reflection.

MEXICAN NIGHTS

At night Mexico valley is a gold and silver carpet of lights. From the observation tower on the old road to Cuernavaca, from several restaurants on the arterial road to Toluca or just from the top floor of the Torre Latinoamericana, there is a marvelous view over the world's third largest city. Almost 300,000 street lamps provide the city's lighting, while more than 35,000 police officers watch over the safety of its population.

Multicolored neon lighting on facades and in shop windows is like make-up on the party face of all the city's squares and secret crannies, giving them its own special charm. Seen from above, the streets with their night-time traffic are shimmering moving streams of light.

An evening stroll through the streets of the Centro Histórico (old town) is a satisfying feast for the eyes and ears. The colonial architecture offers a muted contrast to the glaring neon signs, while from the bars, *cantinas* and cabarets filter music and the babble of voices.

There are few sights more attractive than the Plaza Mayor, the Zócalo, by night. All the historic buildings are carefully floodlit: the cathedral, the Palacio Nacional, the old and new city halls, the Gran Hotel and the Nacional Monte de Piedad.

In the historic city center, people meet for the traditional *merienda* (an early evening snack of pastries and sugary drinks). Popular haunts are the famous **Café Tacuba** for its delicious cakes, sweets and *antojitos* (Mexican appetizers); the **Super Leche**, for biscuits, cakes and milky coffee, and **El Moro**, where you can feast on hot chocolate with sugary *churros*. At this time in the evening there's even an avid audience for lectures and meetings in the Museo Nacional de Arte, the Palacio de Minería, the Palacio de Bellas Artes, the Museo de la Ciudad de México and the Colegio Nacional.

Although the nightlife in Mexico City scarcely compares with New York, Las Vegas or even Paris, it still has its own special charm. The nightspots are no match for Broadway, Acapulco or Monaco in quantity or quality, but nevertheless there is still plenty to do. Some superbly mounted productions, for example, would do justice to great stages the world over. In arts centers and theaters evening performances usually begin from 7.30 p.m. In the nightclubs, business doesn't get under way until around 10 p.m. If you get there early, there'll be nothing happening.

Hotel bars: Most nightclubs are located in the big hotels, and others are scattered across the city – in the center, to the south, in Zona Rosa and Ciudad Satélite. The highest concentration is in the center of Coyoacán, along Avenidas Universidad and Insurgentes, in the shopping precincts and leisure centers like **Perisur**, **Plaza Universidad** and

eceding
ges: the
ty at night.
ft, the
llet
lklórico.
low, Calle
adero and
e "Torre."

Plaza Satélite, on Paseo de la Reforma and, last but not least, Avenida San Juan de Letrán.

Almost every one of Mexico City's hundreds of good hotels boasts an excellent bar. Sometimes, especially at weekends, it can be difficult to find a seat, particularly if the bar also has live entertainment. The prices charged in all these establishments are subject to controls laid down by the Ministry of Tourism and the city administration. It's probably useful to remember that getting drunk is easier at high altitudes and Mexico City is more than 2,200 meters (7,200 ft) above sea level.

Mexico City's nightspots come and go like mayflies. There are always some closing down and others opening up. Sometimes they shut for a short period only to reopen later with a better program of entertainment. *Capitolanos* themselves seem to favor the big hotels which are often the best places for drinking, dining and dancing. Tourists might well consider sampling one of the ubiquitous nightclub tours that offer a taste of several places with minimal inconvenience.

Street life: The city's various districts provide the setting for all kinds of open-air performances. It's fun just to wander through the streets and stumble upon mime artists, bands, artists, fire eaters and market criers, entertaining the crowds. A common sight amidst the colorful nightly bustle are the steaming food stalls selling *tacos*, *tortas*, *tamales*, *atole*, *sopes*, *birria*, *pozole*, and other tasty examples of Mexican cuisine, all at highly affordable prices. There are an enormous number of these stands which seem to flourish mainly at night – on Plaza Garibaldi, for example, the epitome of nightlife in the Mexican metropolis. Renowned for its *mariachi* musicians and *antojitos*, this square is without doubt one of the most popular places in the city, where both locals and tourists can enjoy themselves in a lively party atmosphere. It is where the party-givers hire the musicians for their cel-

Folk night in "Focolare".

ebrations and, although negotiations are always going on, resulting in groups of musicians suddenly leaving, new arrivals constantly swell the ranks of those who remain.

The people of Mexico City are often described as bohemians, because they relish the varied nightlife their city has to offer, the bars, restaurants and clubs where they can listen to romantic songs and sing along if the fancy takes them. In private, too, they organize parties or dances every Friday and Saturday, either in their own homes or in halls or out of doors. The slightest excuse is enough: a birthday, Mother's Day, Father's Day, Godfathers' Day, a christening, a girl's 15th birthday (a special anniversary in Mexico), weddings and even divorces.

The Mexicans love dancing and there are a lot of nightspots in the city where they can indulge night after night to their heart's content. These include the **Los Angeles** and **El Colonial** ballrooms in Cuauhtémoc, the **Riviera** and the **California Dancing Club** in Benito Juárez, various clubs in Zona Rosa and cabarets on the Avenida San Juan de Letrán, Avenida Juárez and Avenida Insurgentes. Finally there are the discotheques in the southern part of the city, in Tecamachalco, Naucálpan and Ciudad Satélite.

World music: The city's many stages offer programmes of Mexican and international music and ballet which are among the very best. These include the **Palacio de Bellas Artes**, the **Auditorio Nacional**, the **Sala Nezahualcóyotl**, the **Sala Ollin**, **Yoliztli**, the **Premier de San Jerónimo**, the **Conjunto Marraquesh**, the **Teatro de la Ciudad**, **El Patio** and the **Magic Circus**.

The **Ballet Folklórico de México** has appeared alongside world-famous artists like Herbert von Karajan, Zubin Metha, Alexander Schnaider, Pablo Casals, Pedro Vargas, Lola Beltrán, Sara Vaughan and Cindy Lauper. The London Symphony Orchestra has also made guest appearances.

International sounds on the dance floor.

The Ballet Folklórico productions, which specialize in regional dances, are events that the first-time visitor to the city should not miss. Tickets – often bought in large batches by tour companies – go early for the three weekly performances, so it is usually advisable to make your plans and book your seats well ahead of time.

In addition, Mexico City has a vast number of museums, galleries, arts centers and cultural meeting places, where every evening a variety of events take place: exhibitions, chamber music recitals, jazz, blues, rock and folk concerts, poetry readings, film festivals and lectures on everything from science to art history.

These venues are scattered throughout the city, but are mainly concentrated in the districts of Cuauhtémoc, Miguel Hidalgo and Coyoacán. The most important are the **Foro Coyoacanense**, the **Hijo del Cuervo**, **El Juglar**, the **Librería Gandhi**, the **Librería del Sótano**, the **Casa de Cultura Jésus Reyes Heroles**, the **Librería Parnaso** and the **Foro Cultural Luis Buñuel**.

Worthy of a special mention is the old-established **Teatro Blanquita** (on Avenida San Juan de Letrán and Eje Central Lázaro Cárdenas), which the people of the city hold very dear. The cabaret there is all that remains of the *Teatro de revista musical* (Mexican revue theater), the last bastion of the magical variety shows from the 1950s, which produced some of the greatest names in Mexican cinema like Cantinflas, Tin Tán and Resortes, to name but three.

Every day a whole assortment of artists appear at the Teatro Blanquita to give of their best in song, dance or comedy routine, to perform a few magic tricks or entertain the audience with humorous sketches. Artists of international repute like Ray Coniff, Juan Gabriel and Vicky Carr have also had top billing here.

Traditional burlesque: The program for the 60 or so theaters dotted around the

Mariachis take a tequila break.

city features Mexican and international plays of all kinds and all periods, on every day of the week except Mondays (theaters closed). Theaters like the **San Rafael**, the **Manolo Fábregas**, **Insurgentes** and **Silvia Pinal** are devoted to Broadway-style musicals.

In other theaters like the **San Jerónimo**, the **Reforma**, the **Hidalgo**, the **Tepeyac**, the **Julio Prieto**, the **Cuauhtémoc** and the **University Arts Center** (in the Sala Juan Ruiz de Alarcón), the classics of world literature are brought to the stage, from Shakespeare and Cervantes, Tirso de Molina and Molière through to Tennessee Williams, Ionesco and Fernando Arrabal. But that's not to say that first-class Mexican playwrights like Sergio Magaña, Vincente Leñero, Hugo Argüelles, Ignacio Retes, Emilio Caballido, Luis Basurto or Victor Hugo Rascón Banda receive short shrift.

Even if the language barrier deters the foreign visitor from a visit to the theater to see a local work, Mexico's leading actors still deserve acknowledgement. Ignacio López Tarso, Hector Bonilla, Ofelia Guilmáin, Carmen Montejo, Rosenda Monteros, Sergio Jiménez, José Alonso, Helena Rojo, Susanna Alexander and Diana Bracho are just a few of the names that strike a chord with Mexican theater audiences.

The majority of theaters in Mexico City, however, cater for the *chilangos'* love of burlesque. There are innumerable second-rate theaters running these kinds of shows from late evening through to early morning. Most of these vaudeville theaters are in the districts of Cuauhtémoc, Miguel Hidalgo and Benito Juárez.

Long lines tend to form, too, outside the city's 150-odd movie theaters, especially at the weekends. There's always a wide choice of movies on offer, Mexican and international, old classics and the latest releases. The best movie houses are in Cuauhtémoc, Benito Juárez, Miguel Hidalgo, Coyoacán and Ciudad Satélite. The second and third-run cinemas tend to be found on the city's outskirts, and in the various outlying districts which have now become part of the metropolis.

Sport, too, plays an important role in the nightlife of Mexico City. Week in, week out, throughout the appropriate seasons, baseball and football matches, boxing and wrestling take place in **Parque del Seguro Social**, the **Estadio Azteca** and the **Estadio Olímpico de la Ciudad Universitaria**, while in the **Arena México** (also known as the Coliseo) and the **Plaza de Toros México**, the toreros and matadors line up for classical bullfights.

Most night-time events are listed either in *The News*, Mexico City's English-language newspaper, or *Tiempo Libre*, which comes out twice a week.

Mexican menu: Despite inflation and the country's perpetual economic crisis, the city's exclusive restaurants are well patronized in the evenings. It's therefore advisable to book your table in advance. No need to worry about parking, though: when you arrive an eager doorman will take your keys and park the car for you.

A wide choice of restaurants covers Chinese, Japanese, Italian, German, French, Polish, Cuban, Arabian and, of course, Mexican cuisine. There are restaurants specializing in vegetarian dishes, others in fish and seafood. The city's oldest and best known eating places are on Paseo de la Reforma and Avenida de los Insurgentes, in Zona Rosa, San Angel and Ciudad Satélite. There are countless top-class restaurants which cater for tourists where you can really dine in style. You shouldn't go home, however, without having tried Mexican cuisine.

As the capital of the country, Mexico City can offer a wide range of night-time diversions every day of the week. Mexico City by night offers an enticing kaleidoscope of images and experiences which you won't find in any other city in Mexico, or even anywhere else in the world.

Plaza Garibaldi: Fiesta Mexicana

Whoever happens to be in the vicinity of Plaza Garibaldi in the evenings is bound to hear the sound of trumpets and violins in the distance. And on the streets musicians appear in *charro* costume, ready to climb into a customer's car for the chance of performing somewhere, no matter what the occasion.

Plaza Garibaldi is one of the most picturesque squares in Mexico City. People come here to listen to the *mariachi* groups who have grown to symbolize Mexican folklore, and engage them to play a traditional *serenata* (a moonlight serenade of seven songs). It's a fascinating square, full of so many nooks and crannies to explore. But its special atmosphere is also due to the *cantinas* and restaurants around its perimeter, where folk groups appear night after night. *Fiesta Mexicana* is celebrated here around the clock, whatever the climate or season.

Plaza Garibaldi offers a cross-section of Mexican folk music. Not only the *mariachi* groups play here, but also *Norteños* (from the north), musicians from Veracruz and *marimba* xylophone players from Chiapas, while balladeers give their renditions of songs old and new by Mexican songwriters like Tata Nachos and Juan Gabriels.

Mexican gastronomy joins in with the traditional chorus. At dusk, all the culinary delights of the Mexican kitchen are brought out into **Camilito Market**. Take a walk through this tunnel-like market hall and snack counters lure you from either side of the long aisle, selling typical Mexican *antojitos* (appetizers) and hot dishes. Everyone can find something to his or her taste in the surrounding restaurants and night-time bars, where the waiters execute the most amazing balancing acts with their trays.

On Plaza Garibaldi you can also sample those famous Mexican drinks: tequila from Jalisco, *mezcal* from Oaxaca – complete with the worm – and *pulque* from the states of Mexico and Hidalgo. They're all distilled from the agave plant and either drunk on their own or served with hazelnuts, walnuts, pine kernels, chunks of celeriac, watermelon or red cactus fruit.

Just as lively as Plaza Garibaldi by night is the adjoining **Plaza Santa Cecilia**, named after the patron saint of musicians. Every year on 21st November a midnight serenade is offered up to the saint by over 1,000 *mariachis*.

The district, which is so typical of Mexico City, has expanded considerably over the years. Today the **Calle de Ecuador** marks its boundary to the north, in the south it stretches as far as **Calle Perú**, in the east to **Calle Allende** and in the west to **Eje Central** (Avenida San Juan de Letrán). Legend has it that the spot on which Plaza Garibaldi now stands was dedicated in pre-Hispanic times to the goddess of the *maguey* (agave art). Later the square was known for a long while as Plaza del Baratillo. It was only in the 1930s that it was given its existing name in honour of the Italian revolu-

tionary Guiseppe Garibaldi, who sided with Mexico during the French invasion.

The square's musical traditions date back to 1925, when the famous *cantina* **Tenampa** opened its doors. Because of the rather scant custom, the bar's owner, a Jalisco man, decided to invite one of the *mariachi* groups popular in Jalisco at the time to the big city. (The word *mariachi* comes from the French *mariage*.) Originally the groups comprised four musicians playing a combination of instruments, including guitar, bass guitar, harp and psaltery. More and more ensembles moved to the capital. In the beginning they used to play in the middle of the

Zócalo to get themselves noticed. But they ran into problems with the police for street music was still illegal at that time. Eventually Plaza Garibaldi was officially sanctioned as their regular performance spot.

At present there are more than 100 *mariachi* groups in Mexico City. They've grown in size over the years with some containing up to 20 players. They've also added more instruments like violins and trumpets, and the traditional threadbare suit has also changed. Modern *mariachis* wear a wide-brimmed *sombrero* and a full *charro* costume with silver buttons on the jacket and trousers.

Following Tenampa's outstanding success with its *mariachis*, other bars moved in around

An essay by the journalist José Alvarado from the 1950s, *Lección en el Tenampa*, succeeds in capturing the atmosphere as no other has done.

"At night the *mariachis* crowd the square, and sounds from Jalisco and Michoacán float on the air. Demure and not so demure young ladies listen from their cars, while in the tavernas young men work themselves up over a few glasses of *Ponche de Granada* with nuts as they discuss life's futility, and old men, fired by a tequila with *perlitas* twig, are still eagerly putting the republic to rights. In the light of the electric bulbs on the stalls selling cinnamon tea laced with alcohol, and by the glowing embers of the charcoal grills on which sit unidentifiable fish and sad-looking burgers, Plaza Garibaldi watches as straggling

Plaza Garibaldi, among them **Guadalajara de Noche**, the **México Típico,** the **Plaza Santa Cecilia** and the **Rincón del Mariachi**. Plaza Garibaldi became the focus of the *alegría mexicana* (Mexican joie de vivre) in the capital.

During its "Golden Age" in the 1940s and 1950s, Mexican cinema contributed to the notoriety of the square, to its worldwide notoriety in fact. Time and again it is used as a setting in movies of this period, sometimes even as the central theme.

<u>Left</u>, serenades in the famous Tenampa. <u>Above</u>, a *mariachi* request spot on Plaza Garibaldi.

recruits, prostitutes, frustrated poets, young tramps, singers of tangos and Yucatec laments, mechanics, existentialist rebels, students and waitresses drift by."

In the 1950s Plaza Garibaldi became known as the Mexican Broadway for theatres such as Follies and the Carpa Margo, where performers like Cantinflas, Palillo, María Victoria and Tin Tán used to appear. Part of this frivolous, lighthearted world persists to this day, for the Plaza's sphere of influence reaches as far as the Lagunilla district, where there are more than 40 nightclubs. Plaza Garibaldi has become the epitome of Mexican folklore.

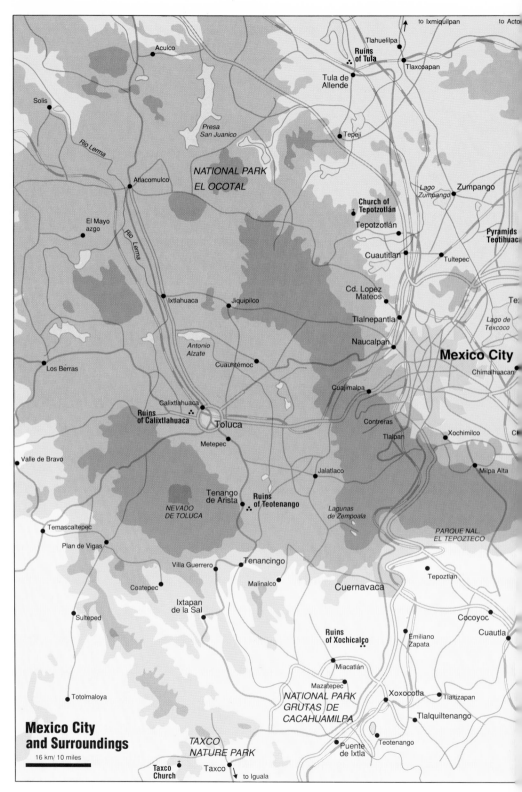

to Ixmiquilpan   to Actо

Tlahuelilpa

**Ruins
of Tula**

Tula de
Allende

Tlaxcoapan

Aculco

Solis

*Presa
San Juanico*

Tepeji

Río Lerma

Atlacomulco

**NATIONAL PARK
EL OCOTAL**

Church of
Tepotzotlán

*Lago
Zumpango*   Zumpango

El Mayo
azgo

Tepotzotlán

Río Lerma

**Pyramids
Teotihuacа**

Cuautitlán

Tultepec

Ixtlahuaca

Jiquipilco

Cd. Lopez
Mateos

Te:

*Antonio
Alzate*

Tlalnepantla

*Lago de
Texcoco*

Cuauhtémoc

Naucalpan

Los Berras

Mexico City

Cuajimalpa

Chimalhuacan

**Ruins
of Calixtlahuaca**

Calixtlahuaca

Toluca

Contreras

Xochimilco

Ch

Metepec

Tlalpan

Valle de Bravo

Jalatlaco

Milpa Alta

Tenango
de Arista

**Ruins
of Teotenango**

*Lagunas
de Zempoala*

*PARQUE NAL.
EL TEPOZTECO*

*NEVADO
DE TOLUCA*

Temascaltepec

Plan de Vigas

Villa Guerrero

Tenancingo

Tepoztlán

Coatepec

Malinalco

Cuernavaca

Ixtapan
de la Sal

Cocoyoc

Sulteped

**Ruins
of Xochicalco**

Emiliano
Zapata

Cuautla

Miacatlán

Totolmaloya

Mazatepec

Xoxocotla

Tlaltizapan

*NATIONAL PARK
GRUTAS DE
CACAHUAMILPA*

Tlalquiltenango

Mexico City
and Surroundings

16 km/ 10 miles

*TAXCO
NATURE PARK*

Puente
de Ixtla

Teotenango

Taxco
Church

Taxco

to Iguala

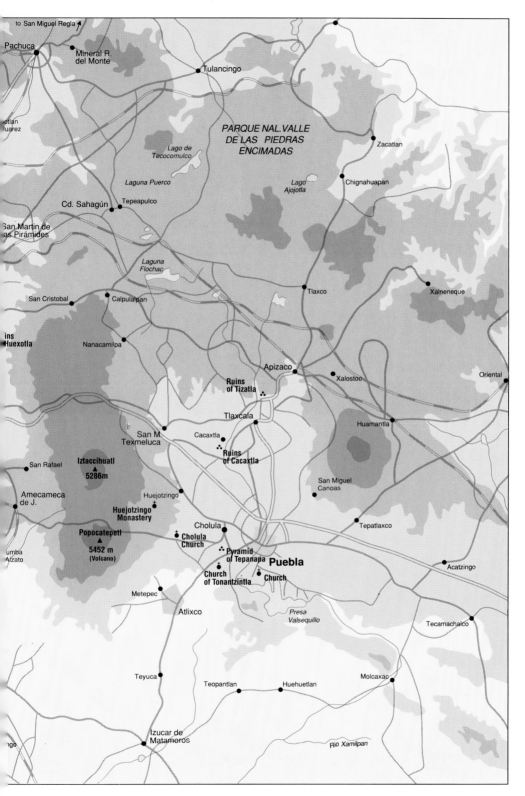

to San Miguel Regla

Pachuca

Mineral R. del Monte

Tulancingo

otlán uarez

PARQUE NAL. VALLE DE LAS PIEDRAS ENCIMADAS

Lago de Tecocomulco

Zacatlan

Laguna Puerco

Lago Ajojotla

Chignahuapan

Cd. Sahagún

Tepeapulco

San Martin de as Pirámides

Laguna Flochac

Tlaxco

Xalneneque

San Cristobal

Calpulalpan

ins Huexotla

Nanacamilpa

Apizaco

Xalostoc

Oriental

Ruins of Tizatla

Tlaxcala

Huamantla

San M. Texmeluca

Cacaxtla

Ruins of Cacaxtla

San Rafael

Iztaccihuatl 5286m

San Miguel Canoas

Amecameca de J.

Huejotzingo

Huejotzingo Monastery

Cholula

Tepatlaxco

Popocatepetl 5452 m (Volcano)

Cholula Church

Pyramid of Tepanapa

Puebla

umba Alzato

Church of Tonantzintla

Church

Acatzingo

Metepec

Atlixco

Presa Valsequillo

Tecamachalco

Teyuca

Teopantlan

Huehuetlan

Molcaxac

go

Izucar de Matamoros

Rio Xamilpan

AROUND MEXICO CITY

Massive pyramids, ornate colonial baroque, snow-covered volcanoes 5,000 meters (16,400 ft) high, sub-tropical gardens, old *haciendas*: whoever chooses the Mexican capital as their base, will find interesting excursions in every direction.

Any organized short program for Mexico City itself normally includes a trip to the pyramids of Teotihuacán. The drive gives an impression of the expanse of the city, the landscape of the high valley of Mexico, and the cultural accomplishments of the pre-Spanish cultures. Our text breathes life into the great city of Teotihuacán with its ceremonial center. On the way to the ruins of the old Toltec capital of Tula in the north of Mexico City, visit the convent of Tepotzotlán, where the Churrigueresco style of architecture is seen at it best.

Have you ever been at an altitude of 3,880 meters (12,500 ft) with an automobile? In Mexico you can. When you drive over the pass between the two volcanoes Popocatépetl and Iztaccíhuatl toward Tlamacas, it almost seems possible to touch the summit of "Popo." The air is quite thin here. To look into the crater of Popo requires a fairly long walk.

One hundred kilometers (60 miles) below Mexico City lies Cuernavaca, a sub-tropical garden paradise. A winding mountain drive takes you from here to the picturesque town of Taxco, where hundreds of workshops turn what silver is still mined into jewelry and vessels.

The art of the Talavera potters is to be found in the city of Puebla. Their work decorates the facades of houses and churches with tile pictures. Once the "City of the Angel," Puebla is today the home of the Mexican Volkswagen factory – the "City of the Beetle." In the vicinity are the climbable pyramids of Cholula and ultra-baroque village churches with pre-Spanish murals.

To the west, take a trip to the highest city in Mexico, Toluca (2,680 meters/8,800 ft). It's worth going there just to see the huge Indian market. The volcano Nevado de Toluca can be negotiated by car as far up as its crater lakes. The *hacienda* hotels surrounding Mexico City are especially recommended to romantics and sports lovers. They are located near extensive, well-maintained parks with golf and horseback riding facilities. Whoever is tired of the city air and beating the pavement can unwind from a visit to the Mexican capital in one of these noble country resorts.

Visitors are allowed to climb the Sun and Moon pyramids of **Teotihuacán**. The task, however, often so completely exhausts them that ugly sunburn is the only souvenir of their visit to Mexico's most popular attraction. This strange landscape of ruins, with the threatening serpent's jaws and the singing jaguars, is initially overpowering. Only after a day or two when one has made the 60-km (37-mile) trip out of the city center to Teotihuacán either by bus or rental car, and

Bordered by mountains on three sides, the valley opened towards the southeast, leading far into the humid plains and to the ocean. Here, more than 2,000 meters (6,500 ft) above sea level, the land is dry and brown. This is true particularly in winter, the high season for tourists. Unfortunately, nothing but a few dismal trees are left from the erstwhile dense forests, and the lakes have disappeared, too. All that remains from the city of Teotihuacán is a skeleton unearthed

when one has explored the archaeological district, guidebook in hand does a faint understanding of what it is all about begin to develop; a visit to the museum at the entrance helps improve that understanding.

Place of pilgrimage: Over 2,000 years ago, pilgrims began to visit this site: most of them came on foot but the rich and noble were carried by sedan, and all those who lived on the banks of the glittering and life-giving shallow lakes that then dotted the high valleys of Mexico came by boat.

Between the lake and the Valley of Teotihuacán there was a fertile marsh area.

by archaeologists, dried and bleached by the sun. We do not even know what the people called themselves or the city they lived in. Teotihuacán, "place of the gods" or "place, where gods are made" is the name the Aztecs gave to this holy and mysterious site which had become a legend for those who themselves were latecomers to the site.

This place of the gods was the first urban development on the American continent, quite distinct from the previous ceremonial centers. Teotihuacán was the unequalled model for all later cities and municipal states. From the peak of the pyramid, the grid of the city's layout is visible: the wide north-south axis, the so-called "Street of the Dead," then filled with the living, leads from the Moon pyramid southward. In the east, the Sun pyramid marks a perpendicular axis. The quarters are separated precisely into smaller and bigger squares. Even the suburbs comply with the pattern and the river traversing the area was divided into matching canals. South of the river were the administration and trade centers. East of the Street of the Dead was the citadel, where the priests and honoraries probably resided. In the west, across the street, stood a walled-in complex of buildings with apartments, stores and

buildings you can see how the Teotihuacáns lived: one-storey apartment houses for several families, arranged around an inner courtyard with a small temple, patios and covered hallways were separated from the street by windowless walls.

The flat roofs were accessible for daily use and fountains and a drainage system were also incorporated. The floors were made of a concrete-like mixture, the walls of stone and mortar or of clay tiles, whitewashed on the inside and the outside.

Many of these apartment complexes served as workshops as well as homes. For example, several artisan families who made

warehouses surrounding the big market square. Today the museum is located here, flanked by numerous souvenir shops and fast food stalls.

Living and working: Few archaeological sites are as thoroughly surveyed and examined as the city of Teotihuacán. No fewer than 2,000 residential sites have been mapped. One and a quarter million ceramic pieces, obsidian splinters, stone tools, bones, and debris have been registered. In some

arrowheads and knives from obsidian would live in one block. The next-door neighbors would specialize in making mirrors and jewelry from black volcanic glass. There were also many household-workshops of potters and ceramic makers who specialized increasingly in delicate figurines which could be used either as room decorations or for domestic worship; or they made fine pottery like the thin, orange-coloured ceramics that were exported as far as what is today Guatemala.

A number of construction workers were constantly needed in the metropolis: carpen-

Left, the Sun pyramid in Teotihuacán. **Above**, view of the "Street of the Dead".

ters, painters, weavers, jewelers, the makers of feather dresses, and stone cutters who carved the typical stone masks of Teotihuacán. Business people and traders lived together, too. Their storerooms, which were filled with goods from everywhere between the Atlantic and the Pacific, can still be identified. Export and import were probably carried out by whole clans who lived together, like the artisans who passed on their craft from generation to generation.

In some neighborhoods, there were even foreigners who would pass their customs down to their grandchildren as in cosmopolitan cities today. The houses of the rich and

dents or tourists as well as thousands of pilgrims during the holidays. All of course had to be housed and fed, which was probably a lucrative source of income for many in those days just as it is today.

The patient research of the archaeologists has unearthed many items of everyday life. Teotihuacán was a center of the arts and crafts as well as of trade. Since the city grew and flourished for more than 600 years, extending its influence ever wider, it served as a model for the construction of other cities and their administrations. There were warriors but no fortresses around the city, and there are no reports of conquests.

prominent were also one-storey buildings with a design not much different than the rest, although more richly ornamented, judging by the colorful lavish murals that have been discovered.

Testimonies of everyday life: In its heyday in the 5th century the city covered an area larger than that of imperial Rome. The archaeologists, their computer-supported research notwithstanding, hesitate to give a final figure on the population: 150,000 or 200,000, maybe even more, they say. In addition, there were all the foreign tradesmen, and people who might have been stu-

The people who made the long journey here even from as far away as the blossoming ceremonial centers of the Mayas in what is now Yucatan came of their own accord, attracted only by the flair of the first and biggest city.

They came so that they might imitate the temples of Teotihuacán and copy the icons and images. There have been archaeologists who tried to explain the copy-cat developments elsewhere solely as a product of a dominant system, but others feel that imitation was based on not much more than flattery. Most visitors who take the time to soak in the atmosphere feel that this is still a special place, a place of power.

The city had approximately 100 temples. Today, the two pyramids dominate the landscape. They stand broad and massive like man-made mountains. The **Sun pyramid** has about the same square base area as the Cheops pyramid in Cairo, but only half its height, 63 meters (200 ft), since the crowning temple and the outer layer of smooth stone has been lost. Its silhouette seems to be modelled after a mountain which appears on the southern horizon.

The **Moon pyramid**, too, in the north, is a diminutive replica of the Cerro Gordo mountain. These cannot be coincidences. Even astronomers have examined the relationships between landscape, celestial phenomena and buildings. They have discovered connexions with the position of the sun and the constellations but without being able to recreate the entire system on which the city worked. We know but very little of the religious life of the Teotihuacán. Even the names Sun and Moon pyramid, date from the Aztec era, 700 years after ancient Teotihuacán had perished.

The oracle of the cave: Further discoveries are still possible. As recently as 1971, during the installation of the nightly sight and sound shows at the foot of the Sun pyramid, a previously unknown entrance was discovered. A natural hallway, about 100 meters (320 ft) long, leads to a cave whose floor has the shape of a four-leaf clover. The cave, which probably used to be partitioned off in four sections, is almost exactly beneath the peak of the pyramid, and contained a spring whose water was channeled to the outside. For centuries a small and simple temple marked the place where people came to consult the oracle in the cave. It is not uncommon to find caves with springs in masses of volcanic stone and often they were used as sacred sites.

In fact this particular cave pre-dates the pyramid. Around AD 100 the Sun pyramid was erected above it. Not much later the

Left, palace architecture in Teotihuacán. **Above**, bird god carvings decorate the stonework of the priests' residence.

Moon pyramid was constructed as the counterpart. When the city continued to grow, the marshy land to the south had to be drained and it was because of this and the clearing of the forests that the spring in the cave dried up. Without the spring the cave lost its significance and it was emptied completely. Nothing but a few clay fragments were left behind when it was sealed. But legends about the cave oracle persisted and were still current when the Spanish came. Had the Teotihuacáns created new gods or had they converted their old ones?

The center of the city extended from the Sun pyramid above the cave to the citadel further south and the great market quarter across from the citadel. A new temple, which is today called the **temple of Quetzalcoatl**, was erected on the empty square in the middle of the citadel.

Human sacrifices: Of the confusing number of old Mexican gods, Quetzalcoatl, the feathered serpent, may be the most confusing of all but also the best known. The name, as with the others, was the invention of the Aztecs; *Coatl* means serpent and *Quetzal* (the 'qu' is simply the Spanish way of writing a 'k') is the shiny green bird of paradise, but it also means "precious". This precious bird-serpent, the plumed serpent, is one of the many symbols for the Mexican dualistic world view in ancient times: heaven and earth, air and flowing water, birth and death are united in one being. In later centuries, the plumed serpent also became the symbol of power and dominance. One theory maintains that in Teotihuacán former fertility deities were complemented by Quetzalcoatl when an elite of priest-politician-warriors built the citadel around the new temple.

The elaborately carved stone sculptures that adorn the steps of the temple of Quetzalcoatl are predominantly of serpents' heads with wide-gaping jaws and threaten-

made", the original name having since been long forgotten.

Compared to the gods of the later city founders like the Toltecs or the Aztecs, the gods of Teotihuacán seem to have been almost benevolent. Nevertheless there are signs here of the future development of a more ominous character with more hunger for sacrifices. Teotihuacán knew human sacrifices, but certainly not to the extent of later eras. The depictions of death, ubiquitous in later centuries, are yet to be found here. On the contrary, on houses in the heyday of Teotihuacán were pictures of happy lives.

Drugs and symbols: Further murals are con-

ing teeth; the eyes are made of obsidian with a feather collar alternating with the mask of the rain god. In between, the bodies of snakes wind around the slabs, and the whole was painted with bright colors. There is a reconstruction on display in the museum near the entrance to the complex. Even in the harsh sunlight the threatening symbols of the gods still emanate their hypnotic power.

Not only is the significance not entirely clear to us today but even in Aztec times Teotihuacán was regarded as an awesome mystery. The very name is an Aztec one meaning "the place where gods (rulers) are

stantly being discovered and restored on the edges of the city. The most famous painting is that which decorates a patio in Tepantitla, a residential and palace complex a little bit outside the current archaeological site. Reconstructions can be seen in the museums in Mexico City and Teotihuacán. A number of competing interpretations exist for the images. At first the masked figure in the center was identified as Tlaloc, the rain god, and the happy scenes in the lower part of the painting accordingly as Tlalocan, the paradise of the drowned and others given to the water. Today, however, experts tend to see the main figure as mother and fertility god. She sits above the sign for a cave, indicating the original site of Teotihuacán.

Above her bird-of-paradise headdress rises a lavish creeper. Those who know how deeply ingrained the usage of hallucinogenic plants is in Mexican cultures will recognize the white leaves of the Rivea Corymbosa bindweed, a plant which prefers humid river banks. Its seeds were the Aztecs' sacred *ololiuhqui*, which is today called the seed of the Virgin Mary. Correctly prepared, the plant creates a change of consciousness which allows the initiated to see the future. The cave, the spring, the oracle, the goddess

signs of serious droughts, probably a result of the destruction of the surrounding forests. The standard of building and craftsmanship sank visibly and the number of inhabitants also decreased.

This decay began to attract nomadic barbarians from the north. After at least six centuries of virtually undisputed power, Teotihuacán had extended its hegemony or influence as far as the Gulf. But a combination of land erosion, drought and plague, and some sort of internal conflict possibly between the religious and the military hierarchy, led to the state's downfall.

Where the surviving original inhabitants

of fertility, these are the foundation elements of the first city on the American continent. Did the painting tell the story of the city's origins at a time when it had long since outgrown its youth and the artisans, tradesmen, priests and warriors who dominated the society had introduced new gods?

Decline and fall: Around the year 650, more than 600 years after the first settlement, the decline of Teotihuacán began. There are

moved to is not known; only about 2,000 peasants, holy men, grave robbers and highwaymen were left once they had gone. Grass grew to cover the temples and houses, and bushes and trees even hid the pyramids themselves until the first serious excavation of the site began in 1905.

The archaeologists found the remains not only of the ancient Teotihuacán civilization but both of the Toltec and Aztec empires which followed it. Today, for those with the imagination to see, it is as awesome as it must have been to those who "adopted" it as their own more than 1,000 years ago.

Left, well-preserved jaguar fresco. **Above**, souvenir merchants (left) and feather-collared serpents' heads on Quetzalcoatl temple (right).

The toll highway from Mexico City to Queretaro passes the village of Tepotzotlán after 40 km (25 miles).

The old Chichimec pyramid in the northern suburb of Tenayuca is well worth a visit before leaving the city – resembling, as it does, a smaller version of the Great Temple of Tenochtitlán. A serpent wall symbolizing the four points of the compass surrounds the structure which once served as the model for the great Aztec pyramid in Tenochtitlán.

Santa Cecilia, a very well-preserved and restored Aztec pyramid, also lies on the same highway. Together with the small museum the entire site manages to give a lively impression of one of the thousands of small village shrines.

Treasures of New Spain: For many *chilangos*, Mexicans from the capital, **Tepotzotlán** is a good destination for a Sunday trip. Families sit in the Plaza enjoying their lunch for hours. Later on, they browse through the market on the village square or doze in the sun. Tepotzotlán is surrounded by rolling hills and the air is cleaner and

fresher than in Mexico City. The elegant steeple of the seminary church reaches into the peaceful sky. Nowhere in Central Mexico does Mexican rococo appear more splendid than in the **church of Tepotzotlán** which is consecrated to St Francis Xavier (San Francisco Javier).

The Franciscans originally founded Tepotzotlán, but already in 1580 the Jesuits owned the town. They started the first school for Indian children and a little later created a seminary for novitiates. During the 17th century, that building was enlarged several times. In 1670, the Jesuits started to build the church whose interior was to be decorated most magnificently in the 18th century, when the Loretto chapel was added, and in 1762 the whole building achieved its ultimate glory with a tower and a facade.

In 1964, when the whole site, including the gardens, was tastefully restored, the **Museo Nacional del Virreinato** (the National Museum of the Viceroyalty) was housed here. The collection of paintings, sculptures, arts and crafts and objects from daily life is displayed in an environment every bit as stunning as the site itself.

Lavish colonial baroque: "Even if all testimonies of the Churrigueresco were to disappear, this room would be sufficient to establish the glory of the ultrabaroque," says art historian Manuel Toussaint about the interior of St Francis Xavier in his work on Mexican colonial art. He continues to describe this masterwork of sacred art in lyrical metaphors, comparing the church to an underwater grotto filled with corals and pearly shells, like a palace created by a fairy's magic wand.

The interior is indeed stunning. The walls are covered by 11 huge wood-carved and entirely gilded altars. Three of them are in the choir, six are in the transept and two in the nave. Toussaint is right in saying that it is the light gushing through the dome onto the glittering, shimmering splendor which breathes life into the statues and ornaments – everything seems to be rising, pulled upward in a whirl of mystical ecstacy. In counterpoint to the gorgeous symphony of the 11 altars in the main church is a delicate but equally impressive chamber-piece in the Loretto chapel. Here, two Indian cherubs smile between the sun, the moon and the stars, and the dome is supported by a blissfully dancing angel.

Toltec warriors: A narrow street branching off the Mexico-Queretaro highway after 55 km (35 miles) leads into the arid highland in the north. Today this region of the country is heavily dominated by PEMEX, the Mexican national oil company.

After the mysterious decline and final dis-

excavation museum right at the entrance to the archaeological site displays examples of the rough-hewn and often threatening sculptures as well as ceramics from the diverse trade contacts of the Toltecs. It also has an illustration of the layout of the maze-like residential quarters in Tula and the Toltec architecture in Chichén Itzá (Yucatán peninsula). Wandering through the dried out cactus-scape of the site to the excavations of the ceremonial district, it is hard to believe that a town of some 10,000 inhabitants could have existed here.

Tula (Aztec *Tollan* which means "place where rushes grow") was probably a small

appearance of the Teotihuacan civilization around the 7th century, the Toltecs began to dominate the Valley of Mexico from their capital at **Tula**, where important remains are still found today.

There are no restaurants – and very little else – at the ruins, so you'll probably stop at the tiny town of **Tula de Allende**, with its 16th-century church and Franciscan abbey, about one kilometer away. The interesting

settlement during the era of Teotihuacan. The beginnings of the ceremonial district probably date from the 9th century. During that time a veritable population explosion took place and many small sub-centers came into existence on which the surrounding hamlets depended. The buildings visible today, however, date from much later, namely from the final phase of the short-lived Toltec empire which disintegrated around the year 1200.

Tula's temple: Although Charney, a Frenchman, reported discovering the ruins in the 19th century, it was unclear quite where Tula was situated up to the 1940s. It was the Mexican archaeologist Jorge Acosta who started in-depth research once Tula had been properly located, concentrating on the city's cult center.

The cult center consists of a sprawling ceremonial square bordered on its east side by a big pyramid and on its west side by a large open field where the sacred ball game was played. On the northern side of the sacred square is Tula's main building, the **Temple of Tlahuitzcalpantecuhtli**. This temple is dedicated to Quetzalcoatl in his representation as the morning star, that is the planet of Venus.

the New World. Padded armor and a shield of undressed leather, which the warriors carried on their backs, offered protection from the enemies' arrows. The headdress consisted of a boxlike hat decorated with Quetzal feathers and a descending bird on the front.

A butterfly pectoral adorned the warrior's chest representing the belief that those who died in battle or as sacrificial victims were changed into birds or butterflies at their rebirth. On the far side of the pyramid is the *coatepantli*, the serpent wall, a wall whose decoration is a string of the same ever-recurring motif: a human skeleton disappearing

The columns and the mighty serpent, which together used to carry the roof, have been restored. A large colonnade, typical of the military period, forms the entrance to the temple where the warriors would gather. The stairs are flanked by two stone columns in the shape of feathered serpents.

Ancient representations of Quetzalcoatl depict him as a Toltec warrior, armed with arrows and the *atlatl*, the throwing board which gave the spear more power and impact, a version of which is still in use today for the hunting of wildfowl. This weapon is typical of the Toltec warrior and unique to

into the wide open mouth of a serpent. It is possible that this is supposed to illustrate Quetzalcoatl's victory over his rival Tezcatlipoca.

Excavations in the residential district by the University of Missouri in the 1960s were as informative as those done in the center. In the late 1970s the Mexican Instituto Nacional de Antropología e Historia continued the work. In 1982, the report on the *Antigua Ciudad de Tula* was published, in which the entire city was effectively reconstructed: over 30,000 people lived on 13 sq. km (5 sq. miles).

Trade and change: Visiting Tula today, it is difficult to imagine the life of the former inhabitants, because the land is now dry and poor. The town used to be on the mountain ledge overlooking the river with the same name, and research has shown that the people used the most simple methods of irrigation to maximise their water: dams slowed the draining off of the rainwater, and the river water was led to the fertile fields on its banks via canals. With this technology the subsistence of the population must have been guaranteed, and their methods of agriculture were followed slavishly by the Aztecs themselves.

clers mention the names of Toltec rulers, we do not know any details about their form of government. It seems that there was a "prince", maybe even several princes of equal standing. The reigning prince (*primus inter pares*, first among equals) was allowed to carry the title "Qu".

According to legend the gentle god-king Quetzalcoatl who abhorred human sacrifice, offering up only snakes, birds and butterflies, was bested by the black magic of his rival Tezcatlipoca ("the dark god of the night sky") which prompted Quetzalcoatl and his followers to move to the east and further to the Yucatán peninsula where they erected

Most recent excavations in Tula, however, also discovered the Toltecs' wide trade network: the tradesmen brought ceramics from Costa Rica, Nicaragua and from the Gulf coast of Campeche; they bought shells from the Pacific coast and turquoise from the most northern parts of Mexico. Bartering and tribute formed the mainstays of their trade-based economy.

Despite the fact that some Spanish chroni-

the ceremonial city of Chichén Itzá (literally "mouth of the well"), an exact replica of Tula. According to later reports this migration supposedly happened just before the year 1000. Archaeological findings corroborate this theory.

Today a fire-damaged palace right next to the main temple in Tula is open to visitors. The heat of the fire has turned the clay into bricks. The fire destroyed Tula to a large extent, but unlike Teotihuacan it was never abandoned and, during the era of the Aztecs, Tula, which was then known as Tollan, rose to some prominence.

Left, the large statues of Tula once carried the roof of the temple of the morning star. **Above**, the warriors of ancient Mexico worshipped the jaguar.

"Popo" and "Izta" – Visiting Volcanoes

In the past, Mexico City's two "local" mountains, **Popocatépetl** ("Smoking Mountain", 5,452 meters/17,890 ft) and **Iztaccíhuatl** ("White Lady", 5,286 meters/17,340 ft) provided the backdrop to the Mexican capital, some 60 km (40 miles) away. Nowadays, the rare occasions when the pair are not obscured by smog are a talking point in the city.

While "Popo" (the Mexican abbreviation) is still an active volcano – albeit the last eruption was in 1802 – "Izta" no longer even has a crater.

In 1519, the Spanish conqueror Hernán Cortéz had to cross the pass that lies directly between the mountains on his way to Tenochtitlán. From the top of what later became Paso de Cortés (2,650 meters/ 11,975 ft), an attempt was even made to reach the summit of Popo, to show the Aztecs that the gods themselves couldn't harm the brave Spaniards. For the Indians believed Popo was an awesome god, and honoured Izta as his wife. Another version of the legend had Popo as the home of the evil spirits, and the earthquakes and the terrible rumblings that accompanied a volcanic eruption were their death throes in its fiery innards. Whatever the tale, the native people fervently believed that an ascent of Popo was physically impossible.

Owing to the fierce volcanic activity at that time, the Spanish in fact only reached just below the edge of the crater, but this was enough to arouse considerable admiration among the population. In the end it was Francisco Montaño who succeeded in reaching the edge of the crater in a second expedition in 1521.

But even that didn't satisfy Montaño. He had his companions lower him down in a basket into the steaming jaws of the volcano, to gather sulphur deposits from the rocky walls. At that time there was urgent demand for sulphur for use in the manufacture of

gunpowder. Cortéz later noted in his report to Emperor Charles V that all in all it would probably be simpler to have had the gunpowder sent out from mainland Spain.

Today the ascent of Popo is far less spectacular, owing to more sophisticated equipment and the minimal volcanic activity. Nevertheless, the whole thing is far from being child's play. There may be fewer technical problems, but there is still the unaccustomed altitude to be accounted for. Anyone

attempting the climb should be physically fit, and have spent a few days beforehand in average to high altitudes to adjust their bodies to the thin air, which is very poor in oxygen. The best time for the trip is during the months from November to January, and those who feel it important to have idyllic solitude on their mountain walks are advised to avoid the weekends, since Popo is also a favorite destination for local walkers and climbers.

How do you get there? There is no shortage of public transport from Mexico City. The famous Cristóbal Colón line and ADO run regular services from the bus station to **Amecameca**. They leave every half hour, and the journey takes about an hour. From there you take a taxi, either to **Tlamacas** (about 25 km/15 miles away) if you're going to Popo, or to **La Joya** if you're heading for Izta. There are also several travel firms in Mexico City where you can book package tours that include guided mountain walks.

Sardine cans: Your starting point for Popocatépetl is Tlamacas, which lies on the edge of the tree line at an altitude of about 3,882 meters (12,740 ft). There are two hostels here: the newer Albergue de la Juventud and the old one some 50 meters (165 ft)

Early start: The usual route, and the simplest, takes you via Tres Cruces. Besides the usual climbing equipment, you won't need anything more than crampons and ski poles. A very early start is advisable for two reasons. First, the fine-grained lava sand and snow will still be frozen hard, which makes the going considerably easier. Second, by midday the mountains are usually shrouded in cloud. So set off from Tlamacas before sunrise, along the gentle path over the lava sand, the lights of the city twinkling away to the northwest.

An awkward steep section follows, where you'll find yourself forever slithering back-

below. Both offer reasonably clean overnight accommodation as well as sanitary facilities, and the new hostel also has hot showers and a restaurant. It's best to bring your own food supplies for the climb, although you can hire crampons and ice picks on the spot.

You are advised not to tackle the trip in a single day but do it in two stages. Bear in mind, however, that the bivouac shelters intended for overnight stops are in an appalling condition and unless you fancy spending the night in a sardine can, your own tent, insulated mat and sleeping bag are essential.

wards and struggling laboriously forwards, until after about three hours, you reach the derelict shelter at **Tres Cruces** (4,400 meters/14,440 ft, tent essential). Just beyond begins the long, monotonous snowy slope which takes you right up to the **Labio Inferior**, the lower lip of the crater (5,254 meters/17,240 ft), a four to five-hour walk.

From here you can look down into the seething volcanic crater, and watch the acrid clouds of sulphur billowing up from the depths of the earth. The yellowish-reddish-black sides of the crater complete the vision of hell. On no account should you attempt to climb down into it as the sulphur-gatherers used to – there's a real danger of suffocating.

From here you can continue for an hour along the rim of the crater to the main peak, the **Pico Mayor**. A shelter has been erected at this point which has since been described as the world's highest bottle bank – and not only for its shape.

The descent is much quicker, if you retrace the same route down, because you can slide you way over the snow and sand back to Tlamacas in two and a half hours. A steeper and more difficult alternative for climbers who feel they haven't worked hard enough is via "Cañada del Venturillo Pico Mayor"

about four and a half hours. The first shelter is at about 4,760 meters/15,620 ft, and there are two others a little further on.

Set off as early as possible the next day for the one and a half hour climb over rough rocky ground to the first peak (5,020 meters/16,470 ft), then onwards via steep paths to the **Rondillas** (two hours). Watching the sunrise from here more than compensates for the effort.

A two-hour walk along the southern ridge brings you to the flat plateau of the main peak, called **Pecho** ("breast"). Allow five hours in total for the descent. Incidentally, there are no buildings in La Joya, but 3 km (2

(allow 5-6 hours), but crevasses make a rope essential while negotiating this route.

The White Lady: The haul to the top of Izta is longer and an overnight stop is therefore inevitable. From La Joya, the path heads in the direction of Amaculécatl across a grassy slope to the first saddle. Follow the red trail up past the Portillo gap, bearing left and then right along the flanks of the main ridge to more tumbledown shelters. This will take

<u>Left</u>, 5,254 meters (17,250 ft) high and a beautiful view down into the deep crater of Popocatépetl. <u>Above</u>, the "White Lady" conquered.

miles) further on at the Torre Rastramisora television station there is an old construction workers' cabin which makes a primitive shelter en route.

Both 17,000 ft peaks are also ideal for those who enjoy hang gliding. From Popo, for example, you can launch off from the edge of the crater hopefully to land at the Tlamacas hostel or on the Paso de Cortés. Needless to say the thinness of the air at high altitudes should discourage all but the fittest from attempting the ascent and all potential visitors should check the weather forecast before setting out.

Lush subtropical vegetation, fascinating colonial architecture, pre-Columbian ruins and fantastic mountain scenery guarantee a varied program for an excursion to the south of Mexico City.

Leaving the urban sprawl by way of the Avenida Insurgentes Sur via the motorway, the 90 km (55 mile) trip to Cuernavaca can be covered in one to two hours, depending on traffic. To the east, the twin volcanoes Popocatépetl and Iztaccíhuatl seem to move

drawn to the garden town, with its brightly colored flowers and hedges. Artists, wealthy citizens and retired Americans have settled here too. At the weekend Cuernavaca is overrun with visitors, trying to escape the smog of the capital for a while. The climate here is temperate through most of the year: sunny but not too hot.

Originally the village here was called Cuauhnáhuac, which more or less means "on the edge of the forest". The Spanish mispro-

closer as the journey progresses. Beyond the Tres-Cumbres Pass, a glorious view unfolds over the wide fertile valley of Morelos. Bordering this to the east are the curious rock formations at Tepoztlán, a picturesque little place with a delightful Sunday market. To the south loom the Guernos mountains, while Cuernavaca sprawls in the foreground.

Montezuma, Cortéz, Emperor Maximilian, the fugitive Shah of Persia – all loved the "eternal spring" that seems to reign at Cuernavaca (1,542 meters/5,060 ft, population 300,000), the capital of the state of Morelos. But not only heads of state are

nounced it *cuernavaca*, meaning "horned cow." After the Aztecs seized the valley in the 15th century, their emperor Montezuma I established his summer palace here, complete with extravagant water fountains and pleasure gardens. Later Cortéz introduced the cultivation of sugar cane to this area. Mexico's "sweet valley" also attracted the unfortunate Emperor Maximilian. After the fierce battles of the Revolution, peace returned to the tranquil provincial town. But Cuernavaca's era of peace and quiet, as captured in Malcolm Lowry's novel *Under the Volcano*, are long gone. At the weekend the traffic is sometimes as bad as it is in the capital.

The most frustrating aspect of this otherwise beautiful city is the way that most of the flower-filled gardens in which residents take such personal pride are tucked away discreetly behind high walls and thus are never seen by casual visitors.

In the main square, the **Plaza de Armas** is dominated by the towering **Cortéz Palace**. It was substantially rebuilt over the years, fell into ruin and in 1970 underwent thorough reconstruction. Today the palace houses a history museum. The main attraction is Diego Rivera's famous frescoes on the walls of

churches in the Americas. It was built to a monumental size to impress the power of the Catholic Church on the indigenous people. The charming courtyard also encloses a little baroque church and a Gothic chapel.

The interior of the cathedral has been tastefully restored to a simple, modern design. During the work, well-preserved 16th-century frescoes were discovered, depicting the long-forgotten voyage of Jesuit missionaries to Japan and their subsequent martyrdom there. A side entrance leads into the quiet cloister of the former Francisan monastery. A *mariachi* **mass** takes place in the cathedral every Sunday.

one of the outside galleries. His portrait of Zapata is particularly well executed. The foundations in front of the building date back to the pre-Hispanic times of Tlahuica and may have been part of an ancient ceremonial ground. Refreshments are on offer in the arcade on the Plaza.

Avenida Hidalgo leads straight to the great **La Asuncion Cathedral**, dating from the early 16th century and one of the earliest

Left, Cortéz Palace stands defiant. **Above**, poinsettia and bougainvillea in the garden paradise, Cuernavaca.

Directly opposite the cathedral are the **Jardines Borda**. These baroque gardens and water fountains were laid out in the second half of the 18th century by Manuel de la Borda, priest and son of Taxco's silver prince and traveler, José de la Borda. Today they are rather overgrown and the fountains are somewhat decayed, but they have lost none of their charm. The Bordas' home later provided a prestigious residence for Emperor Maximilian, who found the climate in Mexico City rather oppressive.

Ancient ball games: On the road from Cuernavaca to Taxco, it's worth making an archaeological detour to the ancient Indian site at **Xochicalco**. Imposingly situated at the top of a hill, the site predates the Aztec period and reached its peak around a thousand years ago. At that time Xochicalco – which in English means "house of flowers" – was the important junction of two major trading routes.

Stylistically, it reveals influences from various ancient Mexican mountain and valley cultures. The ruins, which are only partially excavated, provide a fascinating insight into the past and, surprisingly, reveal two completely separate pitches for ball games. The most important building, the pyramid temple to the feathered snake Quetzalcoatl, is situated on the top square. The superb reliefs have inspired visitors for many centuries.

The journey towards Taxco continues through the pretty but tiny state of Morelos, where fields of sugar cane and roses line the road, and on into the much larger state of Guerrero.

Wild bush and cactus bring to mind scenes from the great Westerns. Eventually the winding mountain road arrives at **Taxco** (1,666 meters/5,466 ft, population 80,000). The Spaniards were mining metal for their cannons here from an early date. At the same time they stumbled on the rich veins of silver in the Cerro Bermeja mountains. Taxco grew out of three mining villages on the steep slope of one of the ridges, Atachi.

Silvertown: It was from these mines that the European adventurer, de la Borda, shovelled his immense fortune. The entrepreneur sank part of the money into improving the town. Later, when production slackened in the mines, the town fell into a fairytale slumber from which it did not awaken until the 1930s, when a North American pioneer brought tourism to Taxco, and with it a new lease of life. William Spratling, known as "Don Guillermo", took advantage of the boom in Acapulco and established a tourist trade and silver craft workshops in the sleepy resort.

Today, the workshops employ almost the entire population of the town, which has become the silver manufacture and retail center of Mexico. Countless shops sell silverware of all qualities and all prices.

The whole town is protected by a preservation order. With its romantic nooks and crannies, whitewashed houses, red tiled roofs and flowers everywhere, this is picture-postcard Mexico, as the foreigners love it. Steep winding alleyways tempt you to go exploring and wandering. Cars are best parked below the town. Contrary to popular belief that mining is a thing of the past in Taxco, the silver miners are now busy once again; modern mining techniques mean that more ore is being extracted than ever before. Mexico is the world's largest producer of silver. The goods on sale in Taxco are priced pretty much the same as in Mexico City but

here competition is fierce because there are so many dealers operating in a small area. Silver is usually 925 sterling, with copper alloy. A word of warning: Alpaca, or nickel silver, contains no silver at all and is made mostly of nickel.

Borda's legacy: Seen from below, Taxco appears to be stuck on the hillside. Avenida J F Kennedy makes a good vantage point. Those in search of a panorama from above should head for the Virgen de Guadalupe church or the Iglesia del Señor de Ojeda. There's a terrific view from the terrace of the Hotel Rancho Taxco, which is particularly impressive after sunset, when the main church, **Santa Prisca**, is spectacularly floodlit. The architectural jewel in Taxco's crown, Santa Prisca, is one of the most beautiful baroque churches in Mexico.

Founded by the wealthy José de la Borda, it was built in the mid-18th century from rose-colored sandstone. The interior is every bit as lavish as the ornate facade. The golden late-baroque altarpieces glisten; the carved figures are of a extraordinary quality of craftsmanship. The whole church is an rare example of genuine baroque, unspoilt by any later additions. De la Borda apparently had this built for his son, who was a priest.

these miniature works of art any cheaper anywhere else. Choose from a large selection in the market outside the church, at its busiest at the weekends and well worth a leisurely visit.

A steep street leads down from the Zócalo, the Calle Alarcón. On the corner is the **Casa Borda**, a lofty building that was once the home of the silver prince, but which now houses the tourist office. Follow the Alarcón which eventually leads to the former Villaneuva Palace, better known as **Casa Humboldt**. The restless German explorer only spent one night behind these hospitable walls, however, in April 1803. The 18th-

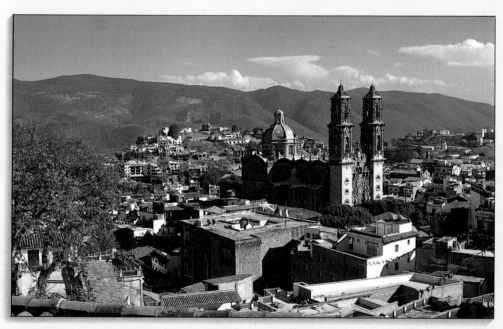

Directly in front of Santa Prisca lies the atmospheric Zócalo with its shady laurels, also known as **Plaza Borda**. The square is lined with hallowed buildings housing restaurants and silver shops. Out in the square, Indian women sell *amates* or pictures on bark. They have often painted the lively village scenes or simple patterns themselves. These enterprising souls come from the neighbouring villages and speak *náhuatl*, the ancient Aztec language. You won't find

century facade with its Andalusian-Moorish decorative work is among the finest of its kind in Taxco.

Above the Zócalo lies the baroque **Casa Figueroa**, a colonial house which has been turned into a small museum by the Figueroas, an eccentric artist couple. From the neighboring terrace, above the Borda fountain, the view opens out over the ever-lively Zócalo. In the afternoon, the square, the heart of Taxco, begins to echo with the sound of the *mariachis* is the nearby cafés.

A pleasant excursion to both towns can easily be fitted into the same day.

Left, Santa Prisca church. **Above**, it's worth a bit of a climb for a panoramic view of "Silvertown."

Puebla has always been one of Mexico's prettiest towns. Around 100 km (60 miles) east of the capital, it lies in an upland lake region at 2,160 meters (7,085 ft) above sea level, surrounded by some of the country's highest volcanoes, notably Popocatépetl, Iztaccíhuatl, Pico de Oricaba and Malinche. Surprisingly, it doesn't suffer much from pollution, despite having a population of over a million and some important industry, including the Mexican Volkswagen plant.

Colonial town: Founded in 1531, the town displays all the features of town planning and architecture which the Spanish adhered to so rigidly in their colonies. Here as elsewhere a network of streets was constructed, forming a series of rectangular blocks or *manzanas*, each about 80 meters (260 ft) wide by 160 meters (520 ft) long. One block was left empty as a central square (**Zócalo**). With its ancient trees, the square is still a favorite meeting place in the town center, especially as it is surrounded on three sides by arcades, full of numerous inviting cafés and restaurants where you can while away the time.

On the south side of the square the **cathedral** rises majestically. Built during the Renaissance in grey basalt, this features Mexico's two tallest church towers, almost 70 meters (230 ft) high. The interior was renovated in fine classical style during the 19th century.

Finding your way around the grid of streets is very simple. Only the streets on the central axis are named. Heading west from the center is Avenida de la Reforma; running east, Avenida Maximino Avila Camacho; to the north, Calle 5 de Mayo and to the south, Calle 116 de Septiembre. All the other streets are known by numbers and points of the compass. Leading off the north-south axis are Avenidas Oriente to the east and Poniente to the west. Streets to the north take even numbers, those to the south odd numbers. By contrast, the Calle 3 (5, 7 etc) Norte and 3 (5, 7 etc) Sur run from the Avenida de la Reforma to the north and south respectively, and Calles 2 (4, 6 etc) Norte and Sur branch off from the Avenida Maximino Avila Camacho.

Although this century has seen some building and renovation in the old town, the architecture is still largely characterized by the colonial-style patio-houses with their flat roofs, mostly three storeys high. The rooms are reached via an inner courtyard (or patio), around which runs a long veranda. The courtyards vary in size, but a glance through the entranceway reveals most are sadly in need of a spring clean. Noted for their particularly spacious courtyards are the former **Archbishop's Palace**, the religious seminary (now the Casa de la Cultura) and the **Biblioteca Palaforxiana**. This 17th-century library merits a visit, not only for its important collection of books but also for the fabulous baroque interior.

Azulejo facades: In spite of the rigid layout of the uniformly straight streets, the townscape is far from monotonous. Innumerable churches and monasteries lend it a special character, not to mention the unique facades, decorated with *azulejos* (ceramic tiles) and red bricks. The art of glazing ceramics in blue (Spanish, *azul*) and other colors was brought over to Puebla from Talavera de la Reina in Spain and is kept alive to this day in several workshops. With the renewal of interest in traditional crafts, demand is growing for these decorative tiles and matching crockery.

Probably the most beautiful *azulejo* facade belongs to the **Casa de los Muñecos** ("House of the Dolls", 2 Norte No. 1), which now houses the University Museum. The individually fashioned, grotesque figures date back to the 18th century. No less splendid is the **Casa del Alfeñique**, the "Con-

embellished, but from the moment of entering the chapel visitors find themselves absolutely dazzled by the opulent gold relief work of this extravagant example of high baroque. As part of the town's recent renovation program, the churchyard was opened up and at the same time the Calle 5 de Mayo was turned into a pedestrian zone.

It says much about the earlier wealth of the Santo Domingo monastery that it occupied two whole *manzanas* within the city's boundaries. As part of the expropriation of church property (1854) these were turned into the main marketplace, which in 1912 was covered with an iron-girdered roof, the

fectioner's House" (4 Oriente), with its white stucco work and a particularly lovely patio. This is now the regional museum.

Churches with decorative tiling include San Francisco, San José, San Marcos and the Iglesia de Guadalupe. But without doubt the most breathtaking of all is the **Capillo del Rosario** (Rosary Chapel) in the Dominican church (5 de Mayo). The ornamental gold work begins in the nave, which is lavishly

Left, tile picture on the side of Casa de los Muñecos. **Above**, the "Confectioner's House" in Puebla looks as if it were decorated with cream.

height of modernity at the time. The market soon outgrew its site, but it was only a few years ago that both the market and the countless itinerant traders from the surrounding streets were successfully moved to new sites on the outskirts of the town. The intention is to use the market hall for cultural events in the future.

Among other, once-important monasteries is **Santa Rosa**, which now houses the state's Craft Museum, and the convent of **Santa Monica**, which survived in secret after secularization in 1857 until its discovery in 1934, when it was turned into a religious museum. The university developed in the 19th century from what had been the **Jesuit college**, built around several patios and a particularly fine baroque hall.

Legendary battle: In the past the eastern boundary of the town was marked by the Rio San Francisco, until in the 1960s the river was diverted through pipes and disappeared under the wide Boulevard Héroes del 5 de Mayo, an urgently needed relief road for the ever-increasing traffic.

On this busy boulevard stands the **Teatro Principal**, which first opened in 1760 and is one of the oldest theaters in the Americas. Nearby is the **Parián**, a market building

Mexican textile industry. Indeed, the first mechanized factory in Latin America, the Constancia Mexicana, was founded in 1835 on the Rio Atoyac to the west of the town. Machinery dating back to 1890 is still operating today in the classical-style buildings.

During the War of Independence at the start of this century, **forts Loreto and Guadalupe** were built on a hill in the northeast of the town. It was here that the Mexicans under General Ignacio Zaragoza won a decisive battle against the invading French army on May 5, 1862. May 5 was declared a national holiday and the official title of Puebla de Zaragoza was thereafter bestowed

dating from the beginning of the 19th century. The succession of bars, distinguished by their barrel-vaulting, were used for a long time as studios until they were turned into a craft market. A section of the old Parián was turned into the **Barrio de Artista**, housing several small artists' studios, whose occupants are often present and exhibiting their works.

In the 19th century, factories were built in the extensive grounds of the former San Francisco monastery on the far side of the river. At that time Puebla was developing into one of the most important centers of the

upon the town.

Jaguar warriors: This hill, and the villa district of Cerro de la Paz to the west, command beautiful views over the town and its environs—which include several interesting sidetrips and excursions.

To the north, the road along the foot of the Malinche leads to **Tlaxcala**, the pleasant, countrified capital of the little state of the same name. The Zócalo is pleasantly leafy and the buildings that open out onto it have recently been renovated. On a raised terrace stands the Franciscan monastery (which features a wonderful cedarwood ceiling in

Mudéjar design) and, high above the town, the **Pilgrimage Church of Ocotlán**, with stucco facade and octagonal chapel (Camarin) behind the altar, a classic example of Mexican Churrigueresque.

From the Tlaxcala road, a road branches off left to San Martin Texmelucan, which leads through **Cacaxtla**, a ceremonial ground which may have flourished as much as 2,000 years ago but had been abandoned for at least 1,000 years until excavated a few years back. Some unusually well-preserved and very striking frescoes depict horrifically realistic and brightly colored battle scenes between Jaguar warriors and their opponents

the corner chapels (*Capillas Pozas*) in the courtyard are very well preserved, complete with pyramid roofs and decorative reliefs.

An attractive avenue of eucalyptus trees leads to **Cholula**, the region's most important pre-Hispanic center. The stepped pyramid may be only 54 meters (177 ft) high, but it has the largest volume of any pyramid in the world. Entering the pyramid along one of several archaeologists' tunnels, you can observe how it was built up in a number of layers. You can also view wall paintings from earlier eras. Next to the Franciscan church in the town's main square you can't miss the mosque-like **Capilla Real** with its

in bird costume (viewing is only allowed in the mornings until 1 p.m., because they must be protected from sunlight).

From Texmelucan (on the Puebla-Mexico motorway) the road continues to **Huejot-zingo**, site of a fortress-like Franciscan monastery. This dates from before 1525 and features some fine Gothic vaulting. Look out in particular for the 16th-century altarpiece. As in the neighboring convent of **Calpan**,

49 domes. At one time, Cholula was supposed to have a temple for every day of the year, and the Spanish invaders promised to build a church on every one.

On the journey back to Puebla, a short detour takes you via two particularly lovely village churches. **Santa María Tonant-zintla** features an overwhelming abundance of brightly painted cherubs and stucco ornamentation in rustic Indian-baroque style. The somewhat more restrained decor of **San Francisco Acatepec** shimmers with gold, against which the *azulejo* facade is all the more gloriously colorful.

<u>Left</u>, a detail from the Capilla del Rosario. <u>Above</u>, the Cholula pyramid towers in the background behind the domes of the Capilla Real.

Vivid bougainvillea blossoms cascade over an ancient wall. Above a large swimming pool curve the arches of an old aqueduct. In the evenings the latest dance sounds blare from what was once a sugar mill. The Mexican *haciendas* of old are every bit as romantic as the chateaux and castles in which you can stay in Europe, offering the paying guest an enviable combination of modern comfort and rustic style.

Visitors to Mexico City who want to empty their lungs of the metropolitan pollution and breathe fresh country air, or unwind with a spot of riding, swimming or golf, will find a choice of *hacienda* hotels within a 200-km (125-mile) radius of the city where they can do just that.

A world of their own: Mexican *haciendas* date back to the 16th century, when the Spanish crown rewarded its conquering heroes with gifts of land. Others sprang up on land appropriated by the monasteries. Until the beginning of this century, the big country houses were surrounded by extensive estates. High walls sheltered a little world of its own: the master's house, the modest quarters of the Indian *peone*, farm buildings, stables, outhouses, a church, a smithy and other workshops, a gaol and a graveyard, as well as a shop where the majority of the laborers used to run up debts. The slate was an effective means of keeping the estate servants under control.

The War of Independence shook the fat, feudal existence of the *haciendas*, which finally came to an end with the Revolution. In the course of the fighting, many *haciendas* went up in flames. Their lands were divided into individual plots and leased out to the *peone* as *ejidos* for them to farm.

Several of the ruined *haciendas* were later tastefully renovated as country hotels. The most famous is probably **Hacienda Cocoyoc** near Cuautla. A visit here can incorporated into a circular tour via Amecameca, past the twin volcanoes Popocatépetl and Iztaccíhuatl (this also allows you a detour to Paso de Cortés). The alternative route is to take the Cuernavaca-Tepoztlán motorway in the direction of Cuautla (about 120 km/75 miles each way).

Cocoyoc was once part of the vast lands held by Hernán Cortéz, who was responsible for introducing sugar cane to the area. He made a gift of the estate to a daughter of the Aztec emperor Montezuma II as a token of his love. In the 17th century the *hacienda* was one of the most important sugar plantations in New Spain. Today the sprawling

grounds are surrounded by mango groves. With 325 rooms furnished in colonial style, the hotel can accommodate even the largest groups, and it also has numerous function rooms which are used for conferences. You can't expect intimacy, though, except perhaps in one of the suites with its own private swimming pool. In the grounds, 12 golf courses (nine and 18-hole), tennis courts, a shooting range and riding stables stand at the guests' disposal.

Hacienda Vista Hermosa on Lake Tequesquitengo is like a fortress. Built in 1529 by Hernán Cortéz, it was later used as a sugar mill. The *hacienda* is a 75-minute drive from the city, only a few miles off the motorway to Acapulco (Tequesquitengo exit). During the Revolution, Villa Hermosa ("beautiful view") was the scene of fierce fighting. The revolutionary leader Emiliano Zapata himself is said to have led the attack which finally brought about its downfall.

Today, the solid walls clad with pewter enfold a miniature subtropical paradise, through which winds an avenue of palms. You can swim beneath the arches of the towering aqueduct and the 16th-century open-air cellar is now a restaurant.

A gift to La Malinche: You'll find other lution, and the hotel was converted from the original buildings. The *hacienda* is built around a series of vast inner courtyards and carefully tended gardens. The church, the old stables and the workshops have all been preserved, as well as the bullfighting arena. The avenues in the surrounding countryside make wonderful bridlepaths.

Drive on past the charming colonial city of Querétaro for 9 km (6 miles) in the direction of San Luís Potosí and you come to the hotel **Hacienda Jurica**, a huge estate with patios, gardens and swimming pools. The former *hacienda* **San Miguel Regla** at Dorf Huasca (past Pachuca) is now used as a silver work-

country homes to put you up in the area to the north of the capital as well. If you take the motorway to Querétaro and exit at the 172 km point, you can't miss the elegant *hacienda* hotel **La Estancia**.

This once belonged to Hotel Galindo, now **La Mansión Galindo**, which is 5 km (3 miles) further up the road. Cortéz used the lands of this *hacienda* to pay off his interpreter and mistress, La Malinche. Amazingly, the estate was spared during the Revo-

shop. Water is everywhere, splashing over aqueducts into lakes which are brimming with trout.

Pachuca itself, a former silver mining town, is a good base from which to visit a couple of nearby colonial monasteries and also the ruins of Tula, from which the god-king Quetzcoatl exerted his sway.

A stay in a *hacienda* hotel makes an agreeable change to the bustle of city life, one which wealthy Mexicans indulge in too. At the weekends these retreats are usually fully booked. It is always advisable to book in advance.

<u>Left</u>, Hacienda Vista Hermosa. <u>Above</u>, Hacienda Cocoyoc's aqueduct and pool.

The highway from Mexico City to Toluca, the Mex 15, is true to Mexican taste: 67 fast km (40 miles), full of curves. Here the drivers of automobiles, buses and lorries can show how macho they are by racing against each other and the natural hazards. The highway is effectively the extension of the Paseo de la Reforma and leads up to the fir forests of the Sierra de las Cruces. It is here that on weekends the masses of recreation-seeking residents of the capital gather. The rest areas are packed with taco and beverage stands. Northwards lies Parque Nacional de Miguel Hidalgo, and to the south is the Parque Nacional Desierto de los Leones, although in this "lion's desert" there are no lions but pines.

Industrial center: From the Paso de las Cruces (3,100 meters/10,170 ft) the highway leads up to the high valley of **Toluca**. The good condition of the road reflects Toluca's significance as a thriving business center.

Mexico's highest big city, Toluca lies 2,680 meters (8,790 ft) above sea level, and has for years been experiencing enormous expansion. Nissan has recently built an automobile factory here, to add to the large chemical factory, the brewery and sundry other production plants. The population of 500,000 continues to grow. The city has good facilities and is well placed to benefit from the decentralization plans of Mexico's politicians. It is near to the capital, and yet the plateau provides much space for growth and can draw on the large supply of workers who are ever anxious to leave the chaos of Mexico City. Since the great earthquake, many companies have shown a strong desire to leave the capital.

Toluca is also the capital of the state of Mexico. The city's name comes from the *náhuatl* word *Tollocan*, which means "place of reeds". Under the influence of Teotihuacan, the region was settled by members of the Nahua tribe, the *Matlatzinca* ("those that have small nets"), in the 13th century. Like many other tribes, they had to submit to the control of the Aztecs – or flee

from their domination. Again and again they rebelled against the violent Aztec rule, finally allying themselves with the Spaniards in their battle against them. In 1529, a Franciscan cloister was founded in Toluca, and it was incorporated as a city in 1667.

Mexico's youngest cathedral: After passing through the industrial section on the edge of the city, visitors to the city are greeted by an equestrian statue of the Revolutionary hero, Emiliano Zapata, as well as a monument dedicated to the Mexican flag. On the Zócalo, which is officially called the **Plaza de los Mártires** (Place of Martyrs), is the neoclassical cathedral. The Plaza is named after the hundred independence fighters who were executed here in 1812.

There is no beauty, but nonetheless there is something special, about the **cathedral**: the cornerstone was laid in 1862, and the construction took many decades. The building only approached completion in the 1950s and was finally finished in 1978. As a result, Toluca can today boast the youngest cathedral in Mexico.

On the north side of the **Zócalo** stands the neoclassical Palacio de Gobierno which was built in 1872. The nearby Palacio Municipal was designed by the same architect. The block of buildings known as the Portales also borders on the Zócalo. It gets its name from the 120 arcades, where a significant and very lovely part of the city's life takes place. Small stands and shops here offer typical delicacies: sweets, green *chorizo* (a sausage specialty of Toluca), fruit or *mosco*, a sweet and heavy liqueur which is sold in long-necked bottles and is said to be "*muy traidor*", quite strong. A few simple but good and reasonably priced restaurants can be found within the quarter.

Colorful markets: Botanical gardens have been planted near the former market hall of the Mercado 16 de Septiembre. Arching over the market is the Mexican artist Leopoldo Flores' vision of the universe depicted in a glass mosaic. Not far away, near the bus station, is the **Indian market**, where

Matlatzinca and Otomí Indians sell food, second-hand items, and handicrafts from stands decorated with flowers. The *mercado* is one of the largest in Mexico and on Fridays it is especially busy. It is also one of the most attractive markets in the vicinity of the capital, but if you have sampled one of the smaller markets in the south, you don't need to drive to Toluca on account of this one.

In 1987 the impressive **Centro Cultural Mexiquense** was opened, on the bypass. The center houses museums for folk art, modern art, anthropology and history which are worth seeing. The adjoining state-controlled shop sells authentic folk art.

Revolts from among the Matlatzinca were put down by the rulers of Tenochtitlán, and the excavated structures nearby indicate Aztec influence.

Calixtlahuaca is renowned for its Quetzalcóatl round pyramid. It has been rebuilt on at least three occasions and shaped in the form of a snail, which supposedly represents a windsock and portrays Quetzalcóatl in his manifestation as the wind god, Ehecatl. Five minutes by foot up the slope among aloe plants is another building complex with a Tlaloc temple. Only one of what was originally four terraces remains. The *tzompantli*, a sort of cross-shaped altar adorned on one

Remains of the Matlatzinca culture: An excursion to the archaeological site of Calixtlahuaca, 11 km (7 miles) north of the city, is definitely worthwhile. The name Calixtlahuaca comes from the *náhuatl* and means "place with houses on the plateau". The site was once an important center of the Matlatzinca culture. It came under the influence of Teotihuacan, Xochicalco, the Toltecs and finally, in 1474, of the Aztecs.

The round pyramid in Calixtlahuaca was dedicated to the wind god. Three smaller pyramids are hidden within its walls.

side with skull ornaments, stands opposite the temple.

Tenango de Arista (or Tenango del Valle) lies 25 km (16 miles) south of Toluca on the Mex 55. It's worth stopping in the pottery town of Metepec (9 km/5 miles south of Toluca) where the tall and colorful clay trees of life are made. On a mountain above Tenango is the archaeological site, **Teotenango**, a very extensive and homogeneous construction whose beginnings are said to reach back to the 7th century. The high double walls could not prevent the Aztecs from occupying Teotenango, which must have been a Matlatzinca city. The place is still practically unknown but is worth inspecting because of its interesting archaeological museum.

By car into the volcanoes: South of Toluca, the 4,570-meter (14,990-ft) high volcano **Nevado de Toluca** towers over the city. Nevado means literally "snow mountain" but it is hardly appropriate for the fourth-highest mountain in Mexico, because there is hardly ever snow around the edge of the crater. The mountain is called Xinantécatl in *náhuatl*, which is probably the better name, since Xinantécatl means "unclothed man", meaning without snow cover.

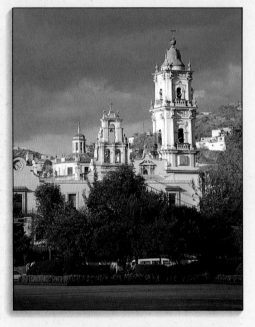

The trip to Nevado de Toluca is spectacular because the road leads up to 4,200 meters (13,800 ft) and into the crater itself. Although the summit is only a good 20 km (12 miles) from the city as the crow flies, it is a 45-km (28-mile) drive. The first 27 kilometers (17 miles) through Capultitlan and San Juan are on a good paved road, but the remainder is unpaved and the traveler won't forget the last 18 kilometers (11 miles) because of the huge amount of dust swallowed in covering them.

The lower slopes of the massive mountains are covered with pine forests, but only a few plants grow in the lava. The last two kilometers of the now narrow road lead into the crater and directly to two lakes, named after the sun and the moon.

It takes an hour and a half to walk around the banks of these lakes. Where the road climbs to the crater's edge, a footpath leads south toward a saddle between the mountains. Anyone can go as far as this point, but whoever wants to get to the main summit, the Pico del Fraile (Monk's Summit) must now do some climbing.

Even if the cliff seems quite ominous from below, the climb is not so difficult, necessitating as it does only occasional use of your hands. The path up to the summit leads clockwise up the crater edges, both on the inside and the outside, over large and sometimes shaky stone masses.

After two hours, you reach the main summit (4,570 meters/14,990 ft), marked with a small cross and if the start was early enough – at 5 o'clock, from Toluca – you will have a magnificent view: of the mountains "Popo" and "Ixta", of the city of Toluca, of the picturesque reservoir in the Valle de Bravo, and of the polluted sky over Mexico City. To descend, the path goes clockwise around the crater's edge for about 10 minutes and then ploughs down a debris furrow to the Sun Lake.

Climbers should be careful: although the Nevado de Toluca is *only* 4,750 meters high, one can still suffer altitude sickness. At any sign of sickness or dizziness, you should return to the valley as soon as possible.

Green valley: Another favorite excursion from Toluca (or direct from Mexico City) leads out approximately 80 km (50 miles) from Toluca over a newly constructed road to **Valle de Bravo**. This beautiful place lies on the bank of a reservoir at about 1,870 meters (6,135 ft) above sea level. It is here that residents of the capital gather on weekends to enjoy the provincial idyll, the lake and the wooded mountain scenery, as well as the very welcome pure, clear air. The lake is ideal for water sports and golf enthusiasts enjoy the area immensely.

Left, the most recent cathedral in Mexico in Toluca. **Right**, crater lake in Nevado de Toluca.

GETTING THERE

BY AIR

As many as 400 flights to Mexico City leave from main cities throughout the US in a single week. Miami is the major gateway. Mexicana and Aéromexico are the two principal national carriers.

Numerous European airlines (Lufthansa, KLM, British Airways etc) fly directly to Mexico City several times a week. Often a cheaper alternative from Europe is to fly with an American airline (Pan American, American Airlines, etc) which travels to Mexico, normally via an intermediate airport in the US for which European travelers will need an American visa, since transfer passengers do not remain in the transit area. British travelers do not need an American visa, provided their passport is valid. Average flight time from Europe is 12–16 hours, non-stop flights take approximately 11 hours.

ON ARRIVAL

Before you get to passport control in Benito Juárez (Mexico City's international airport), you can change money at several government counters. The airport is divided into five areas: A – National Arrival, B – National Departures, C – Airline Counters and Temporary Exhibitions, D – International Departures, E – International Arrivals.

Once in the arrival hall you will be welcomed by a large crowd of wildly gesticulating Mexicans, including taxi drivers and money–changers. Beware of who you agree to do what with: there is an official taxi service into the city (see below) that is safe and reliable.

The airport building also houses a post and telex office (near C), a bank (open from 4 a.m.), car hire companies (near E) as well as a representation of the Mexican hotel association *Asociación de Hoteles des México*

(open from 10 a.m.) where people will help you to make a reservation in one of the city hotels or to get a collective taxi to the hotel. The lost luggage department (*equipaje/objetos perdidos*) is situated on the first floor.

Departure tax: note that there is a departure tax in cash for international departures.

From the airport to the city: A taxi is the quickest way into the city center, which is approximately 13 km (8 miles) away. You simply buy a ticket (different prices for different zones) at the taxi counter in the arrival hall and later hand it over to your driver.

Airline offices: The Mexican airlines Mexicana and Aéromexico have reservation counters in the airport: Mexicana near C, Aéromexico near A.

City and reservation offices:
Aerocaribe, tel: 559 5748.
Aeromar, Leibniz 34, tel: 574 9211.
Aero California, Paseo de la Reforma 332, tel: 514 6678.
Aéromexico, Paseo de la Reforma 445, tel: 525 2722; reservations tel: 207 6311, 207 8233. Further offices all around town.
Air Canada, Hamburgo 108–104, tel: 511 2094.
Aeromorelos, tel: 604 9649, 604 8979.
Air France, Paseo de la Reforma 287, tel: 511 3693, 511 3990 and 566 0066.
American Airlines, Paseo de la Reforma 300, tel: 399 9222.
British Airways, Paseo de la Reforma 333–5th floor, tel: 525 9133.
Iberia, Paseo de la Reforma 24, tel: 592 2988, 566 4011.
KLM, Paseo de las Palmas 735–7th floor, Lomas de Chapultepec, tel: 202 3936, 202 4444.
Lufthansa, Paseo de la Reforma 76, tel: 566 0311; reservations tel: (905) 592 2755.
Mexicana (Compañía Mexicana de Aviación), Av. Xola 535, Col. del Valle, tel: 660 4433. Numerous offices all around town.
PanAm, Blvd M. Avila Camacho 1–702, tel: 395 0077, 557 8722.

BY RAIL

All railway lines from the north and south of Mexico arrive at the main station of Mexico City, the Gran Estación Central de

Buenavista, Calle Insurgentes Norte/ Mosqueta. The Metro stations Guerrero (line 3) and Revolución (line 2) are within easy reach. Take the Metro if you have no luggage, otherwise take a taxi.

Railway information: tel: 547 3190, 547 5819, 547 4114; for sleepers – Thomas Cook: tel: 518 1180, 531 3845 (representation at the hotel Camino Real).

BY COACH

Private coach companies connect Mexico City with the rest of the country. Long overland distances are served by modern Pullman coaches. Shorter journeys can also be made in simpler buses.

Since the bus is one of the most popular means of transport in Mexico, it is not surprising that Mexico City alone has four coach stations for long distance travel, named after the four directions the coaches come from or go to.

Connections to Central and Northern Mexico (e.g. Guadalajara) – Terminal Central de Autobuses del Norte (TAN), Av. Cien Metros 4907; Metro: Autobuses del Norte (line 5), town buses into the center, information stand for hotel reservations (only Spanish spoken – open until 4.30 p.m.).

Connections to the South of Mexico (e.g. Cuernavaca, Taxco, Acapulco): Terminal Central de Autobuses del Sur (TAS), Calzada Tasqueña 1320, at the corner of Tlalpan 2205; Metro: Tasqueña (line 2), town buses into the center, early reservations for journeys to the south absolutely essential.

Connections to the East of Mexico (e.g. Puebla, Veracruz, Oaxaca, Yucatán): Terminal Central de Autobuses del Oriente (TAPO), Calzada Ignacio Zaragoza 200; Metro: San Lázaro (line 1), information stand open from 10 a.m.

Connections to the West of Mexico (e.g. Toluca, Morelia): Terminal Central de Autobuses del Poniente (TAP), Av. Sur 122, at the corner of Av. Rio Tacubaya; Metro: Observatorio (line 1), town buses into the center.

There are taxis at all coach stations waiting to take you into the city center. As in the airport, make sure you buy your ticket at the taxi counter in the hall and hand it to the driver once you are inside the taxi.

TRAVEL ESSENTIALS

VISAS & DOCUMENTS

European and North American travelers need a passport valid for at least 6 months as well as a Tourist Card issued by Mexican consulates or airlines. Tourist Cards (free and valid for up to 6 months) are also available at the border, and in all aircraft arriving in Mexico.

Children must be registered in their parental passports or have their own passport/children's pass. Adolescents under 18 traveling on their own need a written agreement signed by their parents or legal representative. Accompanied by one parent, they still need the written and officially legalized agreement of the other parent.

On arrival, the Tourist Card is stamped. It has to be submitted again on departure. The only place where it can be replaced if lost or extended by a further 90 days is: Oficinas de Gobernación, Calle Albañiles 19; Metro: San Lázaro, Mexico City. Get written confirmation from your embassy first if you have lost your card. An extension will only be granted if you can show your transit or return ticket and – if necessary – prove that you have enough money for the duration of your stay.

MONEY MATTERS

Mexico's currency is the peso and its symbol is $, exactly like the American dollar. Look out for price tags on goods. You may find an additional M. or M.N. (*moneda nacional*).

Bills are in circulation in denominations of $2,000, 5,000, 10,000, 20,000 and 50,000.

Coins are available in values of $20, 50, 200, 500, 1,000 and 5,000.

All banks and bureaux de change (*casas de cambio*) as well as most larger hotels, restaurants and shops will change US$ cash and US$ traveler's checks. European currencies will probably cause inconvenience.

Banking hours for currency exchange are from 9 a.m. to 1 p.m. (sometimes 1.30 p.m.), even if the bank is open in the afternoon. The exception is the bank at the airport which changes money around the clock.

Credit cards: Visa, Eurocard (Mastercard/Mastercharge/Access) and American Express are well known. Hotels and more expensive shops will also accept Diners Card. Certain banks will also pay cash on credit cards.

There are no restrictions on the import and export of Mexican or foreign currencies.

HEALTH TIPS

Vaccinations are not obligatory unless you arrive from yellow fever areas.

Preventive malaria treatment is recommended for all seasons if you intend to travel to rural areas, namely the rather inaccessible regions of Estado de México and Puebla or the humid and tropical regions of the lowlands.

Gamma-globulin injections are also recommended in order to increase personal resistance against hepatitis A. Typhoid, paratyphoid and tetanus injections also protect against any infection of wounds or injuries.

Your nearest tropical diseases institute will be able to give you more detailed and up-to-date information, and some of the major airlines also have medical advisers specialized in these fields.

WHAT TO WEAR

The city climate allows for light summer clothes throughout the year. Business circles, however, insist on formal wear. Churches should not be visited in shorts and bare shoulder tops. Elegant restaurants and hotels prefer more formal wear, but a necktie is not always required.

Always carry an umbrella or raincoat if you are planning any excursions in the late afternoon during the rainy season. A warm sweater is recommended for the cool winter evenings.

CUSTOMS – IMPORT

The following personal items can be imported free of customs duties: 1 camera, 1 film or video camera with 12 films or cassettes, 1 pair of binoculars, 1 portable musical instrument, 1 taperecorder, 1 portable typewriter, one set of used sports and camping equipment for each traveler, 20 books or magazines. Adults over 18 may also import the following: 400 cigarettes or 50 cigars or 250 gms tobacco, 3 liters of wine or spirits, an adequate amount of perfume, medicine for personal use and presents with a value of up to US$300 (no spirits or tobacco).

VAT

Most goods and services in Mexico are subject to 15 percent VAT (some only 6 percent). Retail prices are always tax inclusive (*IVA incluido*). You can save yourself the surprise and hassle of a higher bill in hotels and restaurants by asking in advance whether the meals or services include VAT.

CORRUPTION

It may be difficult for a traveler to know when a small financial "extra", or what is locally known as *la mordida* ("the bite"), will help to obtain a special service, etc. If in doubt, restrain yourself. The government is trying hard to stop corruption.

TIPPING

Restaurant bills almost never include service charges. The total should therefore be generously increased by 10–12 percent.

Hotel employees and porters expect approximately US$1. Taxi drivers do not normally receive a tip.

Getting Acquainted

THE FEDERAL CAPITAL OF MEXICO

Just like the American federal capital of Washington DC, Mexico City, headquarters of the Mexican government, forms a so-called federal district – Distrito Federal – governed by a member of the cabinet. The visitor may therefore hear Mexicans speak of *el D.F.* (pronounced: "el de effe") when they talk about Mexico City. When the boundaries of the Distrito Federal were staked in 1824, it was generally thought that there was plenty of space. Today, however, the city has expanded well beyond these limits. In the west, north and east, partly independent metropolitan settlements spread well into the Federal State of (*Estado de*) Mexico, whose capital Toluca is approximately 65 km (40 miles) away. In the south, the Distrito Federal shares its borders with the Federal District of Morelos (capital Cuernavaca).

In Mexico City the offices of the municipal administration, government and ministries were originally situated in the quarter around the central Zócalo. During the general decentralization campaign, however, the state tried to set an example and has since moved the parliament building and several offices to the periphery.

COAT OF ARMS

On July 4, 1523 in Valladolid (Spain), the emperor Charles V, awarded the City of Mexico, then capital of the colonial overseas empire of *Nueva España* (New Spain), the following coat of arms: out of the center of a blue background (a symbol for the Lago de Texcoco which surrounded the old city) rises a golden tower surrounded by – but not connected with – three stone bridges. The two bridges on either side of the tower carry a lion standing on his hind legs whose front paws rest on the tower. This was seen as a symbol for the victory of the Christian rulers over the Aztecs (the Spanish kings also had lions in their coat of arms). The ten cactus leaves (with green thorns) on the frame of the coat of arms symbolize the vegetation and rural features of the Mexican highlands.

GEOGRAPHY & POPULATION

Mexico City lies some 2,240 meters (7,350 ft) above sea level at the southern corner of the Central Highland in the Valley of Anáhuac. During the very few clear days throughout the year you can see the volcanic cones rising over the eastern borders of the city up to the peaks of Popocatépetl and Iztaccíhuatl, whereas the western hills allow a view of the Nevado de Toluca. Only a plane journey over the northeast reveals the remnants of the former lake on which the city was first built after a clever drainage system completely drained the ground.

The city area has increased to approx 1,483 square km (572 square miles) and the geographical coordinates locate the city as follows: 19°11'53"–20°11'09" northern latitude (cf. Port Sudan near the Red Sea or Bombay in India) and 98°11'53"–99°30'24" western longitude (a little further west than Oklahoma City or Winnipeg in the US).

The urban area is home to approximately 20 million people, one quarter of the total population of Mexico. Although the national increase in population was reduced in the 1980s from 3 percent to 2.5 percent, the annual increase in Mexico City of 5 percent, i.e. one million people per year, still causes major problems – half of them due to the permanent inflow of poor workers from the rural areas of the surrounding federal states.

The average population density of 350 inhabitants per square km (906 per square mile) is comparable to the large urban or industrial centers in Europe. However, this average value is definitely exceeded in the old city center and the areas of extreme poverty; it is said that the old city center houses approximately 20,000 per square km (51,800 people per square mile).

In general, Mexico City shows a clear social decline from west to east within its city boundaries. The well–kept quarters of the wealthy *capitalinos* in the rolling hills of the capital's west and the south of the city are characterized by very few houses and a low population density. The *barrios* on the other hand, partly planned and partly growing uncontrollably, house the lower social classes (more than 50 percent of all inhabitants). The north and east are marked by so-called *colonias populares* or *ciudades perdidas*, i.e. the regions with the largest industrial settlements.

ECONOMY

The capital of Mexico is also the country's economical pivot, both in the private and the government sector. The service industry (banks, insurance companies, commercial enterprises, tourist companies) are concentrated in the center whereas the industrial parks can be found at the periphery in the northeast.

Seventy percent of all Mexican banking activities are carried out in Mexico City alone and more than 50 percent of the total industrial output is manufactured here where 35 percent of the country's industry is located. The decentralization movement stopped the construction of manufacturing plants in the D.F. after 1975 and in the Estado de México after 1980.

New government schemes for the economy offer hope for an industrial boom and the creation of new jobs. At the same time, the influx of people from the country could diminish if the 10-point plan of the Salina government envisaging a revival of agriculture (which employs more than 40 percent of the working population) is successful. The plan envisages extending agricultural areas, improving storage and marketing systems and building up a processing industry.

The lower budget deficit and the "stability contracts" agreed between government and industry in 1987 (and extended until July 1990) over prices, wages and exchange rates has stemmed inflation considerably. Recent inflation rates show a dramatic fall: 1987: 159 percent, 1988: 52 percent, 1989: just under 20 percent. However, the living standards of the population have not improved at the same rate. This is why the large masses of the lower classes – especially in Mexico City – are very suspicious when it comes to the abolition of fixed prices under which their personal standards of living would again deteriorate.

TIME ZONES

Mexico itself is divided into three time zones. Mexico City and all of the highlands adhere to the *hora central*, which is Greenwich Mean Time minus six hours. In summer, one more hour is added.

WEATHER

Air pollution: The geographical situation of Mexico City at the border of the tropical zone, its height above sea-level and its extensive air pollution all contribute to the city's weather.

As is typical for tropical zones, mid–day temperatures vary only slightly throughout the year between 19° C (68° F) in December and 25° C (78° F) in June. Night temperatures may range from 6° C–13° C (43°–55° F) in the same period. The big difference between day and night temperatures is caused by the city's high altitude.

Contrary to the calendar in the northern hemisphere the Mexican year is divided into a dry period from November to April (4–10 rainy days per month) and a rainy period from May to October (17–27 rainy days per month). The rainfall occurs during the summer months because the land absorbs the heat, the heated air masses rise and cause thunder and lightning accompanied by heavy showers lasting only a couple of hours in the afternoon or early evening. These showers, in turn, briefly overstrain the local drainage systems and flood the streets. On the other hand, such air-cleansing showers make it a lot easier to breathe in a city which uses up 20 percent of the total Mexican energy consumption; 20 million liters (4.4 million gallons) of petrol and 5 million liters (1 million gallons) of diesel fuel are consumed by 3 million vehicles, and 5.4 million liters of gas and 5 million liters of oil are used up by approximately 30,000 industrial and service companies.

During the winter months when the highly polluted air masses close to the land surface cannot rise above the warmer air layers, children and older people in particular suffer from the dangerous inversion weather (*inversión térmica*) which produce a smog which is highly detrimental to their health. The lower level of the warmer air layers absorb polluted particles and form clouds which prevent the sun from heating up the ground air. Only the early hours of the afternoon normally see enough thermal currents to break up the city's smog blanket.

Since 80 percent of the air pollution is apparently caused by cars and buses, the local government hopes to reduce exhaust fumes drastically by introducing the scheme of *hoy no circula*, "the day without cars". This program was originally restricted to the winter months but has now been extended indefinitely; it stipulates that certain cars with a certain end digit in their registration plates are not allowed to drive on certain working days. According to official reports, the scheme has reduced exhaust fumes by 10 percent. However, analysis carried out by environmental organizations has not shown any improvement in the values of carbon monoxide, dichloride, nitrogen dioxide and ozone in the atmosphere. Since the beginning of the *hoy no circula* scheme, public transport has been heavily burdened and people have to wait up to one hour for a bus. This is why a lot of private drivers now go out of their way (often traveling two or three times the distance of their original journey) to pick up "carless" friends and relatives. In the meantime, the government has passed a law under which all new vehicles must have a catalytic converter, even the VW beetle which is still manufactured in Puebla!

ELECTRICITY

The power supply is 110 volts; American plugs fit into the sockets. For other plugs, use the same adaptor as for the US.

EARTHQUAKES

Make sure you read the notes on emergency exits displayed in lifts and staircases in many hotels. The doorframe can protect you in extreme emergency.

OPENING HOURS

Banks: Monday–Friday 9 a.m.–1 p.m. (sometimes 1.30 p.m.).

Offices: Open to the public Monday–Friday 9 a.m.–2 p.m.

Shops: Monday–Saturday 10 a.m.–6 p.m. or 8 p.m. Smaller shops close during lunch hours (1 p.m.–4 p.m.). Large shopping centers such as Perisur or Plaza Satélite are open late, sometimes even on Sundays.

Museums, monasteries, archaeological sites: Tuesday–Saturday 9 a.m. or 10 a.m.–5 p.m. or 6 p.m. Sunday only until 4 p.m. Smaller museums may close for one or two hours at lunchtime. Archaeological sites are also open on Mondays.

PHOTOGRAPHY

Everywhere you look in Mexico City there's a picture. However, be reasonably tactful if you take photos of people and ask them for their permission first. Some Indians may be quite shy or even become aggressive when a camera is pointed their way. Museums and archaeological sites normally demand a permission fee to take photographs.

Films in Mexico are manufactured by Kodak and are much more expensive at kiosks than in supermarkets where the prices compare with those in Europe. UV or skylight filter bags are recommended due to the strong sun and intense ultra-violet light.

Beware thieves interested in your equipment: camera bags betray the tourist. Take care on public transport or when waiting for a bus or a taxi.

PUBLIC HOLIDAYS – FIESTAS

NATIONAL BANK HOLIDAYS

1 January – *Año Nuevo* (New Year's Day). Fireworks on New Year's Eve everywhere in the city, parades and fiestas in the streets on New Year's Day.
5 February – *Día de la Constitución* (Constitution Day). In remembrance of the constitution which came into force in 1917.
21 March – *Aniversario* (birthday) of the former president Benito Juárez. Schools and nurseries celebrate a spring festival.
Maundy Thursday to Easter Sunday – People traditionally visit their relatives during the *Semana Santa* (Easter week) so public transport is overcrowded. Passion plays in Iztapalapa, candle processions in Taxco.
1 May – *Día del Trabajo* (Day of Work).

Long parade in the city.

5 May – *Día de la Batalla de Puebla* (Day of the Battle of Puebla). In remembrance of the victory over the French army in 1862.

1 September – National Holiday. The President reports on the nation's situation (traditional since 1824).

16 September – *Día de la Independencia* (Independence Day). On the eve of this day, the bell over the entrance to the Palacio National (at the Zócalo) rings out and at 11 p.m., the President repeats the *Grito de Dolores*, Father Hidalgo's call to the nation against the patronizing Spanish leaders (1810). On 16 September military parade from the Zócalo to the park of Chapultepec.

12 October – *Día de la Raza* (Day of the Race). The day when Columbus discovered America. National holiday in many Latin American countries. Mexico celebrates the merging of the Indian and European races to form the Mexican people.

1/2 November – *Todos los Santos* (All Saints) and *Día de los Muertos* (All Soul's Day). In the night from 1 to 2 November, people take flowers, food, drink and candles to the cemeteries in order to celebrate with the deceased. Particularly impressing in Mixquic, a suburb in the east of the city.

20 November – *Día de la Revolución*. The anniversary of Madero's call to start the Revolution is celebrated with long parades and fireworks in the evening at the Zócalo.

12 December – *Fiesta de Nuestra Señora de Guadalupe*. Long pilgrimages to the Basilica of the Madonna of Guadalupe in Mexico City. Solemn masses, dance performances on the forecourt of the basilica. Processions all over the country.

25 December – *Navidad* (Christmas Day).

31 December – Solemn end of the season of congress meetings.

RELIGIOUS HOLIDAYS & FESTIVALS

Quite a few religious festivals are postponed to the following weekend/Sunday if they fall on a working day.

Most of the city districts mentioned below are in the suburbs of the D.F. and still have all the rural characteristics of former villages: in the north – Gustavo A. Madero and Azcapotzalco; in the west – Alvaro Obregón and Cuajimalpa (de Morelos); in the south – Tlalpan; in the southeast – Xochimilco and Milpa Alta; in the east – Iztapalapa and Tláhuac. The central districts are called Cuauhtémoc (old city), Benito Juárez and Coyoacán (adjacent to the south).

Beginning of January – Festival week in Chalma, a place of pilgrimage approximately 100 km (63 miles) to the south of Mexico City in the direction of Cuernavaca.

6 January – *Fiesta de los Reyes* (Epiphany). People exchange presents.

17 January – *Santa Prisca*. The day animals are blessed in the churches. On the 18th and the following weekend, solemn blessings of animals and fiesta in Taxco.

2 February – *Candelaria* (Candlemas). Fireworks and dances.

Carnival – multi-colored parades and celebrations in all parts of the city. Xochimilco celebrates two weeks later.

Sunday after 9 March – Celebration of Gregory the Great (*Gregorio Magno*) in San Gregorio Atlapulco in Xochimilco (with interesting folk dances).

19 March – Festival of St Joseph in Tláhuac, Iztapalapa and Tlalpan.

25 April – Festival of St Marcus in Milpa Alta and Azcapotzalco. Folk festival with dances and fireworks.

3 May – Festival of the Holy Cross. Building workers erect crosses decorated with ribbons at their building sites. They erect altars in Milpa Alta, Cuajimalpa and Xochimilco where dances and fireworks are also held.

May/June – Corpus Christi. Processions in the church communities. Little donkeys made of maize leaves are given to children. Parents take their children dressed as Indians to the cathedral or the Basílica de Guadalupe.

24 June – Midsummer Day. Folk festival with markets and dances in Milpa Alta, Tláhuac, Coyoacán and Iztapalapa.

16 July – Festival of the Virgen del Carmen in Cuauhtémoc, Cuajimalpa and Alvaro Obregón. Festival and dances around the monastry del Carmen in San Angel.

25 July – Festival of St Jacob (*Santiago*) in the quarters of Azcapotzalco, Cuajimalpa, Cuauhtémoc and Gustavo A. Madero. Folk dances and dance evenings with music.

Sunday after 25 July *(Santiago)* – Large festival on the Plaza de las Tres Culturas, from 10 a.m. dances and market. Fun fair and dance performances in Xochimilco (in the afternoon).

13 August – Holiday in remembrance of the Battle of Tenochtitlán. Wreath-laying at the memorial of Cuauhtémoc on the Paseo de la Reforma. Indian dances on the Plaza de las Tres Culturas.

15 August – Assumption Day. Dances of "Moors and Christians", Indians, shepherds and cowboys in Milpa Alta. Fireworks and dance performances in many parts of the city.

Folk festival in Huamantla (near Puebla) with multi–colored flower and sand carpets in the streets.

28 August – Religious festival in Chalma (see January).

8 September – Nativity of the Virgin. Dances and fireworks in Alvaro Obregón, Benito Juárez, Iztapalapa and Xochimilco.

Festival of the *Virgin de los Remedios* in Cholula. Dances and fiesta in Tepoztlán.

13 September – Day of *Ninos Héroes*, the "young heroes". In 1847, cadets defended the military academy (today the Castillo de Chapultepec) against American troups. The last cadet committed suicide by throwing himself from the high walls.

29 September – Festival of the Archangel Michael. Festivities in the quarters of Gustavo A. Madero, Iztapalapa, Tláhuac and Tlalpan. Folk festival with fireworks and dances in Chalma (the place of pilgrimages).

4 October – Festival of St Francis. Festivals in many communities.

22 November – Festival of St Cecilia, the patron saint of musicians. Festival on the Plaza Garibaldi, in Tláhuac and Xochimilco.

30 November – Festival of St Andrew in Azcapotzalco and Xochimilco as well as Texcoco (in the east of the city).

8 December – Festival of the Immaculate Conception. Religious celebrations in many communities.

16–24 December – time of the *posadas*, celebrations at home in remembrance of Mary and Joseph searching for shelter in Bethlehem. People traditionally serve *ponche* (punch), a cold drink made of various fruits and spirits, and give each other *piñatas* (colored figures made of papier–mâché filled with presents) which are hung up on a piece of string. Some of the visitors are blind-folded and must try to hit and destroy the *piñata* with a stick. The others then grab the contents – sweets, little presents for children – when they fall to the floor.

GETTING AROUND

DOMESTIC TRAVEL

No matter what means of transport you use in Mexico City, your first impression will be dominated by frightening and chaotic traffic. when the traffic is not stationary, it flows with incredible speed and apparent anarchy. However, if you obey certain rules you should be fairly safe.

Pedestrians should take the high kerbs into account when attempting to cross the street and go out of their way to walk to the next set of traffic lights rather than risk an accident with a speeding car. Passing through a line of stationary cars is equally dangerous and should be avoided.

The *hoy no circula* scheme has not really markedly improved the traffic situation. The only difference is that now the public transport system is stretched to the limits. The legendary bus route 100 is said to carry 30 percent more passengers than before.

If you intend to make frequent use of public transport in Mexico City, get yourself an *abono*, a ticket valid 15 days on all Metro routes as well as the buses on "Ruta 100". It is available at Metro ticket counters.

TAXIS

Airport taxis (white with a black plane symbol on a yellow background) take you from the airport into the city. Tickets are available at special counters in the arrival hall.

English-speaking drivers in big and expensive saloon–taxis with the logo *turismo* wait in front of hotels for tourists. They are recommended for sightseeing tours, but it is absolutely necessary to agree on the fare before you set out.

You can wave for cheap cabs (often dark-red Volkswagens with white stripes) but you should take care that the fare-meter is switched on (if it is working at all). Due to the high inflation rate, the final fare is calculated with the aid of the display on the meter and a conversion table. Agree on the price in advance if the meter is broken.

The red *sitio*-taxis are a little more expensive but can be called by phone from their taxi rank (*sitio*).

Cheap *colectivos* or *peseros* (white cars or small buses with dark red stripes) travel on 20 routes along Insurgentes and Paseo de la Reforma. The driver indicates with his fingers how many places he still has available. There are fixed stops along the routes.

METRO

Most Mexicans use the Metro. It carries an average of 4 million passengers per day on its 8 lines, which are constantly being extended. A small exhibition at the Zócalo station displays the plans. The network is displayed on large posters and on Metro maps which are available at the ticket counters in the main stations. Each station is shown by its name and a symbol, the lines are characterized by different colors and the terminal name indicates the direction of the train.

The Metro is open from Monday–Friday between 6 a.m. and midnight, on Saturday until 1 a.m. and on Sunday from 7 a.m. until midnight. Avoid the rush hours on working days (between 6 a.m. and 9.30 a.m. and 4 p.m. and 9 p.m.). During these hours, some compartments are reserved for women and children. At all other times the Metro is quick, reliable and very cheap.

Note: It is prohibited to carry large pieces of luggage in the Metro.

You can purchase single tickets or carnets of 5 or 10 tickets. If you are in possession of an *abono* (see – *Domestic Travel*) you must use the blue Metro entrances.

BUSES

The number of trolleybus and normal bus routes is so confusing that it is much easier to concentrate on a few bus connections, e.g. the "Ruta 100". This leads from the Zócalo via the Calle 5 de Mayo and the Paseo de la Reforma to and through Chapultepec park. Route 13 gets you from Indios Verdes (in the north) via the Avenida Insurgentes to San Angel and the university. Numerous buses

for the Zócalo stop at Chapultepec park or the Paseo de la Reforma and get you back into the old city center. The *peribus* operates on the outer motorway ring route (*anillo periférico*).

The square between the Metro station Chapultepec and the entrance to the park is the main junction for many city bus routes.

COACHES

All destinations in the environs of Mexico City are easily accessible by coach. A list of all four coach terminals for the respective destinations is given in the section *Getting There, By Bus*.

CAR HIRE

You can hire a car with your national driving license; however, an international driving license is recommended. The driver must be at least 25 years old and present a credit card when taking out a contract.

Small national car hire companies are often cheaper than international ones. On the other hand, the latter may have inexpensive offers for longer hire periods and it is also possible to hire the car in advance from home. Many car hire companies distribute their brochures in the city hotels or even run small offices there.

The hire price does not include 15 percent VAT. A return fee is charged if the car is not returned to the same office. Passenger and comprehensive car insurance is recommended. However, stolen spare parts must in all cases be replaced (or paid for) by the hiring party.

Check the main functions of the car and the spare tire before you set out and also ask for a list of repair garages for your particular make and model.

Subsidiaries of international car hire companies:
Avis, at the airport, tel: 762 0099; Dr. Velasco 146, tel: 578 1044; Av. M. Avila Camacho 1830, tel: 572 1611. Reservations: 588 8888.

Budget, at the airport, tel: 784 22 89; Atenas 40, tel: 566 8815.

Hertz, Londres 87–3, tel: 566 0099, 511 5686; Insurgentes Sur 725, tel: 543 1324.

National (InterRent in Europe), Marsella 48, tel: 533 0375; at the airport, tel: 784 2241; agents in the hotels Camino Real and Krystal.

PRIVATE TRANSPORT

Driving a car is not exactly a pleasure in the chaos of Mexico City's streets. For the duration of your stay, you should leave your own car in a parking space at the hotel or in one of the numerous guarded car parks (*Estacionamiento* or simply "*E*"). Often these are temporarily set up in empty lots in the city. Here, you may also have your car washed. You normally have to hand over your keys since the cars are parked by the guards and moved from time to time.

If you intend to use your own car, you should learn the meaning of traffic signs and find out on which days you are not allowed to use your own or any hired car, depending on the last digit of your registration number (the scheme *hoy no circula* is described in the *Weather* section of *Getting Acquainted*). Driving your car on forbidden days may cost you a high fine.

Orientation: A chessboard network of main thoroughfares (*Ejes Viales*) makes it fairly easy to find your way around. They are numbered from the crossroads of *Eje Central* (Av. Lázaro Cárdenas) and Av. Juárez/Fco. Madero towards the north (*norte*), east (*oriente*), south (*sur*) and west (*poniente*). The motorway ring road (*Circuito Interior*) surrounds the city center and the *Anillo Periférico* is the ring road in the western and southern suburbs.

Speed limits: 40 kph (25 mph) in urban areas, 80 kph (50 mph) on dual carriageways and 100 kph (60 mph) on motorways.

On most motorways you have to pay a toll charge (*de cobro*; toll counter – *caseta de cobro*; toll – *cotoa*).

Please beware of *topes* or *vibradores*, artificial road bumps forcing you to reduce your speed in urban areas. They are not always signposted!

Breakdown service: *Angeles Verdes* (Green Angels) of the *Departamento de Información e Auxilio Turístico* (tel: 250 4817, 250 8221) and the yellow cars of the service technicians from the Mexican automobile club (AMA) will help you on the city's motorways and dual carriageways. A

vulcanizadora repairs your flat tires. New ones are extremely expensive.

Petrol (2–star and lead free) is very cheap. Higher octane fuel (4–star) is no longer available.

SIGHTSEEING TOURS

Organized sightseeing tours are on offer in all hotels. Most companies pick up their customers directly from the hotel. Individual sightseeing tours are best organized with a hired taxi. Ask your hotel receptionist for the appropriate fare for the number of hours you want and agree upon it with the driver.

EXCURSIONS

CUERNAVACA

Information office: Av. Morelos Sur 802, tel: 14 39 20.

Coach station 1st class (*Estrella de Oro*): Av. Morelos 900 (in the south of the city).
Coach station 1st class (*Pullman de México*): Abasolo, corner Nezahualcoyotl (center).
Coach station 2nd class (*Flecha Roja*): Av. Morelos 255 (center). Numerous connections from Mexico City, TAS.

First class hotels:
Las Mananitas, Ricardo Linares 107; also excellent garden restaurant.
Posada Jacaranda, Av. Cuauhtémoc 805.

Good hotels:
Posada Xochiquetzal, Francisco Leyva 200; good restaurant.
Most hotels run stylish garden restaurants. There are also several restaurants with European cuisine in the city center.

Shopping: Arts and crafts and souvenir enthusiasts will find a real treasure-trove at the market – *mercado principal* – and the shopping arcades Las Plazas, Pasaje Florencia, Los Arcos and Pasaje Catedral. Particularly beautiful pieces (also furniture) can be found at BIO-ART, Blvd Díaz Ordaz, tel: 14 14 58.

PUEBLA

Information office: Casa de Cultura, Avenida 5 de Oriente 3 (near the cathedral), tel: 46 09 28. Also organizes sightseeing tours.

Coach station: CAPU (*Central de Autobuses Puebla*), Blvd Norte (at the junction to Tlaxcala). Taxi service into the city center; get your tickets in the departure hall. Numerous connections from Mexico City, TAPO.

Several hotels of different classes are situated near the Zócalo.
First class hotels:
Aristos, Av. Reforma, corner of 7 Sur, tel: 42 59 82.
El Meson del Angel, Hermanos Serdán 807, tel: 48 21 00.
Mision de Puebla, 5 Poniente 2522, tel: 48 96 00.
Villas Arqueologicas, 2 Poniente 501, Cholula (near the ruins), tel: 47 19 60/62/63/66.

Good hotels:
Lastra, Calzada de los Fuertes 2633, tel: 35 15 01; reservations in Mexico City tel: 592 8496.
Posada San Pedro, 2 Oriente 202, tel: 46 50 77.
Many good restaurants can be found directly at or near the central Zócalo.

Shopping: Typical souvenirs from Puebla are *talavera* ceramics or onyx. Small shops in the **Mercado El Parian**, Calle 8 Norte, and the **Barrio del Arista** (also with workshops). **Creart**, Av. 2 Oriente 202/204, tel: 46 89 74, and Av. 7 Oriente, corner of Calle 16 de Septiembre, tel: 42 04 59, offers a good choice of arts and crafts.

TAXCO

Information office: at the town entrance from Cuernavaca and Casa Borda, Plazuela Bernal.

Coach station 1st class (*Estrella de Oro*): Av. Presidente John F. Kennedy (in the southwest of the city); several connections daily from Mexico City, TAS.
Coach station 2nd class (*Flecha Roja*): Av.

John F. Kennedy, between the streets Hidalgo and Veracruz.

First class hotels:
Fiesta Monte Taxco, Fracc. Lomas de Taxco (situated above the city, easily reached by cable car, fantastic view); restaurant recommended.
De La Borda, Cerro del Pedregal 2.

Good hotels:
Posada de La Mision, Av. John F. Kennedy 32.
Santa Prisca, Cena Obscuras 1.
Very stylish dinners can be had in the **Hacienda del Solar**, in the southern outskirts of the city. Also recommended are **Cielito Lindo** and **Alarcon**, both near the Zócalo.

Shopping: silver in all variations and prices. The best shops are directly near the Zócalo. Prices are sometimes higher than in Mexico City. Look out for the 925 stamp, a guarantee of the high silver content.

TOLUCA

Information office: Palacio de Gobierno, Lerdo de Tejada Poniente 300, and Lerdo de Tejada Poniente 101, Edif. Plaza Toluca.

Coach station: outside the city center, on the southern ring road Paseo Tollocan. Numerous connections from Mexico City.

Good hotels:
Motel del Rey Inn, at the town entrance from Mexico City.
Also at the same location is the **Cabana Suiza**, a first class restaurant with international cuisine. Recommended in the city center are **La Jaula** and **Nautilus**.

Shopping: Toluca is well known for its Friday market (near the coach station) selling almost everything from fruit and vegetables to pots and pans, pottery and Indian textiles. Some of the fixed stands also sell their goods throughout the week but the main market day is still Friday. **Casart**, Paseo Tollocan 700 Oriente, is a government shop for arts and crafts from the Federal District of México; large choice of good quality products.

COMMUNICATIONS

MEDIA

Mexico City is the largest publishing city in Latin America. In the early hours of the evening, newspaper vendors make an unusual scene in the area of the streets Bucareli and Morelos, riding their bicycles with adventurously high newspaper stacks on the front and back. The most important daily papers are *Excelsior*, *Uno mas Uno*, *Novedades*, *El Día* and *La Jornada*. *La Prensa* is the most widely read national tabloid. The English daily *The News* as well as the American magazines *Time* and *Newsweek* are available in all larger towns and cities of Mexico.

The most comprehensive list of events is found in the weekly magazine *Tiempo Libre*, which is published every Friday.

RADIO – TV

The American stations CBS and NBC broadcast their music, advertizing and sports programs on VHF and medium wave. The Mexican stations only broadcast in Spanish.

Mexican TV is dominated by a touching series called *Telenovela* (in Spanish) whose numerous nightly episodes unite the whole family in front of the television every evening. Even though the national broadcasting stations are trying very hard to convey some culture via the screen, they are always outrun by their private competitors (e.g. *Televisa*) with 24-hour sports programs from the US, shows and music broadcasts, exciting movies, series à la *Dallas* and *Miami Vice*; *Telenovelas* and advertizing, appearing every ten minutes (as in the US).

POSTAL SERVICES

Post office opening hours: Monday–Friday 9 a.m.–6 p.m., Saturday 9 a.m.–1 p.m.

Since the airmail postage for postcards is almost the same as for a letter (up to 20 g), you should put a postcard in an envelope and post it at the nearest post office (safer than a post box). The reception service at the major hotels is normally also reliable. It takes between one and three weeks for a letter to arrive in Europe.

Main post office: Calle Tacuba, corner of Lázaro Cárdenas (opposite the Palacio Bellas Artes).

It is more difficult to send packages and parcels to Europe (special wrapping regulations, several forms to fill in). However, this does not apply to books, brochures, etc. They can be sent from any post office (only weight restrictions). Surface mail (by ship) normally takes three months or longer, airmail is extremely expensive and takes approximately one month. Some shops also offer a courier service.

Post office for airmail packages and parcels: Calle Aldama 218, Col. Guerrero (Metro Revolución), parcel counter open until 2 p.m., packages until 6 p.m.

Surface mail: Aduana Postal, Ceylan 468, in the north of the city. Take a taxi from the Metro station La Raza. Monday–Friday 9 a.m.–1 p.m.

You can receive letters *poste restante* (*lista de correos*) at any post office in Mexico. They will be kept for a period of 10–14 days.

TELEPHONE & TELEX

Normal telephone boxes can only be used for local calls. However, they only cost 1 peso or may even be free of charge. Long-distance and international calls are cheaper from the new *Ladamatico* telephone boxes. Credit card telephones have now also been installed. Make your long-distance calls via an operator from the cheap *Casetas de Larga Distancia* (special telephone boxes marked with a blue telephone symbol, also in shops), or go to the telegraph office.

The luxury tax charged on international calls (units are 3 minutes) makes your phone call home very expensive. Reverse-charge (collect) calls to some countries in Europe are difficult, if not impossible, although reverse-charge calls to the UK provide no problem. Collect calls to the US should be equally trouble-free.

USEFUL TELEPHONE NUMBERS

01 – directory enquiries
02 – international directory enquiries
09 – international operator
91 – code for direct national long-distance calls
98 – code for direct international calls

Telegraph offices (*Oficinas de telégrafos*) are very often separated from normal post offices. International telegrams can be sent from Balderas 14–18, corner of Colón, Metro Hidalgo (near Alameda Park), open 8 a.m.–11 p.m. You can also make international telephone calls from here.

EMERGENCIES

SECURITY & CRIME

A traveler in Mexico City may very easily become the victim of street crime. The crush in overcrowded buses or the Metro and the queues at bus stops are classic danger sites. Even though robbery with violence is relatively rare, you should not tempt fate by walking through deserted streets at night or taking late Metro rides.

EMERGENCY NUMBERS

Contact your embassy as well as the police if you are victim of an accident or crime. They will help find an English-speaking lawyer.

Police (*Policia*): 06; also inner city, tel: 672 0606; Ciudad Satélite, tel: 562 0708; Naucalpan, tel: 560 3813; Tlalnepantla, tel: 565 0758.

Red Cross (*Cruz Roja*): tel: 557 5757.

Fire Brigade (*Bomberos*): inner city, tel: 768 3700; Naucalpan, tel: 560 3868; Tlalnepantla, tel: 565 3638.

Breakdown Services (*Angeles Verdes*): tel: 250 8221.

LOCATEL (*service for tracing missing persons*): tel: 658 1111.

HEALTH

For vaccinations, etc., see under *Travel Essentials* above. We recommend travel insurance policies including repatriation since many health insurance policies only cover limited costs for medical treatment or drugs (enquire before you set out).

Travelers dependent on special drugs should carry an adequate amount with them. It is also recommended that you take medicines for gastric illnesses, migranes or colds. Some Mexican medicines (e.g. Acanol) are much more effective in curing "Montezuma's Revenge", a gastric disease which can have various causes. For preventive measures, avoid drinking tap water or consuming ice cubes or icecream from street vendors. *Agua purificada*, filtered water, replaces tap water in many hotels. If not, you can always buy mineral water (e.g. Tehuacán).

Be careful when choosing raw fruit or vegetables (including salads) in your restaurant. Ice-cold drinks or extremely spicy dishes may also cause severe stomach upsets.

Do not plan exhausting outings for the first few days. Your body needs time to get acclimatized to the time difference and the altitude.

PHARMACIES – DOCTORS

A "first class" pharmacy, supervized by a doctor and well equipped, can be recognized by its green cross symbol.

"Second class" pharmacies only store basic medicaments.

Recommended pharmacies: *El Fenix* (chain of pharmacies), e.g. in Av. Fco. Madero 39, corner of Motolina; Isabel La Católica 15; Iturbide 6, corner of Plaza Hidalgo;

Also *Farmacias* in the supermarket chain *Sanborns*, e.g. Paseo de la Reforma 45 and 333.

Contact your doctor if your diarrhoea lasts longer than a couple of days or if you develop a temperature. The hotel or the embassy/consulate will help you find an English-speaking doctor.

Medical services are always paid for in cash. Some countries have reciprocal health agreements which will allow for reimbursement at home, but check this with your embassy before you go.

HOSPITALS

The American British Cowdray Hospital (called ABC), Sur 136, corner of Observatorio, Col. América, tel: 277 3434; emergency telephone (only for this hospital): 515 8359, has the best reputation.

WHERE TO STAY

HOTELS

Arriving in Mexico City without a hotel reservation is not a great problem. The information stands at the international airport, the station and the national coach stations will help you get a room.

International hotel chains, such as Best Western, Hilton, Holiday Inn and Sheraton, accept reservations from Europe. According to their equipment and services, hotels are characterized by one to five stars. First class luxury hotels are allowed to display "GT" (Gran Turismo) after their name.

The hotel prices given below include accommodation only, sometimes referred to as EP (European Plan). More comprehensive services are abbreviated as follows: MAP (Modified American Plan) – half board. AP (American Plan) – full board.

The peak season lasts from mid–November/beginning of December through to the end of May. Prices are usually 20–30 percent up on the other months.

Prices for a double room in all categories, based on 1990 charges, are as follows:

Luxury hotels (GT) and five-star hotels	US$100–150
four-star hotels	US$60/70–100
three-star hotels	US$25/30–60
one and two-star hotels	from US$10

The big luxury hotels in Mexico City are concentrated in the area of Zona Rosa and Chapultepec whereas medium range hotels can also be found along the Paseo de la Reforma and around the Alameda park. Simpler hotels are situated in the old city around the Zócalo and north of the Plaza de la República towards the station.

CHAPULTEPEC

Luxury/first-class hotels
Camino Real, Mariano Escobedo 700, tel: 203 2121 and 250 5144, reservations: 203 1133.
Del Prado, Marina Nacional 399, tel: 254 4400, reservations: 255 4222.
El Stouffer Presidente Chapultepec, Campos Eliseos 218, tel: 250 7700, reservations: 255 4242.
Nikko, Campos Eliseos 204, reservations tel: 203 4020, 203 4000.

ZONA ROSA

Luxury/upper-class hotels
Galeria Plaza, Hamburgo 195, tel: 211 0014.
Krystal, Liverpool 155, tel: 211 0092 and 211 3464, reservations: 511 8779, 525 2650.
Maria Isabel Sheraton, Paseo de la Reforma 325 (near the Independence Memorial), tel: 525 9060.

Upper/medium-range hotels
Aristos, Paseo de la Reforma 276, tel: 211 0112.
Calinda Geneve, Londres 130, tel: 211 0071, reservations: 525 9184.
Century Zona Rosa, Liverpool 152, tel: 584 7111.
El Presidente Zona Rosa, Hamburgo 135, tel: 525 0000.
El Romano Diana, Rio Lerma 237, tel: 211 0109.
Del Angel, Rio Lerma 154, tel: 533 1032.
Marco Polo, Amberes 27, tel: 511 1839.
Royal, Amberes 78, tel: 525 4850.

Medium-range hotels
Maria Cristina, Rio Lerma 31, tel: 564 9880.

REFORMA/INSURGENTES CENTRO

Luxury/first-class hotels
Crowne Plaza Holiday Inn, Paseo de la Reforma 80, tel: 566 7777, reservations: 559 3233.

Upper/middle-class hotels
Emporio, Paseo de la Reforma 124, tel: 566 7766.
Plaza Reforma, Insurgentes Centro 149, tel: 535 0556, 535 0777.
Placa Florencia, Florencia 61, tel: 211 0064.

OLD CITY (ALAMEDA PARK/ZOCALO)

Upper/medium-range hotels
Ambassador, Humboldt 38, tel: 518 0110.
Casa Blanca, Lafragua 7, tel: 566 3211.
Estoril, Luis Moya 93, tel: 521 1466, 521 1226, 521 9762.
Gran Hotel (Howard Johnson), Av. 16 de Septiembre 82, corner of Zócalo, tel: 510 4040.
Hotel de Cortéz, Av. Hidalgo 85, tel: 518 2121.
Majestic, Av. Madero 73, tel: 521 8600.
Ritz, Av. Madero 30, tel: 519 1340.

Medium-range hotels
Fontan, Colón 27, corner of Paseo de la Reforma, tel: 518 5460.
Metropol, Luis Moya 39, tel: 510 8660.

AT THE AIRPORT

Luxury/first-class hotels
Fiesta Americana Aeropuerto, Blvd Puerto Aereo 502, tel: 762 4088.

Upper/medium-range hotels
Holiday Inn Aeropuerto, tel: 762 4088.

YOUTH HOSTELS

To get accommodation in Mexican youth hostels you should be in possession of an international youth hostel card. An international student's card would also be useful.

The youth hostels are run by several different organizations which will send you written information on request:
Asociación Mexicana de Albergues de la Juventud (AMAJ): Madero 6, Of. 314, México 1, D.F.

Consejo Nacional de Recursos para la Atención de la Juventud (CREA): Oxtocopulco 40, Colonia Oxtocopulco, App. Postal 04310, México, D.F.
Youth hostel CREA: Insurgentes Sur, corner of Camino Sta. Teresa, Deleg. Tlalpan, south of the university, in the former Olympic village, tel: 573 7740 and 655 1416.
The **Mexican students' association** (SETEJ) runs a guest house south of the Zona Rosa, Calle Cozumel 57 (Metro Sevilla), tel: 514 9240, 514 4210. You need a student card which is available from the SETEJ office in Hamburgo 273 (Zona Rosa, also Metro Sevilla), tel: 514 4213 and 511 6691.
The **Casa de los Amigos**, the Quaker guest house, resembles a youth hostel: Ignacio Mariscal 132, near Plaza de la República (Metro Hidalgo), tel: 705 0521. Reservation recommended.

CAMPING

Camping sites are relatively rare in Mexico but you will find numerous caravan parks, mainly used by Americans. Caravan parks in Mexico City:

Cabello Calle Hortensia, corner of Av. Universidad.

El Caminero, Ruta 99, Tlalpan, in the south of the city shortly before the toll barrier (*caseta de cobro*) of the motorway towards Cuernavaca.

Food Digest

RESTAURANTS

Capitalinos enjoy eating foreign food from time to time and so the Zona Rosa houses a good selection of European or even Asian restaurants. The grand hotels normally also serve an international menu. There are plenty of alternatives if you do not want to indulge in Mexican cuisine right from the start.

However, once you have experienced good Mexican food, you are likely to stick to *guacamole*, *pollo con mole poblano* or *tortillas* in abundance. A juicy steak and *frijoles* in a simple restaurant with a 1950s formica decor is as enjoyable as dining extensively in one of the romantic *hacienda* restaurants. Try the different regional specialities, particularly fish *à la veracruzana* or pork *à la yucatán*.

In many of the bigger restaurants, meals are accompanied by music at weekends and reservations are necessary.

Mexicans are hardly ever late for their meals; meal times are the same as in Spain, i.e. lunch between 1 p.m. and 3 p.m. Dinner, which normally starts at 8.30 p.m., may last two hours or even longer.

Many restaurants are closed on Sundays or public holidays. Please check opening times before setting out.

Below you find a small selection of recommended restaurants and cafés, the latter sometimes also serving food during the day. With a few exceptions, we have not listed the many excellent Mexican and international restaurants that you will find in hotels.

ZONA ROSA & REFORMA

A – expensive, B – average, C – cheap.

The Pasaje Jacaranda between Génova and Londres is a shopping arcade with several street cafés and restaurants, such as the Italian restaurants **Alfredo's** (B), tel: 511 3864, 511 6740, and **La Trucha Vagabunda** (B), tel: 533 3178.

Anderson's (B), Paseo de la Reforma 382, tel: 525 1006. Good Mexican and international cuisine, great choice. Popular with young Mexicans, casual atmosphere.

Antigua Fonda Santa Anita (B), Londres 38, tel: 514 4728, 528 8439. The owners have been cooking traditional Mexican food for the last 40 years.

Bellinghausen (A/B), Londres 95, tel: 511 9035, 511 1056, 525 8738. Specializes in fish and steak dishes. The quiet patio is full of businessmen at lunchtime.

El Parador de Jose Luis (A/B), Niza 17, tel: 533 1840. Excellent Spanish cuisine, good daytime menu. Overcrowded at lunchtime but quieter in the evening.

Focolare (A), Hamburgo 87, tel: 525 7468, 511 2679. Excellent Mexican and international dishes. Elegant rooms around a patio in neo–colonial style. Piano music at lunchtime, *marimbas* in the evening. Interesting folklore performances. Special Sunday brunch. Cantina bar **El Trompo** at the entrance to the restaurant.

Fonda el Refugio (B), Liverpool 166, tel: 525 8128, 207 2732.
Traditional Mexican restaurant with very pleasant atmosphere. Reservation recommended.

La Marinera (B), Liverpool 183, tel: 511 2466. Fantastic fish and seafood *à la Mexicana*. Very popular with Mexicans.

La Cofradia de Loredo (A/B), Hamburgo 32, tel: 533 6869–71. Classic Mexican cuisine, particularly their *sabana*. Many business people amongst their guests.

Meson del Perro Andaluz (B), Copenhague 26, tel: 533 5306, 528 8939. Spanish cuisine. Very popular with young Mexicans, also well known in artists' circles; also a street café.

Toulouse Lautrec (B/C), Génova 74, tel: 533 4786. Mexican and international dishes. Young clientèle. Live music after 8 p.m. Bar.

Yug (C), Varsovia 3, tel: 574 4475. Good vegetarian menu. You have to queue but it is well worth it.

CHAPULTEPEC – COLONIA POLANCO

A – expensive, B – average, C – cheap.

Del Lago (A), at the large lake near the new, western part of the Chapultepec park, tel: 515 9585, 515 9350. *Haute cuisine*, served in an architecturally extravagant building. Very formal, reservation necessary.
Fonda del Recuerdo (B), Bahía de las Palmas 39, Col. Anzures, near hotel Presidente, tel: 545 7260-62, 545 1652. Best example of Veracruzian cuisine, e.g. *huachinango*, live music every day (*jarocho*); open from 1 p.m., reservation necessary.
Kino Mexikatessen (A/B), Campos Eliseos 363–A, corner of Goldsmith, Col. Polanco, tel: 540 5970, 202 5343. Apart from classic Mexican dishes this restaurant also serves exotic specialities prepared according to pre–Spanish recipies.
La Hacienda de los Morales (A), Vázquez de Mella 525, Col. del Bosque, tel: 540 3225, 202 1973. Mexican and international cuisine; beautiful *hacienda* (17th century) with covered patio. Very elegant, ties must be worn after 6 p.m. Reservation necessary.
Lincoln Grill (B), Amberes 64, tel: 511 0308. Classical Spanish cuisine.

OLD CITY

A – expensive, B – average, C – cheap.

Bar Opera (B), 5 de Mayo, corner of Filomeno Mata. Recommended if you intend to drink and eat a snack in quiet and historic surroundings (Pancho Villa took the bar by storm).
Danubio (C), Uruguay 3. Simple Mexican menu, particularly fish dishes.
El Vegetariano (C), Filomeno Mata 13, tel: 521 1895; and Madero 56, tel: 521 6880. Cheap vegetarian meals, open Monday–Saturday 8 a.m. – 8 p.m.
Hosteria de Sto Domingo (C), Belizario Dominguez 72, at the Pl. Sto. Domingo, tel: 526 5276. This restaurant, probably the oldest in Mexico City, has been serving local dishes since 1860.
Las Cazuelas (B/C), Rep. de Colombia 69, tel: 702 1140, 702 0535. Traditional Mexican restaurant, particularly crowded at lunchtime.
Lincoln Grill (B), Revillagigedo 24, near Alameda park, tel: 510 3317. Stylish old Spanish restaurant.
Majestic (Hotel) (B), Av. Madero 73, tel: 521 8600. Beautiful roof garden restaurant, especially good for breakfast, with a fine view over the Zócalo, the cathedral and the National Palace.
Prendes (B), Av. 16 de Septiembre 10, tel: 521 1878. One of the oldest restaurants in the city (founded 1892) whose famous guests, from Pancho Villa and the revolutionary generals to Walt Disney, are displayed on murals. Reservation necessary at lunchtime.
Sanborns (B/C), Av. Fco. Madero 17, Casa de Azulejos, tel: 521 6058. From small breakfast to extensive lunch, the service is fast and efficient. The tiled patio serves as a dining hall.

ELSEWHERE

A – expensive, B – average, C – cheap.

Antigua Fonda Santa Anita (B), Insurgentes Sur 1038, tel: 559 8061, 539 8140. Sister restaurant to the long-established business is Zona Rosa; traditional Mexican food.
Antigua Hacienda de Tlalpan (A), Calzada de Tlalpan 4619, south of the Anillo Periférico, tel: 573 9933, 573 9959. Exquisite Mexican and international dishes, elegant atmosphere in a restored 18th-century *hacienda*, beautiful gardens, music performances in the evenings. Open after 1 p.m.
Circulo del Sureste (C), Lucerna 12, tel: 535 2704. The best restaurant in the whole of the D.F. for Yucatacan specialities, e.g. *cochinita pibil* or *papatzules*. Casual atmosphere, overcrowded at lunchtime.
Hosteria del Trovador (C), at the main square in Coyoacán. Friendly Mexican restaurant, very crowded at lunchtime, many white-collar workers and business people.
Hosteria Sta Catarina (C), Jardín Sta. Catarina 10, tel: 554 0513. Inexpensive and good Mexican food, pleasant atmosphere.
Loredo San Angel (B), Av. Revolución 1511, tel: 548 6717, 548 9296. Classic Mexican cuisine.
Los Comerciales (A/B), Av. Insurgentes Sur 2383, tel: 550 6000, and Circuito Ingenieros 39, Ciudad Satélite, tel: 572 3323. Full of posters and other funny advertizing memorabilia, these two restaurants are ex-

tremely popular with young people. The international menu is served by waiters on roller skates.

Meson del Caballo Bayo (B), Av. del Conscripto 36, Lomas Hipódromo, Naucalpan, in the west of the city, near the race course, tel: 589 3000. Among the many Mexican specialities are *cabrito* and *sabana*; this is a former *hacienda* with a relaxed family atmosphere; *mariachi* music, also breakfast service. Reservation recommended.

San Angel Inn (A), Palmas 50, corner of Altavista, San Angel, tel: 548 6746. Exquisite Mexican and international food; very upscale atmosphere in a former *hacienda* (built in the 18th century), surrounded by romantic gardens. One of the best restaurants in Mexico. Live music. The proprietor insists on formal wear; tie obligatory. Early reservation recommended.

RESTAURANT CHAINS

Lynis's, fast-food chain (with service) for Mexican and international dishes. Subsidiaries: Newton 7, Col. Polanco; Gutenberg 231, Col. Nueva Anzures; Paseo de la Reforma 423; Insurgentes Sur 866, Col. del Valle.

Potzolcalli, simple and clean restaurants with a large menu of Mexican food. Popular with Mexican families. Subsidiaries in the city center: Xola 32; Molière 325; further subsidiaries in the outskirts.

Sanborn's, well-organized restaurants located in department stores of the same name. Mexican and international food, cheap daytime menu.

CAFÉS

Café la Blanca (C), 5 de Mayo 40, city center, tel: 510 0399, 585 1529. Traditional coffee house which serves Mexican breakfast but also plain dishes.

Café Tacuba (C), Tacuba 28, city center, tel: 518 4950. Traditional Mexican Café–Restaurant (est. 1912), most famous for its *enchiladas*. Very crowded at lunchtime.

Café Tacuba (C), Newton 88, Col. Polanco, tel: 250 2633. Offspring of the restaurant with the same name in the old city center.

Café Viena, Cacahuamilpa 8, Col. Hipódromo Condesa, tel: 528 6029. The

right place if you are craving for cakes.

Konditori, Genova 61, Zona Rosa, tel: 514 4828. Open daily from 7 a.m.–midnight, deliciously fresh puff pastry, cakes and small dishes.

Konditori, Euler, corner of Masaryk, tel: 250 1032, 250 0881. As above.

RESTAURANTS WITH EVENTS

Restaurant Focolare, Hamburgo 87, tel: 525 7468, 511 2679. Flamboyant folklore shows in the evenings.

Hotel de Cortéz, Av. Hidalgo 85, tel: 585 0322. Saturdays 8 p.m: The fixed price includes dinner and a show in the patio. Reservation recommended.

MENU GLOSSARY

desayuno – breakfast
comida – lunch
comida corrida – dish of the day
merienda – tea break
cena – supper
aguacate – avocado
agua mineral (con/sin gas) – mineral water (with/without fizz)
aguas naturales – fruit or flower water made with tamarind, melon, lime, guava or hibiscus
albondigas – meat balls
antojitos – starters based on tortilla
arroz – rice
arroz con leche – rice pudding with cinnamon
atole – maize meal drink
atún – tuna
azúcar – sugar
barbacoa – meat cooked in a clay oven
bistec – steak
bolillos – bread rolls
cabrito – kid goat
café americano – weak (sometimes instant) coffee
café con leche – milk coffee
café cortado/con crema/con un poquito de leche – white coffee
café de olla – coffee brewed together with cinnamon
café negro/solo – strong, black coffee
calabacita – courgettes
calabaza – pumpkin
calamares – octopus
caldo – clear meat soup

caldo tlalpeño – chicken soup with Mexican vegetables

camarones – prawns

carne (de res) – meat (beef)

carne asada – roasted meat

carnitas – small pieces of meat fried in lard or dripping

cebolla – onion

cerdo – pork

cerveza (clara/oscura) – (light/dark) beer

ceviche – raw pieces of fish, marinaded in lime juice, chili and onions

chicharrón – crackling

chilaquiles – stripes of *tortillas* in hot chili sauce

chiles en nogada – chilis in nut sauce with pomegranate pips

chiles rellenos – green chilis filled with meat, fish or cheese

chirimoya – "sugar pear"

chocolate – hot chocolate

chuleta – pork chop

cilantro – fresh coriander

cochinita pibil – very hot pork dish

conejo – rabbit

consomé – clear meat soup

cordero – lamb

dulce de almendra – almond pudding

elote – grilled corn on the cob

enchiladas (suizas) – *tortillas*, covered in a meat or cheese paté and then rolled up (refined with cream)

ensalada – salad

ensalada de nopales – salad of steamed cactus leaves

epazote – herb resembling parsley

flan – caramel pudding

flor de calabaza – steamed pumpkin buds, served as a vegetable

fresa – strawberry

frijoles (refritos) – brown beans, half whole and half puree (fried in a pan)

gorditas – small filled *tortillas*, deepfried or fried in a lot of oil

guacamole – avocado puree with sliced onions, chilis and red tomatoes (called *jitomate*)

guajolote – turkey

guayaba – guava

gusanos de maguey – agave worms, crisply fried (Aztec speciality)

helado – ice cream

higos – figs

hongos – mushrooms

huachinango – rosefish

huevos – eggs

huevos á la mexicana – scrambled eggs with tomatoes and finely chopped chilis

huevos estrellados – fried eggs

huevos rancheros – fried eggs on *tortillas* with *frijoles* and a spicy chili sauce

huevos revueltos – scrambled eggs

huevos tibios – boiled eggs in a glass

jamaica – hibiscus

jamón – ham

jícama – tuber, containing starch

jitomate – red tomato

jugo – fruit juice

langostas – crayfish or lobster

lechuga – lettuce

licuado de agua/de leche – fruit juice mixed with water or milk

limón – lime

mantequilla – butter

margarita – *tequila* with lemon juice

mariscos – seafood

melocotón – peach

merluza – cod

mezcal – crystal clear agave schnapps

mojarra – seafish

mole poblano – slightly thick and dark sauce which gets its sweet–hot taste from a mixture of chilis and chocolate

naranja – orange

nopal – leaves of the fig cactus, served as a salad or vegetable

ostiones – oysters

pampano – seafish

pan – bread

pan dulce – yeast pastry

pan tostado – toast

papas – potatoes

pepino – cucumber

pescado – fish (dish)

pez espada – swordfish

pimienta – pepper

pina – pineapple

pipián – sauce, similar to *mole*, but lighter and milder, with pumpkin seeds and chili

pitaya – cactus fruit

plátano – banana

pollo – chicken

postre – dessert, pudding

puchero – stew dish

pulque – fermented agave juice, national drink of Mexico

queso – cheese

quesadilla – baked *tortilla*, filled with cheese

refresco – refreshing drink, lemonade

romeritos – vegetable, similar to spinach

sabana – slice of beef

sal – salt

salsa verde/roja/mexicana – cold spicy sauce (green/red/Mexican), served with meat, fish, etc.

sandia – watermelon

sopa de arroz – dry rice with vegetable pieces (e.g. as an intermediate course)

tacos – filled *tortillas*, rolled up and fried

tamales – spicy maize semolina puree, wrapped up in maize or banana leaves and boiled

té de manzanilla – camomile tea

té negro – black tea

tequila (con sangrita) – agave schnapps (with a tiny glass of spicy tomato juice)

ternera – veal

tocino – bacon

toronja – grapefruit

tortas – oval or round bread rolls, filled with cheese or meat, salads and chilis

tortilla – flat maize bread

tortilla de huevos – omelette

tostadas – crisply fried *tortillas*, covered in lettuce, *frijoles*, cheese and meat

tuna – fruit of the fig cactus (*nopal*)

venado – venison

verduras – vegetables

zanahoria – carotts

NIGHTLIFE

ENTERTAINMENT

Mexico City, the cultural mecca of the country, offers a wide spectrum of evening entertainment even to the non–Spanish speaker. The weekly magazine *Tiempo Libre* (which appears on Fridays and is available at newsagents) publishes comprehensive information about cultural events (also modern pop music). It lists the individual events, locations, telephone numbers for reservations and the nearest Metro station.

Advance tickets for theater performances, concerts, sport and other events are available from ticket machines (*boletronicos* or simply "*B*"). They are situated in the Palacio de Bellas Artes and the main Metro stations.

The **Ballet Folklorico** has been the most famous night show for years. The dance group, swirling across the stage to traditional music in frilly and brightly colored costumes, gives a memorable display of the variety of Mexican music and dance.

Performances: Palacio de Bellas Artes, see below, tel: 512 3633, Sundays 9.30 a.m. and 9 p.m., Wednesdays 9 p.m.

Museo de la Ciudad, Pino Suárez 30, Centro, tel: 542 0487, 542 0671; Sundays 9.30 a.m., Tuesdays 9 p.m. (or 9.30 p.m.).

The **Teatro de la Ciudad**, Donceles 36, tel: 510 2197, also has excellent folklore performances.

Below is a listing of the addresses of the most important music and concert halls, cultural centers and theaters as well as discos and pubs with live music.

MUSIC & CULTURAL CENTERS

Anfiteatro Simon Bolivar, Justo Sierra 16, Centro, former Colegio de San Ildefonso, Metro: Zócalo.

Auditorio Alejo Peralta, Unidad Cultural López Mateos, Zacatenco (in the north), tel: 586 2847, Metro: Lindavista.

Auditorio Nacional, Paseo de la Reforma, corner of Campo Marte, Chapultepec, tel: 520 9060, Metro: Auditorio.

Biblioteca Publica de Mexico, Plaza de la Ciudadela 4, Centro, Metro: Balderas.

Casa de Cultura del Periodista, Eje Central Lázaro Cárdenas 912, Col. 2a del Periodista.

Casa de la Cultura Jesus Reyes Heroles, Francisco Sosa 202, Col. Coyoacán, tel: 658 5223, Metro: Viveros.

Casa del Lago, Bosque de Chapultepec, tel: 553 6318, Metro: Chapultepec.

Centro Cultural Unversitario, Ciudad Universitario, Insurgentes Sur 3000, tel: 655 6511, Metro: Universidad. Several halls for cultural events.

Centro Cultural/Foro Coyoacánese, Allende 36, Col. Coyoacán, tel: 554 6030/ 36, 658 4891.

El Desvan de las Quimeras, hall in the Fritz restaurant, Dr. Rio de la Loza 221, Col. Doctores, tel: 709 2305.

El Hijo del Cuervo, Jardín Centenario 17,

Col. Coyoacán, tel: 658 5306.
El Juglar, Manuel M. Ponce 233, Col. Guadalupe Inn, San Angel, tel: 660 7900.
Foro de la Libreria Luis Bunuel, Insurgentes Sur 32, tel: 592 8204.
Foro Gandhi (Libreria), Miguel Angel de Quevedo 134, Col. Chimalistac/Coyoacán, tel: 550 2524, 548 1990, Metro: M.A. de Quevedo.
Museo Universitario del Chopo, Enrique González Martínez 10, Col. Sta. María la Ribera, tel: 535 2186, 544 4698, Metro: Revolución.
Palacio de Bellas Artes, Av. 5 de Mayo, at the Alameda Park, Metro: Bellas Artes.
Palacio de Mineria, Tacuba 4, Centro, tel: 510 1668, Metro: Bellas Artes.
Polyforum Cultural Siquerios, Insurgentes Sur, corner of Filadelfia ("Hotel de México"), tel: 536 4521/22.
Premier, Av. San Jerónimo 190, Pedregal de San Angel, tel: 652 6933, 652 5066.
Sala Carlos Chavez, in the Centro Cultural Universitario, see above.
Sala Manuel M. Ponce, in the Palacio de Bellas Artes, see above, tel: 512 5676, ext. 203.
Sala Miguel Covarrubias, in the Centro Cultural Universitario, see above, tel: 655 6511, ext. 7071.
Sala Nezahualcoyotl, in the Centro Cultural Universitario, see above, tel: 655 6511, ext. 7051.
Sala Ollin Yoliztli, Periférico Sur 5141, Tlalpan, tel: 655 3311.
Teatro de la Ciudad, Donceles 36, Centro, tel: 510 2942, 521 5083, 510 2197, Metro: Allende.
Teatro de la Ciudadela, Tresguerras 91, Centro, tel: 710 2942, Metro: Balderas.

THEATERS

Benito Juarez, Villalongín 15, Col. Cuauhtémoc, tel: 546 0820, ext. 48, Metro: Insurgentes.
Hidalgo, Av. Hidalgo 23, Centro, tel: 521 5859, Metro: Bellas Artes.
Insurgentes, Insurgentes Sur 1587, Col. San José Insurgentes, tel: 660 2304.
Juan Ruiz de Alarcon, Centro Cultural Universitario, Cd. Universitario, Insurgentes Sur 3000, tel: 655 1344, 655 7956, Metro: Universidad.
Julio Prieto, Xola, corner of Nicolás San Juan, Col. del Valle, tel: 543 3478, Metro: Etiopía or Xola.
La Blanquita, Plaza Serdán 16, Eje Central Lázaro Cárdenas, near the Plaza Garibaldi, tel: 747 0357, Metro: Bellas Artes.
Reforma, Paseo de la Reforma, corner of Burdeos, tel: 211 3622, Metro: Chapultepec.
San Rafael, Virgínia Fábregas 40, Col. San Rafael, tel: 592 2142.
San Jeronimo, Periférico Sur, corner of San Jerónimo, Unidad Habitacional del IMSS, tel: 595 2117.
Tepeyac, Calzada de Guadalupe, corner of Victoria, tel: 517 6560.

DISCOS

Cero Cero, in the hotel Camino Real, Leibnitz 100, tel: 203 2121. Elegant and expensive. Open 9 p.m.–4 a.m. Reservation recommended at weekends.
Club 84, in the hotel El Presidente Stouffer Chapultepec, Campos Eliseos 218, Col. Polanco, tel: 250 7700. Modern disco with a lot of musical flair. Open 9 p.m.–4 a.m.
Le Chic, in the hotel Galería Plaza, Hamburgo 195, Col. Juárez, tel: 211 0014. Most extravagant disco with the latest hits.
Lipstick, in the hotel Aristos, Paseo de la Reforma 276, tel: 211 0112. Mixed clientèle, casual atmosphere. Open Wednesday–Sunday, after 9 p.m.
Valentinos, in the Marrakesh, Florencia 36, Zona Rosa, tel: 525 2020. Choose between the fantastic (and expensive) disco, the bar and two nightclubs.
Zazzy, in the hotel Nikko, Campos Eliseos 204, Col. Polanco, tel: 203 4020. Hypermodern disco. Open 8 p.m.–4 a.m.

MUSIC & NIGHTCLUBS

Some of the music clubs below also run a restaurant and provide folkloric music. Others are casual, bar-like pubs with small musical groups playing everything from hard rock to Caribbean reggae. Most of the grand hotels have very elegant nightclubs.

The *cantinas*, similar to pubs, are normally only for men. Some of them, however, now admit women:
Aantillano's, Francisco Pimentel 74, San Rafael, tel: 592 0439. Mainly Afro–Caribbean music (salsa, etc.) relaxed atmosphere. Open after 9 p.m.

Cantina la Guadalupana, Calle Higuera 14, Metro: Coyoacán, tel: 554 6542

Cantina la Valenciana, Av. Brazil 29, tel: 747 2404

Casa Blanca, in the Marrakesh, Florencia 32, Zona Rosa, tel: 525 7319. Nightclub with show after 10 p.m.

Disco Bar 9, Londres 156, Zona Rosa, tel: 514 4387, 514 4148. Gay club.

El Corral de la Moreria, Londres 161, Zona Rosa, tel: 525 1762. Nightclub with dinner service, Spanish music, flamenco show. Open after 10 p.m., show begins at midnight.

El Patio, Atenas 9, Zona Rosa, tel: 535 3904. Traditional, elegant nightclub, dinner service, dance (two orchestras). Open 9 p.m.–4 a.m.

Gatsby's Musical Bar, in the hotel El Stouffer Presidente Chapultepec, tel: 250 7700. Elegant nightclub, performances by international stars. Reservation recommended. Open 7 p.m.–3 a.m.

Hosteria del Bohemio, former Convento San Hípolito, Av. Hidalgo, west of Alameda park. Relax in the beautiful patio. Lively music pub, young people. Open 5 p.m.–10 p.m.

La Bodega, Popocatépetl 25, Col. Hipódromo Condesa, tel: 525 2473. Bohemian restaurant, pleasant for eating out, mixed and unconventional crowd.

La Escena, Ameyalco, corner of Insurgentes Sur, Col. del Valle, tel: 687 7893. Bar with club atmosphere, music and show performances in turns. Open 7 p.m.–3 a.m.

La Mancha, in the hotel Aristos, Paseo de la Reforma 276, tel: 211 0112. Stylish hotel bar. Popular with Mexicans, *mariachi* music.

Las Sillas, in the Hotel Crowne Plaza, Paseo de la Reforma 80, tel: 705 1515. The "bar of the funny chairs" (*sillas*), entertaining live music and shows. Closed on Sundays.

L'Baron, Insurgentes Sur 1231. Gay club.

L'Fameux, Hamburgo 41, Zona Rosa. Gay club, many transvestites.

Muralto, in the Torre Latinoamericana. Bar with live music included in the price. Beautiful view over the city lights.

New Orleans, Av. Revolución 1980, San Angel, tel: 550 1908. New Orleans by name and by nature. THE classic jazz bar in Mexico City.

Pena de Gabriel del Rio, Pasaje Balderas 33. Latin-American music.

Pena el Condor Pasa, Calle Rafael Checa 1, tel: 548 2050. Latin-American music.

Pena el Payador, Rio Amazonas 36, north of the Zona Rosa. Latin-American music, popular with young Mexicans.

Rockotitlan, Insurgentes Sur 953–202, Col. Nápoles, tel: 584 4730, 687 7893. Sophisticated rock music program, interesting atmosphere.

Rock Stock Bar, Paseo de la Reforma, corner of Niza, Zona Rosa, tel: 533 0906. Rock groups constantly changing.

(Plaza) Santa Cecilia, Callejon de la Amargura 30 (Plaza Garibaldi), tel: 526 1804, 529 1102. Restaurant cum bar with lively *mariachi* music and folklore performances. Open 9 p.m.–3 a.m.

Tenampa, Plaza Garibaldi

Tenampa (Salon), Plaza Garibaldi 12, tel: 526 6176. THE classic *cantina* (also for women) at the Plaza Garibaldi. Non-stop *mariachi* music.

Yesterday's, in the hotel Aristos, tel: 211 0112. Disco and live music on alternating days, pleasant atmosphere. Open after 8 p.m.

CULTURE PLUS

MUSEUMS

Alvar y Carmen T. de Carrillo Gil (Museo de Arte), Av. Revolución 1608, San Angel, open Tuesday–Sunday 10 a.m.–7 p.m. Selected collection of modern (and contemporary) paintings from Mexico and Europe.

Anahuacalli/Diego Rivera (Museo), Calle del Museo 150, Coyoacán, open Tuesday–Sunday 10 a.m.–2 p.m., 3 p.m.–6 p.m. Unconventional building, designed by Rivera. Contains Rivera's former collection of pre–Spanish art (60,000 pieces) and folk art as well as the painter's own works. Celebrations in remembrance of Rivera during the first week of November.

Antropología (Museo Nacional de), Paseo de la Reforma, corner of Gandhi, Bosque de Chapultepec, open Tuesday–Friday, 9 a.m.–7 p.m. Saturday, Sunday, bank holidays 10 a.m.–6 p.m. Simply a must when you are in Mexico City. The two floors offer the best and most comprehensive display of Mexico's Indian culture from pre–Spanish to modern times.

Arte (Museo Nacional de), Tacuba 8, open Tuesday–Sunday 10 a.m.–6 p.m. Comprehensive collection of arts and crafts, paintings, etchings and sculptures from pre–Spanish to modern times.

Arte Contemporaneo (Centro Cultural), Campos Eliseos, corner of Jorge Eliot, Col. Polanco, open Tuesday–Sunday 10 a.m. –6 p.m. Departments for contemporary arts, the history of photography (largest collection in South America) and pre–Spanish art. Also cultural center with a library, theater, cinema, etc.

Arte Moderno (Museo de), Paseo de la Reforma, corner of Gandhi. Open Tuesday–Sunday 10 a.m.–6 p.m. Permanent exhibition of modern Mexican painters such as Orozco, Tamayo, Frida Kahlo, Cuevas, Coronel and Toledo. Numerous cultural events, temporary exhibitions.

Artes e Industrias Populares (Museo Nacional de), Av. Juárez 44 Open Tuesday–Sunday, 10 a.m.–2 p.m. and 3 p.m.–6 p.m. Exhibition of Mexican arts and crafts from all over the country, also for sale.

Carmen (Museo Regional del), Av. Revolución 4–6/Avenida de la Paz, San Angel. Open Monday–Sunday, 10 a.m.–5 p.m. Former Carmelite monastry (17th century), collection of religious paintings from the 17th and 18th century, e.g. Villalpando and Correa. The basement houses some mummies which were conserved by a special combination of humidity and soil.

Casa del Risco (Museo de la), Plaza de San Jacinto 5 y 15, San Angel. Open Tuesday–Friday 10 a.m.–3 p.m., Saturday and Sunday 10 a.m.–2 p.m. Typical mansion of an aristocratic family in the 18th century, collection of European paintings from the 14th to the 18th century, Mexican paintings from colonial times, luxurious rooms on the upper floor. Cultural center.

Castillo de Chapultepec, see (Museo Nacional de) Historia.

Cera de la Ciudad de Mexico (Museo de), Londres 6. Open Monday–Friday 11 a.m.–7 p.m., Saturday and Sunday 10 a.m.–7 p.m. Interesting waxworks in an equally interesting art nouveau city palace (by the same architect who designed the Revolution Memorial).

Charreria (Museo de la), Isabel la Católica 108. Open Monday–Friday 9 a.m.–6 p.m., Saturday 3 a.m.–1 p.m. Convent church of the late 16th century, interesting collection of clothes from the *charros* and other artefacts used at the *charrería* (Mexican rodeo). On special display: Pancho Villa's saddle and revolver.

Ciudad de Mexico (Museo de la), Pino Suárez 30. Open Tuesday–Sunday 9.30 a.m.–7.30 p.m. Former city palace of the Earl of Santiago Calimaya (18th century). The documentation of the city's development since pre–Spanish times (geography, history, art) is well worth seeing.

Cuicuilco (Museo Arqueológico de), Insurgentes Sur (south of the junction with the Periférico Sur). Open Tuesday–Sunday 10 a.m.–5 p.m. Small museum next to the circular pyramid explaining the role of what was the most important ceremonial center in the highlands and the social order at the time of its building 4,000 years ago. Pretty figurines.

Culturas (Museo Nacional de las), Calle Moneda 13. Open Tuesday–Friday 9.30 a.m.–6 p.m., Saturday and Sunday 9.30 a.m.–4 p.m. In the northwestern corner of the National Palace, ethnographical collection about many tribes of the world. In the entrance hall mural by Rufino Tamayo.

Culturas Populares (Museo Nacional de), Hidalgo 289, Coyoacán. Monday, Thursday 10 a.m.–4 p.m., Wednesday, Friday, Saturday 10 a.m.–8 p.m., Sunday 11 a.m.–5 p.m. Museum in the style of a colonial house, temporary exhibitions on different aspects of Mexico's culture.

Diego Rivera (Museo Estudio), Calle Diego Rivera, corner of Altavista, Col. San Angel Inn. Restored residence and studio of the painter Diego Rivera.

Franz Mayer (Museo), Av. Hidalgo 45, north of the Alameda park. Open Tuesday–Sunday 10 a.m.–5 p.m. Former hospital (16th century), excellent museum for applied arts in colonial times, fantastic paintings, furniture, textiles as well as arts and crafts from Mexico and Spain.

Frida Kahlo (Museo), Londres 247, Coyoacán. Open Tuesday–Sunday 10 a.m.–2 p.m. and 3 p.m.–6 p.m. Former residence and studio of the artist couple Kahlo–Rivera, very stylish and at the same time unconventional interior. Death mask of Frida Kahlo, the urn with her ashes and some clothes in her bedroom.

Historia (Museo Nacional de), **Castillo de Chapultepec**, Bosque de Chapultepec. Open Tuesday–Sunday 9 a.m.–5 p.m. In the west wing of the castle of the viceroys (18th/19th century): ground floor – exhibition of Mexico's history (from the conquest to the Revolution in 1910); first floor – documentation of the social and economic development from 1759–1917. Also valuable art and murals by great artists (Orozco, Siqueiros, and others).

Intervenciones (Museo Nacional de las), 20 de Agosto, corner of Xicotencatl, Coyoacán. Former Churubusco monastery; history of the period from the War of Independence until the Revolution in 1914, when Mexico had to defend herself against the interventions (*intervenciones*) of foreign powers. Also a collection of religious art from colonial times.

Leon Trotsky (Museo), Viena 45, Coyoacán. Open Tuesday–Friday 10 a.m.–2 p.m. and 3 p.m.–5.30 p.m., Saturday and Sunday 10.30 a.m.–4 p.m. Former residence of Leon Trotsky and his wife, in which the Russion revolutionary was murdered by a Spanish Communist on April 20, 1940. The garden houses a monument with the couple's urns.

Palacio de Bellas Artes (Museo del), Av. Juárez, corner of Lázaro Cárdenas. Open Tuesday–Sunday 10.30 a.m.–6.30 p.m. Works of the most famous Mexican muralists in the entrance hall and upper floors. Collection of Mexican paintings from the 19th century and etchings by José Guadalupe Posada.

Pinacoteca Virreinal de San Diego, Dr. Mora 7, at the Alameda Park. Open Tuesday–Sunday 9 a.m.–5 p.m. Some rooms and the church of the former convent of San Diego (17th century) house one of the most valuable collections of paintings from the time of the viceroys (16th–18th century), mainly religious motifs. The Pinacoteca also includes the new building for the 15 meter (50 ft) painting *Sunday Afternoon Reverie in the Alameda* by Diego Rivera which was part of the entrance hall of the hotel Del Prado until the earthquake in 1985.

Polyforum Cultural Siqueiros, Insurgentes Sur, corner of Filadelfia. Open Moday–Sunday 10 a.m.–9 p.m., also *Son et Lumière* show. Exhibitions of Mexican folk art and works of Siqueiros' school in the *Foro de las Artesanías*, of contemporary art in the *Foro Nacional*. Finally, in the *Foro Universal*, Siqueiros' masterpiece – *The Way of Mankind*, a 2,400 sq. meter (26,000 sq. ft) picture with collages.

Revolucion (Museo Nacional de la), Plaza de la República, below the Revolution Memorial. Open Tuesday–Friday 10 a.m.–5 p.m., Saturday and Sunday 9 a.m.–5 p.m. Clear and impressive display of the history of the Revolution.

Rufino Tamayo (Museo), Paseo de la Reforma, corner of Gandhi, Bosque de Chapultepec. Open Tuesday–Sunday 10 a.m.–6 p.m. Extraordinary collection of modern art, including several works by Tamayo himself.

San Carlos (Museo de), Puente de Alvarado 50, west of the Alameda park. Open Wednesday–Sunday 10 a.m.–3 p.m. and 4 p.m.–7 p.m. Former city palace of the Earl of Buenavista (designed by the famous Spanish architect Manuel Tolsá). Collection of paintings by the most famous European painters from the 16th to the 19th century. Also contemporary paintings.

Templo Mayor (Zona Arqueológica del), Seminario 8, at the Zócalo. Open Tuesday–Sunday 9 a.m.–5 p.m. Excellent presentation of pre-Spanish finds, including the stone of the moon goddess Coyolxauhqui, at the border of the archaeological site of the Templo Mayor.

MURALS

Locations of the most famous murals in Mexico City:

IN THE OLD CITY

Palacio Nacional, Plaza de la Constitución. In the stairwell the most famous mural by Diego Rivera, *La Historia de México*; in the gallery on the first floor a picture sequence about the ancient tribes of the country and their way of life, also by Rivera.

Suprema Corte de Justicia, Plaza de la Constitución, Pino Suárez, corner of Corregidora. In the stairwell is the very expressive cycle of paintings by J.C. Orozco: *Justice* and *The National Weal*. At the library entrance is *War and Peace* by George Biddle.

Museo de la Ciudad de Mexico, Pino Suárez 30. *Vision of the Defeated* by Francisco Moreno Capdevilla. On the upper floor the studio of Joaquin Clausell, where the painter created unconventional patterns on the wall by wiping his brush.

Iglesia del Hospital de Jesus Nazareno, Pino Suárez, corner of Av. Rep. de El Salvador, opposite the Museo de la Ciudad. On the ceiling and the choir wall an apocalyptic and cruel version of the *Spanish Conquest* by J.C. Orozco.

Anfiteatro Simon Bolivar, Calle Justo Sierra 16. In the hall is *The Genesis*, Diego Rivera's first masterpiece; also Fernando Leal's *Festival of the Lord of Chalma*.

Escuela Nacional Preparatoria, San Ildefonso 33. Famous cycle of socio-critical paintings by J.C. Orozco in the great hall, e.g. *La Trinchera* ("The Trench"), *La Huelga* ("The Strike"), *El Juicio Final* ("The Last Judgement"). Also *Allegory of the Virgin of Guadalupe* by F. Revueltas, *The Elements* and *The Worker's Funeral* by D.A. Siqueiros, *The Massacre of Templo Mayor* by Jean Charlot.

Secretaria de Educacion Publica, between the streets of Rep. de Argentina, Luis González Obregón and Rep. de Venezuela. In two patios a sequence of 235 paintings by Rivera (more than 1,600 square meters/17,200 square feet) about Mexican life. In the second court paintings by Jean Charlot and Amado de la Cueva. In the library, *Red Riding Hood* by Carlos Merida.

Antigua Aduana, Plaza de Santo Domingo. In the stairwell, *Patrician and Patricide* by David A. Siqueiros.

Antigua Camara de Senadores, Xicoténcatl 9. In the stairwell, a sequence of paintings about Mexico's history by Jorge González Camarena.

Palacio de Bellas Artes, Eje Central Lázaro Cardenas, corner of Av. Juárez. On several floors, in the great hall and in the corridors, works by the great muralists José Clemente Orozco, David Alfaro Siqueiros, Diego Rivera, J.G. Camarena, M. Rodríguez Lozano and Rufino Tamayo.

Casa de los Azulejos, Fco. Madero. In the stairwell of the patio-restaurant the huge painting *Omniscience* by J.C. Orozco.

Pinacoteca Virreinal de San Diego, Dr. Mora 7, at the Alameda Park. In a new building, especially designed for Diego Rivera's *Sunday Afternoon Reverie in the Alameda*, originally painted for the reception of the Hotel del Prado which was demolished after the 1985 earthquake.

ON THE PASEO DE LA REFORMA

Sindicato de Electristas (Electricity Company), Antonio Caso 45. In the stairwell, the extremely critical *Picture of Bourgeoisie* by David Alfaro Siqueiros.

Instituto Mexicano del Seguro Social (Mexican Institute for Social Security), Paseo de la Reforma 476. A concrete wall became a work of art: *Mexico* by Jorge González Camarena.

Secretaria de Salubridad y Asistencia, Paseo de la Reforma, corner of Lieja, shortly before the Chapultepec Park. Several paintings by Rivera showing the different cycles of life.

Comision Federal de Electricidad (National Electricity Commission), Rio Rodano 14. Here, Jesús Guerrero Galvan painted his interesting *Allegory of Electricity*.

Castillo de Chapultepec, Bosque de Chapultepec. A representative cross-section: *The History of Mexican Independence* by Juan O'Gorman, *Juárez, the Church and the Imperialists* by J.C. Orozco (in the room *Reforma e Imperio*), *The Conquista Crush Indian and Spanish Culture* (in the room *Conquista*) and *Venustiano Caranza* (in the room *La Constitución*), both by J.G. Camarena. *From the Porfiriate to the the Revolution* by D.A. Siqueiros (in the room *Revolución*).
Also: *The Revolutionary Leaders* by Eduardo Solares, *The Landscape* by Gerardo Murillo (Dr. Atl) and *The Return of Benito Juárez to Mexico on 15 April 1857* by Antonio González Orozco.

Museo Nacional de Antropología, Paseo de la Reforma, corner of Gandhi. Murals complement the exhibits, e.g. The *World of the Tzeltales and Tzotziles* by Leonora Carrington or *The Fantastic World of the Yucatán Peninsula* by Rafael Coronel (both in the Maya room). *The Expression of Culture in Mesoamerica* by José Chavez Morado (in the Mesoamerica room).
Also works by Arturo Covarrubias, Arturo Garcia Bustos, Matias Goeritz, Iker Laurrauri, Leopoldo Mendez and others.

Hotel Camino Real, Mariano Escobedo 700. *Man confronted with the Infinite* by Rufino Tamayo, in one of the entrance halls. Life is seen as a street where human beings can only be saved by hiding behind illusion and hope.

Lerma–Bassin, in the new, western part of the Chapultepec Park. Imaginative underwater relief by Diego Rivera in the large pool.

ON THE AVENIDA INSURGENTES

Polyforum Cultural Siqueiros, Insurgentes Sur, corner of Filadelfia, next to the Hotel de México. The 12 outer walls display historical scenes, painted by 30 artists according to Siqueiros' design. Inside the building, *The Way of Mankind*, Siqueiros' huge masterpiece. Next to the Polyforum you can find another huge work by Siqueiros, showing the artist himself together with several other muralists such as Dr. Atl (Gerardo Murillo), Clemente Orozco and Diego Rivera.

Teatro Insurgentes, Av. de los Insurgentes Sur 1587. A huge mosaic in mural style according to Diego Rivera's design. The actor Cantínflas is in the center of a group of artists.

Ciudad Universitaria, Insurgentes Sur. One of the most impressive mosaic façades in the style of a mural can be found in the library. It was created according to the design of Juan O'Gorman and covers the following subjects: The cosmologies of Ptolemy and Copernicus (south), Mexico's history before the Spanish conquest (north) and the New Age (west) as well as a future vision of the country (east).
In the rectorate, Siqueiros designed a mural in partly three-dimensional form, *People for the University – the University for the People*. The designs for the glass mosaics at the façade of the lecture hall for natural sciences (*Conquering Energy*) and at the plaza of the same faculty were created by José Chávez Morado.
Life, Death and the Four Elements is the name of a gigantic mosaic created by Francisco Eppens which is housed in the medical faculty.

Estadio Olimpico, Insurgentes Sur, opposite the Ciudad Universitaria. The glass mosaic showing an allegory of sport was designed by Diego Rivera.

IN THE NORTH

Instituto Politechnico Nacional, Prolongación Carpio/Lauro Aguirre. Mural by David Alfaro Siqueiros: *Man – Master of Technology, not its Slave.*

BOOKSHOPS

In the publishing world, Mexico City assumes the first position in the whole of Latin America. This is why there are numerous book shops in the capital. English literature about Mexico can also be found in the book departments of many museums.

Larger book shops often serve as cultural meeting points and offer readings by the authors.

Information in the weekly magazine *Tiempo Libre*.

Deutsche Buchhandlung, Benjamin Hill 193, Col. Condesa.
American Bookstore, S.A., Madero 25, tel: 512 0306.
Libreria Hamburgo, Insurgentes Sur 58, tel: 514 5086.
Libreria (Foro) Gandhi, Miguel Angel de Quevedo 134, Col. Chimalistac/Coyoacán, tel: 548 1990, 550 2524. Monday–Friday 10 a.m.–11 p.m., Saturday and Sunday 10 a.m.–10 p.m. The largest bookshop in Mexico and a cultural meeting place.
El Juglar, Calle Manuel M. Ponce 233, Col. Guadalupe Inn, tel: 660 7900, 548 2697. Beautiful rooms in an old villa with literary café, cultural meeting point.
Parnaso de Coyoácan, Av. F. Curillo Puerto 6, Coyoacán, tel: 658 5718. Also open on Sundays. In the style of a university bookshop, wide range of books, readings.
Libreria (Foro) Luis Bunuel, Insurgentes Sur 32, tel: 592 8204. Cultural meeting point.
Sanborn's. Book departments in all subsidiaries of the chain.

SHOPPING

It does not matter whether you are interested in buying arts and crafts (*artesanías*), jewelry or elegant clothes – you will find everything in the Zona Rosa. **Sanborn's** department stores also offer a comprehensive choice of high quality goods.

The choice of exotic spices and chilis at the old **Mercado de la Merced** is great. The *mercado* covers a complete quarter with small greengrocers and spice shops reaching from the southeast of the Zócalo to the Merced market hall (Metro: Merced).

Many galleries specializing in modern Mexican art or folk art (such as naive paintings or *papel amate*) are also situated in the Zona Rosa. However, quality and famous names demand a high price.

ARTS & CRAFTS

Arts and crafts and folk art (*arte popular*) are best bought and sold at one of the larger markets (where haggling is possible) or in special shops such as:

FONART (Fondo Nacional para el Fomento de las Artesanías), a government organization to promote arts and crafts. The subsidiaries sell goods from all over the country:
Av. Patriotismo 691 (headquarters with store);
Avenida Juárez 89, near the Alameda Park;
Londres 136, Zona Rosa;
Av. Insurgentes Sur 1630, Col. del Valle;
Av. de la Paz 37, San Angel;
Av. Manuel E. Izaguirre 10, Cd. Satélite.

Artesanias del Polyforum, in the Polyforum Siqueiros, Insurgentes Sur, corner of Filadelfia; open 10 a.m.–9 p.m. An all-round arts and crafts shop subsidized by the government, good prices.

Casart, Av. Juárez 18–C, near the Alameda Park. Wide choice of beautiful folk art and sophisticated arts and crafts from the Estado de México. Subsidiary at the Plaza Satélite, main shop in Toluca.

Artesanias Finas Indios Verdes, Insurgentes Norte, corner of Acueducto 13. A department store for arts and crafts and souvenirs, also silver, leatherware and clothes.

Galeria Reforma, Reforma Norte, corner of Gonzáles Bocanegra (at the second roundabout north of the junction of Av. Juárez). Excellent choice of arts and crafts of all kinds; also jewelry, leatherware and textiles.

La Carreta, Insurgentes Sur 2105, near Sanborns, San Angel. A kind of market with many stalls and small shops where the artists themselves sell their works.

Muller's, Florencia 52, corner of Londres, specializes in onyx. Many items, such as games, are made and sold in Puebla.

You should stick to specialized silver or jewellery shops if you want to buy items made of silver. Many of these can be found in the Calle Amberes in the Zona Rosa, amongst them also the well–known shops **Tane** and **Los Castillo** (the latter being a subsidiary of the most famous silversmith in Taxco).

A wide choice of high quality arts and crafts is also available at the **Museo Nacional de Artes e Industrias Populares**, Av. Juárez 44, close to the Alameda Park.

Some **markets** specialize in arts and crafts (and kitschy souvenirs), on others you just have to look out for *artesanía* amongst the daily necessities.

La Ciudadela, (Mercado Central de Artesanías), Av. Balderas, Metro: Balderas or Juárez; open Monday–Saturday 9 a.m.–6 p.m., Sunday 9 a.m.–2 p.m. One of the most comprehensive ranges of arts and crafts items from all over the country. Many small workshops offer jewelry and hammocks amongst other things. The prices are appropriate.

Mercado San Juan, C. Ayuntamiento, corner of Dolores, Metro: Salto del Agua, or by foot from the Alameda Park. Open on working days 9.30 a.m.–6 p.m. Huge build-ing with small shops, arts and crafts and kitsch, appropriate prices.

Calle Londres, market in the Zona Rosa; good choice of silverware, but not cheap.

El Bazar Sabado, Plaza San Jacinto, San Angel; every Saturday; bric-a-brac and arts and crafts (good quality).

La Lagunilla, Calle Allende/Rayón; Sundays; a typical flea market with second-hand clothes, junk and rubbish as well as arts and crafts.

ARTS & CRAFTS SUMMARY

The following are areas of Mexico which specialize in particular products:

Ceramics, pottery: *loza bruñida*, unglazed but highly polished, fine ceramics from Tonalá (near Guadalajara, Jalisco), often decorated with plants or animals (grey, brown, white)

Green-glazed ceramics (e.g. in the shape of a pineapple, *piña*) from Patamban, San José de Gracia and other Taraska villages in the state of Michoacán.

Black and shiny ceramics from San Bartólo Coyotepec (Oaxaca).

Animal figures made of clay for growing cress from Santa María Atzompa (Oaxaca).

Various clay figures, e.g. nativity figures from Tlaquepaque (near Guadalajara, Jalisco).

Conifers mainly from Metepec (near Toluca, Est. de México) and Acatlán de Osorio (Puebla).

Talavera-ceramics, glazed, multicolored ceramics of Spanish origin (e.g. crockery and tiles) from Puebla.

Lacquerwork: many items are decorated with elaborate lacquerwork: gold-leaf decorations from Pátzcuaro (Michoacán), inlaid work from Urápan (Michoacán), pumpkin vessels or boxes in scratch technique (multicolored) and jaguar masks from Olinalá (Guerrero), black pumpkin vessels with painted flower decorations from Chiapa de Corzo (south of San Cristóbal, Chiapas)

Textiles: embroidered blouses from San Pablito Pahuatlán and Cuetzalan (Puebla) as well as Oaxaca and Chiapas.

Woven fabrics (also belts) from Oaxaca and Chiapas.

Woven wool carpets from Mitla (Oaxaca). Finely woven *rebozos* (scarves) in black and grey from the villages of the Estado de México and Oaxaca.

Dresses and blouses in modern designs with traditional embroidery come from the states of Jalisco and Michoacán as well as other places.

Glassware: handmade glassware is mainly manufactured in the region of Guadalajara.

Onyx: beautiful chess and domino sets, bowls or vases – mainly from Puebla.
Papel amate (painted raffia paper): the paper is produced in San Pablito (in the north of Puebla) and then painted in various villages such as Xalítla, Toliman and San Agustín de las Flores in the state of Guerrero.

Wickerwork, basketwork: hammocks from Yucatán, sisal bags and mats from Yucatán.
Reed mats, baskets from Michoacán.
Palm wickerwork from the state of Puebla.
Finely woven hats from the Gulf coast, Campeche.

Woodwork: animal figures made of ironwood, carved by the Seri Indians, from Bahía de Kino (Sonora).
Colonial style furniture from Cuernavaca (Morelos) and Michoacán.
Mahogany and cedar wood furniture (also chests and other small pieces of furniture) from Yucatán, Tabasco and Campeche.
Guitars from Paracho (Michoacán).

Jewelry, metalwork: silver (jewelry, bowls, vases, cutlery) comes mainly from Taxco.
Masterpieces of art made of copper are found in Santa Clara del Cobre (Michoacán).
Coral jewelry from the Gulf and Caribbean coast.
Gold jewelry created after designs found in pre-Spanish tombs (e.g. imitation of jewelry from Mte. Albán) in Oaxaca.

SPORTS

For more details on specific sports see the chapter *Off Duty in Mexico City*.

Soccer is the most popular sport in Mexico. Children kick their footballs in courtyards and parks, whereas the professionals play in the Ciudad Deportiva (Insurgentes Sur), in the Estadio Azteca (Aztec stadium, 110,000 places; near the junction of the Periférico Sur with the Calzada Tlalpan) or in the Estadio Olímpico (80,000 places) at the Insurgentes Sur. Matches are every Thursday evening at 9 p.m., Saturday at 5 p.m. and Sunday at 12 noon.

Jai alai: A *frontón*, as the *jai alai* halls are called, is situated near the Revolution Memorial. Games take place daily after 6 p.m., except Mondays and Fridays.
Horse races are held in the Hipódromo de las Américas in the southwest of the city. Travelers pay less on presentation of a tourist card. The races start at 3 a.m. (Tuesday, Thursday, Saturday, Sunday). Betting is also an integral part of the races. Pretty restaurant in the Derby club, reservations tel: 557 4700.

Charreadas: organized by Charro clubs, mainly on Sundays, e.g. in the Rancho Grande de la Villa, Insurgentes Norte (north of the Metro station Indios Verdes); Lienzo del Charro, at the Periférico, west of San Angel; Charros del Pedregal, Camino a Sta. Teresa 305, Tlalpan, tel: 655 9353; Lienzo Rancho del Charro, Av. de la Constituyentes 500. Information and reservations at: Asociación Nacional de Charros, A.C., tel: 277 8706 and 277 8710.

If you want to play **tennis** in Mexico City, there are a few hotels with adjacent tennis courts. The Club Reyes near the Chapultepec Park is also open to non–members. Reservation recommended, tel: 277 2690.

Golf is played in the Club Campestre (est. 1906) in Mexico City (Churubusco). This club, as well as the Club de Golf de México (in Tlalpan), the Club de Golf Chapultepec and the clubs Bellavista, Hacienda and Valle Escondido (situated to the west of the city in the Estado de México), are only open to visitors when accompanied by a club member. On presentation of a membership card and for a green fee, you can play in the following clubs: Chiluca, Bosques del Lago (also in the west) and Acozac (in the east, towards Puebla). (Please enquire before setting out. Playing conditions may change from season to season.)

Bullfighting is a hotly debated issue all over the world but it has many fans (*aficionados*) in Mexico. The largest arena in the whole of Latin America, with 50,000 seats, can be found in the Ciudad Deportiva (Insurgentes Sur).

FURTHER READING

General
Insight Guide: Mexico. Apa Publications (HK) Ltd, 1991.

History
Bernal Díaz del Castillo: *Conquest of New Spain.* Penguin, 1969.
Bernal: *The Vanished Civilizations of Middle America.* Thames & Hudson, 1980.
Octavio Paz: *Pre-Columbian Literatures of Mexico.* University of Oklahoma Press, 1986.
Raat (ed.): *From Independence to Revolution, Mexico 1810–1910.* University of Nebraska Press, 1982.

Politics & Society
Alan Riding: *Inside the Volcano.* Hodder & Stoughton, 1989.

Art, Culture & Cuisine
Zamora: *Frida Kahlo – The Brush of Anguish.* Art Data, 1990.
Hayden Herrera: *Frida.* Bloomsbury Publications, 1989
Octavio Paz: *Convergences.* Bloomsbury Publications, 1987.
Octavio Paz: *Eagle or Sun?* Prose Poems. P. Owen, 1990.
Detroit Inst. of Arts: *Diego Rivera – A Retrospective.* WW Norton, 1986.
Rochford: *Murals of Diego Rivera.* Journeyman Press, 1987.
Schmeckebier: *Modern Mexican Art.* Greenwood Press.
Marian Harvey: *Mexican Crafts and Craftspeople.* Philadelphia Art Alliance Press, 1988.
Charlot: *Mexican Mural Renaissance*, 1920–1925. Hacker Art Books, 1980.
Lawrence Anderson: *The Art of the Silversmith in Mexico*, 1519–1936. Hacker Art Books, 1974.

Literature
Carlos Fuentes: *Where the Air is Clean.* Deutsch, 1986.
Carlos Fuentes: *Costancia and Other Stories for Virgins.* Deutsch, 1990.
Celia Correas de Zapata (ed.): *The Magic and the Real.* Short Stories by Latin American Women. Arte Publico, 1990.
Irene Nicholson (ed.): *Mexican & Cental American Mythology.* Newnes Books, 1983.
Campos (ed): Mexican Folk Tales. University of Arizona Press, 1977.

Maps
The most detailed map of Mexico City is the *Guía Roji* which is available as a book or foldable map everywhere, sometimes even at street stalls. The *Mapa Turístico de Carreteras* (free of charge) contains a street map on its back. It is available from the Mexican Tourist Authority overseas or in Mexico from the tourist information centers.

Special Information

TOURIST INFORMATION OFFICES IN MEXICO

Dirección General de Servicios Turísticos, Presidente Mazaryk 172 (corner of C. Hegel), Colonia Polanco, tel: 211 0099, 250 8555.

Lodge your complaints by telephone at 250 0123 from 8 a.m.–8 p.m. The same number also gives out tourist information.

Further tourist information offices are at the airport, the coach stations and the main station as well as in the Zona Rosa, Amberes 54, tel: 525 9380–85.

Information leaflets and maps are available from Cámara Nacional de Comercio (Chamber of Commerce), Paseo de la Reforma 42.

Every Friday, the weekly magazine *Tiempo Libre* (in Spanish) publishes information about cultural and tourist events in the city. The title, issued by the same company which also publishes the daily newspaper *Uno más Uno*, is available from all newsagents.

EMBASSIES

Mexican embassies abroad:
Austria: A–1010 Vienna, tel: (02 22) 535 1776; Bernastrasse 57,
Great Britain: 8 Halkin Street, London SW1, tel: (071) 235 6393.
Germany: D–5300 Bonn 1, tel: (02 28) 218043/46, Adenauerallee 100, Konsularabt. 219561; Renngasse 4,
Los Angeles: 125 Paseo de la Plaza, tel: (213) 624 3261.
New York: 8 East 41st Street, tel: (212) 689 0456.
Spain: Paseo de la Castellana, 93, tel: (091) 456 1263
Switzerland: CH–3005 Bern, tel: (0 31) 434060.

FOREIGN EMBASSIES IN MEXICO CITY

Austria: Campos Eliseos 305, tel: 540 3415, 540 3651.
Canada: Schiller 529, tel: 254 3288.
France: Havre 15, tel: 533 1360/65.
Germany: Calle Lord Byron 737, Col. Polanco Chapultepec, tel: 545 6655.
Netherlands: Montes Urales Sur 635–2nd floor, tel: 540 7788–92.
Switzerland: Hamburgo 66–4th floor, tel: 533 0735.
United Kingdom: Rio Lerma 71, tel: 207 2089, 207 2288.
USA: Paseo de la Reforma 305, tel: 211 0042.

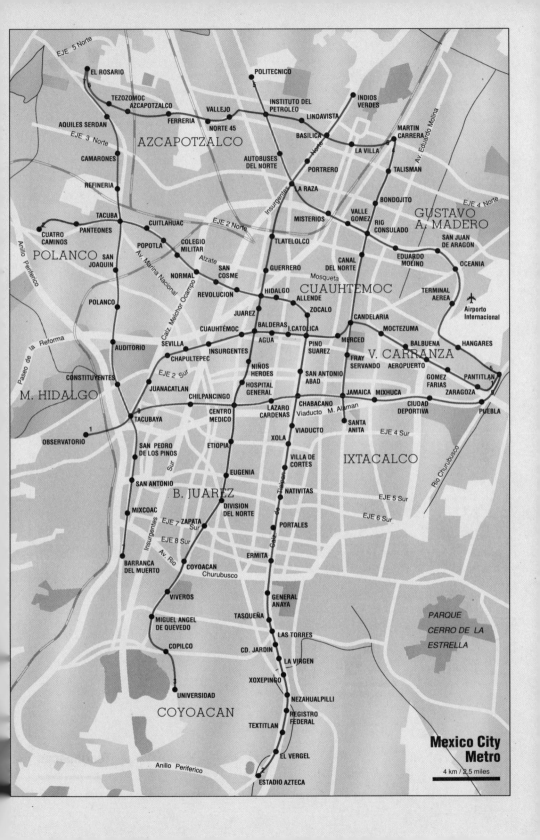

EJE 5 Norte

EL ROSARIO

TEZOZOMOC
AZCAPOTZALCO

AQUILES SERDAN

EJE 3 Norte

CAMARONES

REFINERIA

Anillo Periferico

TACUBA

CUATRO
CAMINOS

PANTEONES

POLANCO

SAN
JOAQUIN

POPOTLA

CUITLAHUAC

COLEGIO
MILITAR

Av. Marina Nacional

Alzate

POLANCO

NORMAL

SAN
COSME

AUDITORIO

Calz. Melchor Ocampo

REVOLUCION

SEVILLA

JUAREZ

CHAPULTEPEC

CUAUHTÉMOC

INSURGENTES

Paseo de la Reforma

EJE 2 Sur

CONSTITUYENTES

NIÑOS
HEROES

M. HIDALGO

JUANACATLAN

CHILPANCINGO

HOSPITAL
GENERAL

TACUBAYA

CENTRO
MEDICO

LAZARO
CARDENAS

OBSERVATORIO   1

SAN PEDRO
DE LOS PINOS

ETIOPIA

Sur

XOLA

VILLA DE
CORTES

SAN ANTONIO

EUGENIA

B. JUAREZ

NATIVITAS

MIXCOAC

ZAPATA

DIVISION
DEL NORTE

Insurgentes

EJE 7
Sur

PORTALES

EJE 8 Sur

Av. Rio

ERMITA

Calz. de

BARRANCA
DEL MUERTO

COYOACAN

Churubusco

VIVEROS

GENERAL
ANAYA

MIGUEL ANGEL
DE QUEVEDO

TASQUEÑA

Calz. de Tlalpan

COPILCO

CD. JARDIN

LAS TORRES

LA VIRGEN

UNIVERSIDAD

XOXEPINGO

COYOACAN

NEZAHUALPILLI

REGISTRO
FEDERAL

TEXTITLAN

Anillo Periferico

EL VERGEL

ESTADIO AZTECA

POLITECNICO

INSTITUTO DEL
PETROLEO

INDIOS
VERDES

VALLEJO

LINDAVISTA

MARTIN
CARRERA

FERRERIA

NORTE 45

BASILICA

Av. Eduardo Molina

AUTOBUSES
DEL NORTE

LA VILLA

TALISMAN

AZCAPOTZALCO

PORTRERO

Norte

LA RAZA

Insurgentes

BONDOJITO

EJE 2 Norte

MISTERIOS

VALLE
GOMEZ

RIO
CONSULADO

GUSTAVO
A. MADERO

EJE 4 Norte

TLATELOLCO

SAN JUAN
DE ARAGON

GUERRERO

CANAL
DEL NORTE

EDUARDO
MOLINO

OCEANIA

Mosqueta

HIDALGO

CUAUHTÉMOC

TERMINAL
AEREA

ALLENDE

ZOCALO

Airporto
Internacional

BALDERAS

I.CATOLICA

CANDELARIA

MOCTEZUMA

AGUA

PINO
SUAREZ

MERCED

BALBUENA

HANGARES

V. CARRANZA

FRAY
SERVANDO

AEROPUERTO

5

SAN ANTONIO
ABAD

GOMEZ
FARIAS

PANTITLAN

JAMAICA

MIXHUCA

CHABACANO

Viaducto

M. Alaman

ZARAGOZA

CIUDAD
DEPORTIVA

PUEBLA

VIADUCTO

SANTA
ANITA

EJE 4 Sur

IXTACALCO

EJE 5 Sur

Rio Churubusco

EJE 6 Sur

PARQUE

CERRO DE LA

ESTRELLA

**Mexico City
Metro**

4 km / 2.5 miles

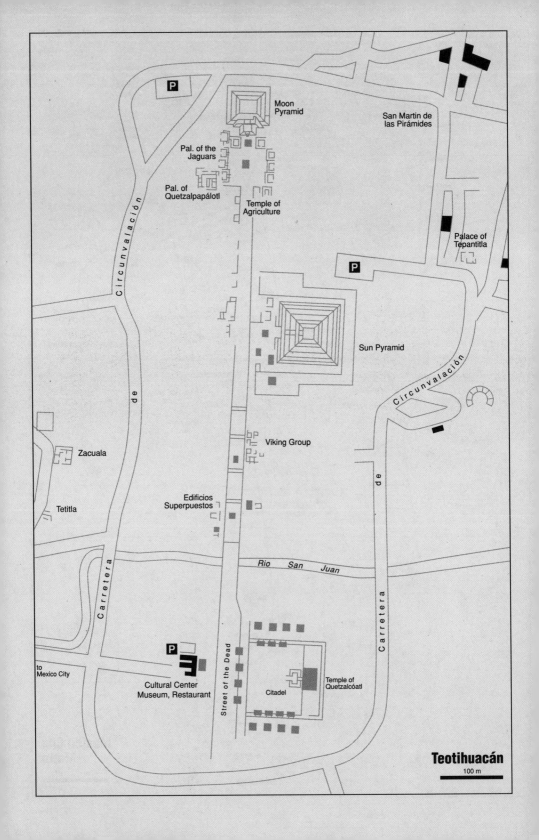

P

Moon
Pyramid

San Martin de
las Pirámides

Pal. of the
Jaguars

Pal. of
Quetzalpapálotl

Temple of
Agriculture

Palace of
Tepantitla

P

Circunvalación

Sun Pyramid

de

Circunvalación

Zacuala

de

Viking Group

Tetitla

Edificios
Superpuestos

Carretera

Rio   San   Juan

Carretera

P

to
Mexico City

Street of the Dead

Cultural Center
Museum, Restaurant

Citadel

Temple of
Quetzalcóatl

Teotihuacán

100 m

ART/PHOTO CREDITS

INDEX

Q – R

S

T

A
C
D
E
F
G
H
I
J
a
b
c
d
e
f
h
i
j
k
l